THE FALL OF THE HOUSE OF HUTTON

DONNA SAMMONS CARPENTER

THE FALL OF THE HOUSE OF HUTTON

AND JOHN FELONI | HENRY HOLT AND COMPANY
NEW YORK

Published by Henry Holt and Company, Inc.,
115 West 18th Street, New York, New York 10011.
Published in Canada by Fitzhenry & Whiteside Limited,
195 Allstate Parkway, Markham, Ontario L3R 4T8.

Library of Congress Cataloging-in-Publication Data
Carpenter, Donna Sammons.
   The fall of the house of Hutton / Donna Sammons Carpenter
   and John Feloni—
1st ed.
      p.   cm.
   Includes index.
   ISBN 0-8050-0946-9
   1. E.F. Hutton & Company. 2.Stockbrokers—United States.
I. Feloni, John. II. Title.
HG4928.5.C37   1989
364.1'63—dc19   89-1768
                                                        CIP

Henry Holt books are available at special discounts
for bulk purchases for sales promotions, premiums,
fund-raising, or educational use. Special editions
or book excerpts can also be created to specification.

   For details contact:

   Special Sales Director
   Henry Holt and Company, Inc.
   115 West 18th Street
   New York, New York 10011

First Edition

Designed by Katy Riegel
Printed in the United States of America
10   9   8   7   6   5   4   3   2   1

In the end, your legacy is,
did you know what the hell you were doing?

—LEE IACOCCA

CONTENTS

THE FALL OF THE HOUSE OF HUTTON

PROLOGUE

Whatever else he was—lonely, driven, insecure, generous, loyal, self-destructive—Robert M. Fomon was a man dedicated to E.F. Hutton.

He envisioned the firm's new, pink marble world headquarters in Manhattan as a prominent symbol of the giant corporation that Hutton had become under his leadership. Everything about the building—its forty-five-foot marble columns, floor-to-ceiling tinted glass walls, and commanding views of the city—bespoke success. Unfortunately, by the end of 1987, when Bob Fomon's twenty-nine-story memorial to his own achievement was finished, so was the firm.

In December of that year, Hutton was forced to auction itself off to the highest bidder. Shearson Lehman Brothers offered nearly $1 billion and swallowed the venerable eighty-three-year-old firm whole. And so, more quickly than the capital and reputation that had sustained it, Hutton itself was lost.

The new Hutton headquarters still stands as a prominent symbol—but of the rewards of hubris, the consequences of pride, the achievements of greed, and the blindness of arrogance. It is testimony to what happens when people forget how and why they rose to prominence in the first place.

Hutton—one of the oldest and best-known names on Wall Street—did not fall victim to the stock market crash or the industry's relentless drive toward consolidation. Rather, the story of E.F. Hutton is a reminder that human shortcomings—more often than market forces or financial acumen—determine the success or failure of a company.

1981

The singular sequence of events that would culminate in E.F. Hutton's pleading guilty to 2,000 counts of mail and wire fraud— a plea that would contribute mightily to the ultimate destruction of the firm—began in December of 1981.

The Batavia branch of the Genesee Country Bank is, as its name suggests, a small bank in a small town. Batavia, New York, a city of some 16,703 souls, lies near the Genesee River, thirty-three miles west of Rochester in rich fruit and truck-farming country.

For more than a year, the bankers at Genesee had courted Hutton executives, trying to convince them to move the brokerage firm's Batavia account from giant Marine Midland Bank to their own modest institution. Finally, they won the prize.

But right from the start, the relationship proved troubling for the small bank. And for the big brokerage firm, it marked the beginning of an ignominious end.

When Hutton opened its account with Genesee on December 1, it deposited two checks, which turned out to be minuscule by

*The per share closing price of Hutton common stock.

5

Hutton standards. One was for $128,648.73, the other for $206,249.85. The new account's initial total balance stood at $334,898.58.

WEDNESDAY, DECEMBER 2

41 7/8

The next day, Hutton deposited two more checks in its Genesee account—one for $123,067.58, the other for $760,000.00. Its balance was now $1,217,966.16. The Genesee bankers were pleased. Winning the Hutton account away from Marine Midland, they were convinced, would prove a shot in the arm for their institution.

In fact, Ned F. Chatt, manager of the Batavia branch, was so pleased that he telephoned his boss, A. Keene Bolton, president and chief executive officer of the $74 million Genesee, at its headquarters in nearby Le Roy, New York. Hutton, he told Bolton, was making huge deposits.

The two men couldn't believe Genesee's good fortune. But they were also puzzled as to why Hutton would put so much money in their tiny bank. "Who could have guessed then," Bolton says, "what Hutton was up to." Keep your eye on the account, Bolton instructed Chatt, and the two men hung up.

THURSDAY, DECEMBER 3

42 1/8

Hutton deposited yet another check in its Genesee account— this one for $2,655,384.51—bringing the account balance to $3,873,350.67.

That day, at the bank's Le Roy headquarters, Bolton bumped into Stephen G. Milne, one of Genesee's internal auditors. Bolton told him, too, to keep close tabs on the Hutton account.

FRIDAY, DECEMBER 4

41 ⅛

The activity in Hutton's account, impressive for a bank of Genesee's size, continued. The firm made another deposit, and this one was the biggest yet—$8,088,613.37.

The same day, another check reached Genesee. Hutton had written a check to itself for $334,000, which Genesee honored. Hutton's balance was now a healthy $11,627,964.04.

MONDAY, DECEMBER 7

40 ⅜

Hutton deposited two more checks—for $61,999.32 and $2,020,439.85—in its Genesee account. At the same time, three checks written on the account arrived at the bank. All three —one for $884,000, another for $2,666,000, and the third for $8,100,000—were payable to E.F. Hutton.

Genesee honored them—a total of $11,650,000—and Hutton's balance fell to what now seemed like a meager $2,060,403.21.

TUESDAY, DECEMBER 8

40

Robert P. Lowe, a young municipal-accounts officer at the Genesee bank, was doing what he regularly did during part of every business day. He was studying the report of customers' deposited checks that had not yet cleared when an eye-popping figure jumped off the page at him.

Genesee had paid out $8 million on checks written by Hutton *before* it had received credit from the Federal Reserve for the checks that Hutton had deposited from other banks. Lowe quickly alerted Steve Milne to the problem, and Milne began an investigation.

The danger of the situation was obvious to both Lowe and Milne. The checks Hutton was writing and depositing were larger than the total capital of the bank.

Meanwhile, the cashier in Hutton's Batavia office phoned the Genesee and asked for the firm's account balance. No one at the bank could give it to her, since it depended upon whether individual checks had cleared.

WEDNESDAY, DECEMBER 9

40 7/8

What was most striking to Steve Milne about the Hutton account was the amount of money involved. The number of dollars deposited was clearly way out of line with the amount of business generated by the brokers at Hutton's four-man Batavia office. Since opening its account just nine days earlier, Milne calculated, Hutton had deposited a total of $26,427,507.

All eleven deposits consisted of large checks written *by* Hutton *to* Hutton on its accounts at two banks in Pennsylvania—United Penn Bank in Wilkes-Barre and American Bank & Trust Co. in Reading. Hutton was moving money back and forth between the two Pennsylvania institutions and Genesee.

Also, during these first nine days of December, Hutton had drawn checks on its Genesee account totaling $26,432,000—or $4,493 *more* than the firm had deposited.

Why? Milne didn't know, at least not yet.

As he looked closer into the account, something else caught Milne's eye: Many of the checks deposited in the account and many of the checks drawn on it carried the same date. For example, Genesee had paid off an $8.1 million check, which was dated December 4. The *same* date appeared on an $8.1 million check that Hutton had deposited with Genesee. Finally, Milne noted, the checks deposited in Hutton's account carried the signatures of employees at the local brokerage office, while the checks drawn on the account did not.

Milne wasn't sure, but what he had found so far led him to suspect a classic check kite—that is, he suspected that Hutton was depositing money in Genesee via check, then withdrawing the cash before the check it deposited had time to clear.

The question for Milne was, what should he do next? He decided to telephone the United Penn Bank in Wilkes-Barre. Were there sufficient funds in Hutton's account to cover two $6 million checks deposited at Genesee on December 8 and 9? Milne asked. A clerk at United Penn put him on hold. When she returned, she told him that one check was good, the other was not.

That same Wednesday, Hutton deposited still more money in its Genesee account. This deposit—for $110,000—was a check payable to Hutton and drawn on a Hutton account at the American Bank & Trust Co. in Reading. Milne called that bank, too, and was not surprised to learn that there was not enough money in the account to cover Hutton's check.

That same day, the cashier in Hutton's Batavia office telephoned the Genesee and again asked for the balance in Hutton's account. Again, she was unable to get a figure. But no one with whom she spoke even hinted that there might be trouble brewing with the Hutton account.

THURSDAY, DECEMBER 10

41 ¼ ·

E.F. Hutton continued depositing money into its Genesee account. The December 10 deposit, a check for $500,000 payable to Hutton, was also drawn on the firm's American Bank & Trust Co. account. Again, Milne phoned the bank, and again it confirmed that this check was no good.

He decided to give United Penn Bank another try. Had the $8 million check drawn by Hutton on its account there and deposited by Hutton in its Genesee account on December 4 cleared? A clerk put Milne on hold, but this time she dialed E.F. Hutton. When she returned to the phone, she told Milne that she had spoken to a Hutton manager, who had said that, although the funds were not there now, they soon would be.

Milne now knew for sure that something was up. He and other bank officers discussed the situation and agreed that it would be best to stop all activity in the account "until the dust settles." Consequently, the bank refused to honor the next Hutton check to come through—one for $2,071,000.

For the third day in a row, the Hutton cashier phoned the Genesee bank and asked for an account balance. Still the bank was unable to provide one. And still no one at the bank said anything about Genesee's suspicions.

FRIDAY, DECEMBER 11

40 ¼

Genesee had bounced the $2,071,000 check, and, on Friday, it refused to honor another check—this one for $8,000,000 written by and payable to Hutton.

According to documents and reports made public in a later congressional investigation of Hutton, Ned Chatt notified the local Hutton branch manager, Michael J. Ryan, an old friend, that the checks were being returned unpaid. Ryan apologized for any problems the bank was experiencing. A little later, he called Chatt back and told him that Hutton would wire $8 million to the bank immediately. By noon, Chatt still had not received the money.

Ryan remembers a different scenario. According to the Batavia brokerage manager, Chatt never phoned him. Instead, for the fourth straight day, he had his cashier call Genesee and request Hutton's account balance. The bank employees again couldn't— or wouldn't—comply. Nor, as he recalls, did they say a word about the bounced checks.

Three men from the Genesee Country Bank—among them, Rob Lowe and Keene Bolton—visited Hutton's Batavia office, where they met with Michael Ryan. According to Bolton, the bankers got right to the point, which was that now they wanted Hutton to take its business elsewhere.

As Ryan remembers events, the meeting wasn't initiated by the bankers. In fact, he says, it was prompted by a phone call from him to Ned Chatt.

"We're going to pull our account," said Ryan, "if we don't get some answers about our balance." At that point, the bankers decided to pay their visit.

At the meeting, Ryan heard the word *kiting* for the first time in relation to Hutton's activities. "Something's going on here," Ryan recalls Bolton saying. Bolton then told Ryan about the bounced checks.

"Well," Ryan replied "if you thought something was going on, why didn't you call me? Damn it," he continued, "I've lived in this town for more than twenty-five years. Everybody knows I'm honest. Why couldn't you take the time to call?"

Then the brokerage manager turned to Bolton and said, "If you don't want our business, we'll take it elsewhere."

"Well," Bolton replied, "we don't want it."

Fine, Ryan said, then turned to the cashier and instructed her to start depositing the brokerage's funds back into Marine Midland.

The Genesee bankers would release Hutton's money, they said, once the bank was sure all the funds had been collected. Ryan, Bolton says, was "very businesslike" about the bankers' decision.

Later that same day, Genesee bounced three more Hutton checks—one for $7,000,000, one for $4,393,000, and one for $2,000,000—a total of $13,393,000.

Before he went home for the day, Steve Milne wrote a memo to John Lounsbury, vice president and auditor of the Security New York

State Corporation, the Genesee Country Bank's parent. In it, he laid out everything he knew about Hutton's check-writing practices.

TUESDAY, DECEMBER 29

39 3/4

As the auditor of the Security New York State Corporation, John Lounsbury made it a point to know the law—at least as it pertained to banks. The law said that "every organization organized, licensed or registered under the banking law shall submit a report to the superintendent [of banking] immediately upon the discovery of any of the following events: holdups, thefts, burglaries, and check-kiting schemes."

Since Lounsbury was convinced, as were Milne and Bolton, that Hutton was kiting, he reported Hutton's activities to Donald J. Kavanagh, deputy superintendent of banks for the state of New York. Then he sent copies of his letter to the Federal Reserve Bank and the Federal Deposit Insurance Corporation.

THURSDAY, DECEMBER 31

39 1/4

At the close of Hutton's fiscal year, the firm reported record revenues of $1.4 billion—up from $1.1 billion the previous year. Despite the boost in revenues, net income actually declined—from $82.6 million to $78.8 million. Earnings per share came to $4.31— down from $4.93 in 1980. The dividend was 60 7/8 cents a share— up from 39 1/2 cents a share. Book value rose from $15.52 a share to $19.40 a share.

No one knew it at the time—and Hutton's results certainly didn't reflect it—but the firm was already on its way to becoming a corporate ghost. Within months a pack of federal and state regulators would be sniffing at the cuffs of its pin-striped trousers— a prelude to the debacle to come.

1982

No one who rises to the top of a giant corporation is ordinary, and Robert M. Fomon of E.F. Hutton conforms to that rule, if to no other.

Soon after he arrived in New York City from Los Angeles to assume the post of chief executive officer, he installed in his ficus-filled office his pet birds—two large, colorful hybrid Catalina macaws with powerful beaks and thirty-six-inch wingspans.

Fomon kept the birds for about a year—which was quite long enough for other Hutton executives and people he did business with to start squawking themselves. The macaws had a habit of walking through the hall in front of Fomon's office and, if people got too close, reaching over and taking a chunk out of them.

The other problem was the birds' limited vocabularies—they knew only obscenities. Often, while Fomon was on the telephone, the person on the other end could hear the birds in the background screeching "Shit, shit, shit!" "As you can imagine," says Thomas W. Rae, then Hutton's general counsel and an executive vice president, "it didn't go over too well."

Of course, Fomon might have argued that he had to make a dramatic impression, since few people at the firm even knew who he was. He had held the title of senior vice president for less than two months before he was elevated to CEO and, in the official corporate history, wasn't even included on the list of five young up-and-comers.

To hear Fomon and other Hutton executives tell it, the new CEO became head of the firm almost by accident. Sylvan C. Coleman, Hutton's chairman and chief executive officer, was slated to retire in September of 1970, when he reached age sixty-five. Two executives were rivals for the job. One was John S.R. Shad, head of the firm's East Coast corporate finance department, who twelve years later would be appointed chairman of the Securities and Exchange Commission by President Ronald Reagan. The other was Keith S. Wellin, the president of Hutton, who later became chairman of Reynolds & Co., the forerunner of Dean Witter Reynolds.

The two lobbied for support within the firm but succeeded only in dividing Hutton into two camps. Fomon, head of Hutton's West Coast corporate finance department for the past eight years, was a friend of both men. Despite his close relationship with Wellin, Fomon had opted to support his counterpart on the East Coast, not out of any particular allegiance to Shad but because he found Wellin so weak.

"Wellin was a charismatic guy," Fomon recalls. "He was good-looking, tall, charming. He remembered everybody's name. But he just couldn't make decisions on his own."

When the executive committee of Hutton's board met in February to select a new chairman and chief executive officer, it surprised everyone. Instead of going for either Shad or Wellin, board members turned to Alec R. Jack, Fomon's colorful, popular, California-based boss and mentor.

"Al Jack," says Tom Rae, "was our version of the Godfather." In other words, nothing happened at Hutton without Jack's approval. A short, plump, genial Scotsman with thick hands and a thick torso, Jack was a powerful man not only at Hutton but also in Fomon's life. The two were like father and son. "I loved him," Fomon says simply.

Jack, sixty-three years old, agreed to assume the title of chairman, but he argued that the CEO's job should go to a younger man—in fact, to Fomon.

Nobody—neither Jack nor anyone else on the board—could have known then what would follow from putting Fomon at Hutton's helm. Ten years later it appeared to have been a brilliant decision. Seventeen years later one could have had some doubt.

Once he assumed his new post, Fomon wasted no time proving himself a forceful and iconoclastic chief executive. One of his first acts was to chop the firm's payroll by some 600 people. That action earned him a reputation for toughness that stayed with him throughout his career. He wasn't afraid, at times, to ignore the rules of convention, either.

The Hutton chief, for example, sat on the board of the New York Stock Exchange, a status achieved only by bona fide heavyweights in the financial community. Traditionally, all board members attend each meeting. Not Fomon. Not only was he a perpetual no-show, but he was bored by one of the few meetings he did attend. So halfway through it, he just stood up and walked out.

While Fomon's behavior in this instance didn't endear him to his colleagues, some of his other actions drew only admiration.

In 1972, for instance, when Hutton moved its offices from One Chase Manhattan Plaza to One Battery Park Plaza, all the securities in the Hutton vault had to be moved, too. "We had received some bids from Wells Fargo, people like that," says one former account executive. "It would have taken a half-million dollars to have armored guards move the securities. Well, Fomon had the balls to put all those securities in boxes and call a regular moving company. They moved it all during the night. They had no idea what they were moving."

In years to come, Fomon wasn't always so thrifty, but his ability to be tough would prove useful in helping him survive the 1980s. On this wintry Wednesday, the New York State Banking Commission summoned Hutton to appear at its offices at Two World Trade Center.

The five-acre World Trade Center complex in Manhattan is

dominated by two 110-story, steel-and-glass towers that rise some 1,350 feet above sea level. On the ninety-second floor of the second of these twin towers is the office of the banking commission.

Three Hutton executives—Senior Vice President and Deputy General Counsel Loren Schechter and Senior Vice Presidents Thomas P. Morley and Robert M. Ross—were dispatched to the meeting. The Hutton executives arrived promptly and were immediately shown to the commission's immense boardroom, where they were peppered with questions about the Genesee Country Bank in particular and the firm's banking practices in general.

"When the government calls you on the carpet," says one of the Hutton executives who attended the meeting, "you like to see very young people behind gray metal desks. That means it's nothing serious. We walk in, and there are a dozen or so guys, all in their fifties, sitting on one side of this huge table. I knew then," he adds, "that we were in deep trouble."

After the meeting, the executives walked back to Hutton's headquarters, a boxlike structure that overlooks New York's historic Battery Park and the Statue of Liberty. (The building is also adjacent to what in colonial days was Wilson's Tavern, birthplace of the martini, one of Fomon's favorite libations.)

Schechter broke the news to Thomas P. Lynch, Hutton's de facto chief financial officer and a twenty-year veteran of the firm. Then the two men walked down the hall to Fomon's office and told him that Hutton was under investigation by the state banking commission for kiting checks.

Fomon looked somewhat startled but quickly dismissed the problem as nothing more than a minor annoyance. In his mind, the Genesee Country Bank was to Hutton what a fly is to an elephant. "Find out what's going on," he told Lynch and Schechter, "and take care of it."

TUESDAY, APRIL 13

27 7/8

Albert R. Murray, Jr., assistant U.S. attorney for the Middle District of Pennsylvania, sat in his office on the fourth floor of the U.S. Post Office Building in Scranton, a city of about 88,000 on the Lackawanna River in northeastern Pennsylvania.

The telephone rang. It was Postal Inspector Richard E. McGee, in Harrisburg. Murray knew McGee well. The two had worked together to nail more than thirty local politicos in Luzerne County for election fraud.

Now McGee was calling to read to the thirty-two-year-old Murray a memo that the Federal Deposit Insurance Corporation had sent to postal inspectors in New York State and Pennsylvania. "You're not going to believe this," McGee said.

Dated January 19, 1982, the memo was written by Gerald B. Korn, an examiner in the Rochester, New York, office of the FDIC, to B. J. McKeon, regional director of the FDIC office in New York City. The subject was the big brokerage firm, E.F. Hutton.

Korn was convinced that the brokerage giant was kiting checks. "At first glance," Korn wrote, "it could appear that Hutton was playing the float, but further investigation revealed evidence of an apparent deliberate kiting operation almost textbook in form."

A week or so later, McGee and Murray met in Murray's office. "Hutton may be up to something," McGee told Murray. "You may want to look into it." Murray agreed. The young prosecutor was intrigued—especially since the case involved such a household name—and he resolved to find out what he could about the case. New York State bank regulators, Murray discovered, had already begun investigating Hutton, and the paper trail had led them to two large New York institutions—Manufacturers Hanover Trust (Manny Hanny, as it is familiarly known) and Chemical Bank. Hutton maintained its central checking accounts at these institutions, and the New York regulators had decided to audit four days of account activity. The audit revealed large, inexplicable transfers of funds between Hutton accounts at the two banks. At Manufacturers Hanover, regulators uncovered withdrawals that left the bank exposed overnight to Hutton overdrafts of as much as $1.3 billion.

What was Hutton up to? The brokerage firm, some of the regulators believed, was engaged in an elaborate—and some said illegal—game of *check crossing*, a form of check kiting. The scheme, they hypothesized, worked something like this:

Say that on Monday the balance in Hutton's account at Manny Hanny stood at $50 million and its Chemical Bank account balance totaled $10 million. Hutton would write a check for $75 million on its Manny Hanny account—an amount well in excess of its balance—and deposit this check in its account at Chemical Bank.

Now its Chemical Bank account balance would climb to $85 million—the $10 million already there plus the $75 million deposited. Hutton would write a check on this Chemical Bank account and invest the amount in some interest-bearing instruments, such as U.S. government Treasury bills—even though the check had not yet cleared Manufacturers Hanover. What's more, Hutton would cover its $25 million overdraft at Manny Hanny with yet another check, written on its Chemical Bank account. "In other words," says Murray, "Hutton was covering its overdrafts with overdrafts."

Since the firm gained use of the money not by a traditional loan but by overdrafting its account, it would pay Manufacturers Hanover *no* interest on the $25 million by which it overdrew its account. In other words, it would have use of the money *interest free* and without Manny Hanny's okay.

Hutton, some of the auditors suspected, was playing its check-crossing game not only at Manufacturers Hanover and Chemical Bank but at other institutions as well. But check crossing, these auditors determined, wasn't the only type of kiting in which the firm was engaged. Perhaps the most difficult check-kiting practice for them to trace was the one carried on in banks outside New York City. It was the practice first detected by officials at Batavia's Genesee Country Bank.

The activity at Genesee led the auditors to suspect that Hutton was involved in what is known in financial circles as *chaining*. The brokerage would write enormous checks on its Manufacturers Hanover and Chemical Bank accounts and deposit the money in small local banks all across the country. Because these institutions were in remote areas, the checks Hutton deposited took longer than the usual one to two days to clear. (Similar kinds of "chains" existed with other banks, for example, between the United Penn Bank in Wilkes-Barre, Pennsylvania, the American Bank & Trust Co. in Reading, Pennsylvania, and tiny Genesee in Batavia.)

What Hutton was doing in all these cases was creating float, and thus pocketing millions of dollars of interest profits it wasn't entitled to. In 1981, for example, 70 percent of the profits generated by Hutton's retail sales arm came from interest.

Many of the investigators thought that Hutton was up to something unsavory, and that these activities extended well beyond the borders of New York State. But they bumped into the limits of their jurisdiction. The law prevented them from following the Hutton paper trail beyond New York's borders.

The New York regulators, says a Justice Department official, "were afraid of Hutton. They were afraid of disrupting the stock market. So they covered up." (To this day, their report has never been released.)

Meanwhile, the size of the overdrafts took the top brass at Manufacturers Hanover by surprise. Nonetheless, the bank's chairman, John F. McGillicuddy, told regulators that he was satisfied with his institution's overall relationship with Hutton. What McGillicuddy said to regulators, however, and what he did back at the bank were entirely different. Soon after he was questioned, the chairman imposed new restrictions on Hutton, restrictions so tough that the firm had no choice but to take most of its accounts elsewhere.

Like McGillicuddy, Chemical Bank Chairman Donald C. Platten insisted to regulators that he was not disgruntled with his bank's relationship with Hutton.

What he chose not to mention was that the head of Chemical Bank's brokerage unit, Stephen Laserson, had pressured Hutton all through 1981 to stop overdrafting its accounts. Chemical Bank, Laserson told Hutton, was not in the business of making interest-free loans. Eventually, he forced Hutton to leave excess funds on deposit—without interest—to compensate for the $440,000 of interest that the bank had paid on overdrafts.

But, as Barbara Donnelly wrote in *Institutional Investor*, these problems, as far as the banks were concerned, "were all in the family." In their minds, there was no need to involve bank regulators. The regulators, they figured, would only end up creating headaches for them—not for Hutton.

MONDAY, MAY 3

31 ¼

By the middle of spring, the New York State Banking Commission had put the finishing touches on its report and was debating what action, if any, to take against Hutton. While the commission members deliberated, Al Murray lifted the decision out of their hands.

Murray, on this cloudless Monday, asked the commission for a copy of its report on Hutton. The New York banking regulators responded with a firm no. Murray, they argued, was overstepping his authority as a federal prosecutor. The federal government, they maintained, does not have jurisdiction over banking matters.

But Murray was unpersuaded and simply, in his capacity as a federal prosecutor, called a grand jury in Scranton and asked it to subpoena the study. The grand jury agreed.

And the young prosecutor worked diligently over the next eight months to gather evidence—from internal bank audits and federal audits to New York State audits, and Hutton's own records—that he thought would help prove a case against Hutton.

In many respects, Murray was a man unlikely to go on a crusade against E.F. Hutton. When he began his investigation, he knew nothing about banking or banking practices. In fact, he says, he could barely balance his own checkbook. But Murray was resourceful. He discovered that the Federal Reserve publishes "Fed Funnies"—comic books that teach children about banking. So he ordered copies of the comics, and one night stayed late at the office and read each one. It was from these publications that he learned how checks clear through the federal system—and got a handle on what Hutton was up to.

After his initial immersion in the subject, Murray became more sophisticated in his approach. He went to the library and checked out books on accounting, economics, and the brokerage industry—these would be his late-night reading for the next few months. Finally, he visited the Federal Reserve Bank for a briefing. "I ended up knowing as much as they did," he says.

Still, there was no question that Murray was totally unfamiliar with banking practices when he began his investigation. Murray wasn't familiar with Hutton's long and distinguished history, either. If he had been, he might have been even more shocked at what he saw as the brokerage's flagrant disregard of financial ethics.

Like most big companies, E.F. Hutton had started out small. Its founder and first president, Edward F. Hutton, was born and raised in New York City, the son of a failed entrepreneur. (His grandfather, a vegetable farmer in Ohio, was also a man of modest means.)

At the age of ten, Edward was left fatherless. At fifteen, he quit school and signed on as a laborer with the Diamond Truck and Car Gear Co. in Kingston, New York. A year later, frustrated with the work, he accepted a position with a Wall Street mortgage company. Edward didn't last very long in his new job, either. When he flaunted the firm's no-vacation policy, he was promptly fired. Hutton's next post—with the Manhattan Trust Co.—ended unhappily as well. Asked by his boss to go to school and learn how to write better, Edward wrote his resignation instead.

By 1901, when he was twenty-five, Hutton, as a result of his previous employment, had made two important discoveries: He wanted to make his mark in the financial world, and he wanted to work for himself. So, with a partner, Arthur Harris, he bought a seat on the old Consolidated Stock Exchange.

For a poor boy, it wasn't a trivial achievement. But it wasn't enough to impress Harry L. Horton. An influential member of the New York Curb Exchange—forerunner of the New York Stock Exchange—Horton wasn't about to let his daughter Blanche marry a Consolidated Exchange member.

So for love—or because his prospective father-in-law paid for it—Edward, who had met Blanche in 1902, acquired a seat on the Curb Exchange. It was the first time—but not the last—that the aggressively ambitious Edward would combine romance and finance.

With a new partner, George Ellis—his old partner, Arthur Harris, held on to their Consolidated Stock Exchange seat—Edward founded E.F. Hutton & Co. in 1904 in New York City. It would be, the partners decided, a brokerage that stressed service above all else.

It would also be the first brokerage to offer services on both coasts. Hutton had traveled to California in the winter of 1904 and was so impressed with business prospects in the state that he wanted to open a branch office there. Ellis wasn't convinced. He wanted to take some time, think it over.

But near the end of 1905, with a handful of employees and $150,000 in the bank, the two men set up an office in two small rooms on the ground floor of 33 New Street in San Francisco. (Entertainment wasn't part of Edward's game plan, but it was provided anyway: Next door to their offices was a popular shoe-shine parlor where customers were serenaded by Caruso records.)

The competitive advantage that E.F. Hutton cultivated—aside

from the hands-on quality of its service—was its rapid and reliable communications system. It was the first brokerage, for instance, to boast a private telegraph wire connecting its San Francisco and New York offices.

The legendary John W. ("Bet-You-a-Million") Gates tested the Hutton wire in 1905 during a San Francisco visit. He gave Hutton's West Coast office a purchase order, which the firm transmitted, executed, and reported in less than three minutes. Gates, impressed, began a lifelong relationship with Hutton that brought the firm hundreds of thousands of dollars in commissions. (In time, Hutton would have its share of famous investors. During the 1970s, for example, John Paul Getty appeared in a Hutton advertisement endorsing the brokerage's services. It was the only time Getty ever posed for an ad for a company he didn't own.)

A better test of Hutton's system came the following year. When the powerful 1906 earthquake struck San Francisco, Richard Mulcahy, Hutton's West Coast manager, was on his way to work. By the time he arrived, the Hutton offices were almost demolished. Yet, miraculously, the records and books were intact.

Mulcahy and several assistants rented a fishing boat and, with their records, headed for Oakland, where they persuaded the Western Union office chief to open Hutton's direct line to New York. E.F. Hutton & Co. in Manhattan became the first Wall Street firm to learn of the devastation.

The firm quickly sold off its clients' holdings in companies with San Francisco operations and raised cash for its San Francisco clients—all before news of the quake reached the markets back east. In the aftermath, Hutton acquired the envious admiration of many of its competitors on the Street—and a good number of their clients, as well.

Hutton and Ellis's leadership of the firm as it grew—in volume and in reputation—was visionary and at the same time cautious. The two men continued to add to and extend the company's wire-service facilities. In 1925, Hutton became the first firm to install quotation tickers in California.

Hutton also made it a point to go where its clients were. For instance, it opened branch offices in certain hotels—Saratoga Springs "in season"—and in suburbs where the wealthy lived. And Hutton was the first firm to publish a market newsletter for investors and to pioneer financial services advertising.

Yet in its core business E.F. Hutton & Co. remained carefully conservative, never succumbing to the expansionary fever of the late 1920s. Instead, it required its customers to adhere to strict margin requirements.

The practice cost Hutton dearly in unrealized commissions, but when the market crashed on October 29, 1929, Hutton lost less than $50,000 on unsecured accounts. Its profits that year came to $8.2 million—second only to those of the venerable Lehman Brothers, which traced its roots to pre–Civil War days. (Hutton's successful weathering of the 1929 disaster would stand in sharp contrast to its fate in the crash of 1987, an event that contributed significantly to the eventual demise of the firm.)

In the early 1930s, when other firms were struggling, and failing, to stay alive, E.F. Hutton & Co. continued to post regular profits. It may have earned only $773,293 in 1931, but that was more profit than any other Wall Street firm reported for that gloomy year.

Strategic relationships—marital and other—worked to the firm's advantage. Hutton, for instance, was a major underwriter when F.W. Woolworth went public in 1911. It's true that Edward may have been one of the first financiers to recognize the growing strength of retail chain stores, but it also helped that his brother and partner, Franklin L. Hutton, had married one of the Woolworth daughters.

Likewise, Edward's second marriage, to Marjorie Merriweather Post, put the firm in line to take the Postum Co. public. After the stock offering, Hutton himself took a leave of absence to become president and chairman of Postum, transforming, through acquisition, the former Post family business into the giant General Foods Corp. (Hutton and Post's daughter, the actress Dina Merrill, would become a Hutton board member in 1986.)

Edward went on to pursue other business interests, later returning to Hutton as a limited partner. Nevertheless, the personal relationships he cultivated directed more desirable business Hutton's way. Walter Chrysler, for instance, became a friend of Hutton's, with the result that Hutton would be the firm that took Chrysler public. (There would be a time in the 1980s when Chrysler and E.F. Hutton would briefly touch each other again, but under far different circumstances.)

Under the direct management of other men now, E.F. Hutton & Co. survived the perilous 1930s and emerged from World War II poised to expand. It began a series of acquisitions that continued through the postwar decades, and although its investment-banking activities grew, the greatest growth was in its retail brokerage accounts. Its customer base expanded geographically and demographically as individual investors entered the market during the 1950s and 1960s.

The 1970s would be golden years, years of explosive growth, for Hutton. And much of the credit for that success goes to Bob Fomon and his handpicked successor, George L. Ball. By 1972, Hutton ranked second among New York Stock Exchange member firms in revenues and first in return on equity. By 1975, no one could argue with Hutton's success.

But something significant happened that year. Congress passed legislation that deregulated brokerage commission rates. When the new law took effect, Hutton and other Wall Street firms would enter a new competitive world and a different business environment.

No firm entered this new era with as much potential as E.F. Hutton—and no firm would fail as miserably. In 1975, though, who could have known?

Hutton continued to introduce innovative investment programs for its customers. It created one, for instance, that allowed them to purchase gold bullion and another that allowed small investors to participate in the purchase of corporate bonds through a mutual fund.

Its prestige had grown as well. Hutton ranked fourth in *Insti-*

tutional Investor's "All American" research survey, and it topped all other full-service, nationwide securities firms in the influential magazine's poll. Now a highly visible, national firm, it began underwriting public television's "Washington Week in Review."

It is also testimony to Hutton's reputation that it was able to attract three of the country's top specialists in tax-exempt municipal bonds from the then leading firm in that market, Blythe Eastman Dillon Inc. The three—Dick Locke, Jim Lopp, and Scott Pierce—were thinking of setting up their own firm.

Instead, they decided to move to Hutton, because of the sort of ship Fomon and Ball ran. "We decided," says Pierce, "that Hutton, with its retail distribution, its unstructured management, its lack of politics . . . was probably our best opportunity. Coming from a firm that had lots of committees," Pierce says, "where the decisions of those committees didn't necessarily get carried out, it was a great relief to come to Hutton, where at that point there were no committees—at least none that I knew of. You were allowed to build your business. The decisions that required approval from senior management were fairly few."

At the end of 1975, Hutton was able to report its best financial year ever. Revenues of $253.1 million yielded profits of $20.1 million. The firm was riding high, and no one was riding higher than Fomon, who, in just one more year, would ascend to the chairmanship.

By the end of 1978, Hutton stood second among publicly owned securities firms in revenues and profits and at the top in return on sales and return on equity. Fomon continued his efforts to reduce Hutton's dependency on its traditional ticker-tape business. Income from sources other than securities sales that year had grown dramatically. For example, its combined commodity—$49 million—and option—$37 million—revenues exceeded the firm's total annual revenues in a year as recent as 1970. Hutton's share of the investment-banking business was growing more rapidly than most other underwriters'. In 1978 it managed or co-managed a record 212 offerings, totaling $9.1 billion. Merger and acquisition fees accounted for about 40 percent of its corporate finance revenues.

What Fomon did during those days was give his executives plenty of leeway—too much, as hindsight reveals. Furthermore, he had dozens of people, far too many, reporting to him. "Whenever there was a conflict between two people in the same area of the business," says one former senior executive, "Bob would split the business in two and have both people reporting to him." The scandal that later tarnished Hutton's image as well as Fomon's made very clear that there is a dark side to this style of management. But at the time, Fomon looked brilliant, and Hutton, to all appearances, could do nothing wrong.

In December 1980, Fomon's mentor, Al Jack, died, but Fomon could find some solace in the firm's financials. Record revenues of $1.1 billion yielded $82.6 million in profits.

Jerome H. Miller, who had joined Hutton in 1963 and was tapped for the senior management team in 1970, just about the time Fomon took control, remembers Hutton's glory years with more than a touch of wistfulness. "Those," Miller says, "were the good years at Hutton—from around 1970 to 1980. There was a small group of very young senior officers running the firm, and the firm did very well at that time. There were about six or eight of us. . . . We were very aggressive at the time when it looked like the whole industry was going down. We expanded, and we were right in doing so. I think that was a time when Hutton was looked at as the most effectively run brokerage house.

"The senior management," he continues, "had a very strong interest in what the firm was going to do, because everybody had all their capital in the firm. . . . If we were going to build any wealth, we were going to build the wealth from the growth of E.F. Hutton. Therefore, we were completely connected, not only jobwise, but economically and everything else, with E.F. Hutton. We liked it that way.

"No one knew what an eight-hour day was. Our life was E.F. Hutton. We acted that way, and the firm reacted that way. . . . It was a terrific place to work, and everyone loved to come to work in the mornings. That atmosphere permeated the company," says Miller. "That changed in the eighties." Dramatically.

TUESDAY, MAY 18

28 1/8

Thomas F. Curnin is something of a hotshot in legal circles. A partner at the Wall Street law firm of Cahill Gordon & Reindel, he specializes in handling the problems of big brokerage houses and investment bankers. (He is now a counsel for troubled Drexel Burnham Lambert.) A native of New York City and a graduate of Fordham Law School, Curnin was retained by Hutton soon after the New York examiners called the firm on the carpet. "He seemed like the right man at the time," says Fomon. "He had a reputation for being tough."

Putting Curnin in charge—some former Hutton executives argue—turned out to be all wrong. In fact, they say, his selection would prove key in shaping the unfortunate outcome of the Hutton case. Curnin became Goliath; Al Murray, the young prosecutor in Pennsylvania, a wily David. Curnin's first mistake, these executives claim, was in underestimating Murray. His initial impression of the young assistant attorney was correct; Murray *was* ignorant of corporate banking practices. But once Murray got a handle on the case, he proved a worthy—some would even say deadly—opponent. "I was ignorant," he says, "but I was *not* afraid."

THURSDAY, JUNE 3

25 1/8

George Ball is one of those men who could be any age—thirty, forty, or fifty. Compactly built with wispy blond hair, Ball possesses a rare gift for motivating people. He can talk anyone into doing practically anything. His own determination is extraordinary. As a young man, for example, he had a serious stutter that he overcame by sheer will.

In 1973, Bob Fomon plucked Ball—the son of a college professor—from his post in the Atlantic region and appointed him president of E.F. Hutton & Co., the firm's retail sales arm. Ball had a talent for getting people to work harder than they thought they wanted to. For instance, he would call Hutton's retail salespeople early in the morning, not to speak to them, just to leave a message: "Would you tell him that George Ball called at twenty to eight?" "It was," says a former Hutton account executive, "his subtle way of letting people know that he was at work, and maybe they should be at work, too."

In 1977, when Fomon became chairman, he elevated Ball, a graduate of Brown University, to the post of president of the parent company, the E.F. Hutton Group.

Fomon had never dealt with anyone quite like Ball. He was, in a word, Fomon's opposite. Ball was an extrovert, Fomon an introvert; Ball was articulate, Fomon often ineloquent; Ball was friendly and outgoing, Fomon was frequently gruff. While Fomon liked to arrive at the office in midmorning and work late into the night, Ball came in at dawn. When Fomon offended an employee, Ball apologized for him. Whereas Fomon couldn't recall a broker's name, Ball remembered the broker's wife's birthday and sent her flowers.

While Fomon gave his underlings plenty of freedom in their decision making, Ball ran a tight ship. "It was political suicide if you didn't clue Ball in on your plans," says Norman M. Epstein, Hutton's former head of operations. "Fomon didn't hold it against you if you didn't tell him every little thing."

Despite their differences—or perhaps because of them—Ball became Fomon's alter ego. The two men, in other words, made a good team. They grew close, and, with Fomon fourteen years Ball's senior, like father and son, some said. Ball contends that he felt more like a younger brother. But whatever the analogy, Ball was clearly in line to succeed Fomon, which meant that the upper reaches of Hutton management were, for the most part, free of the backbiting politics normally practiced when rivals contend for the same corporate throne.

Ball's latest idea was to reorganize Hutton completely. In early June, Fomon agreed to the plan. It would turn out to be one of the biggest mistakes of his career. Ball's reorganization would weaken Hutton's mighty retail sales force organization and take the firm farther down the path to self-destruction.

A few days after he persuaded Fomon to endorse the plan, Ball floated his ideas past Scott Pierce, then an executive vice president in Hutton's capital markets group. Fifty-one years old, tall and trim, with Ivy League good looks, Pierce had grown up in the affluent New York City suburb of Rye, gone to public, then private schools, and graduated from Miami University in Oxford, Ohio. His father, Marvin, was publisher of *McCall's* magazine, and his mother, Pauline, the daughter of an Ohio Supreme Court justice.

One key to Ball's plan was persuading Pierce to take over Hutton's retail operation. He wanted Pierce there, he says, because he had very good people skills and a keen strategic sense of the business.

Another key was to shift Jerry Miller, one of the top men in retail, to capital markets. Because of all Miller's experience in retail, Ball argued, the move would be good for Miller's career; it would give him additional expertise.

Pierce hadn't objected to the proposed plan, but Miller, regional vice president in charge of the Atlantic region (Hutton's largest), had.

"I thought it was ludicrous," Miller says.

But Ball and Fomon worked on Miller for weeks. Jerry, they said, Hutton needs you in capital markets. What was important, they stressed, were Miller's management skills. He could pick up the technical knowledge later. The move was for the good of the firm and for Miller's career. Miller knew that capital markets was in trouble, and eventually, the firm's chairman and CEO won him over.

When Ball announced that Pierce would become president of the brokerage's retail arm, the response—especially from brokers—was harshly critical. Brother of then Vice President George Bush's wife, Barbara Bush, Pierce was well connected in social, business, and political circles. Executives and stockbrokers at Hutton generally liked him, but they found him longer on charm and sincerity than on talent and competence.

The brokers opposed Pierce's appointment for one reason above all others. Although he had spent most of his adult life on Wall Street, Pierce had never held a responsible position—or any position at all, for that matter—in retail sales. Now he would be running Hutton's huge retail operation, with its 344 sales offices and 5,309 account executives.

Pierce knew as well as anyone that he lacked the usual prerequisites for the job, but the job change hadn't seemed like such a farfetched idea earlier, when Ball had proposed it. "As he painted the picture," Pierce says of the time Ball first suggested the reorganization, "the job was quite appealing, because it was new and different, and he would be there to gradually break me into it." But, as it turned out, he wasn't.

MONDAY, JULY 12

26 ⅛

It is difficult to exaggerate the importance of George Ball to E.F. Hutton's success. "He provided the psychological glue that held the place together," says one former account executive.

The retail salespeople adored him, and for good reason. No matter where in the country Ball traveled, he always recognized his brokers immediately and greeted them by name. The brokers were delighted—and astounded.

What they *didn't* know was that before Ball visited a branch office, his secretary would hand him a folder containing pictures of all the people he was likely to see. He then carefully studied their names and faces, so he could put the two together on the spot.

Ball was also admired for never forgetting birthdays—those of his brokers *and* their spouses. Again, he had an aide-memoire, this time in the form of a computerized database. His secretary would punch in a date and up would come the correct batch of names.

Ball's techniques worked wonders. It also didn't hurt that he treated his brokers like royalty. Ball's philosophy was simple enough. He believed that if he did right by his brokers, his brokers would do right by Hutton. It was as simple as that, and it worked. Whatever Ball wanted the sales force to do, they did and without question. They were devoted to him and to Hutton.

Bob Fomon began increasingly to rely on his top lieutenant. In fact, by the late 1970s Fomon had withdrawn from the day-to-day management of the firm and virtually turned the reins over to his protégé. But what Fomon gave Ball was power, not visible authority. Ball, an immensely ambitious man, wanted both. When it became clear, at least in his mind, that Fomon was not going to surrender the CEO title until he stepped down, Ball decided to look elsewhere.

FRIDAY, JULY 16

26 ¾

On Friday, Ball broke the news to Bob Fomon and then to Scott Pierce and Jerry Miller that he was weighing an offer to defect to rival Prudential-Bache, a subsidiary of the Prudential Insurance Co. Ball did not say he had accepted the job, although later it would become clear that by this time he had already signed on with the rival firm.

"George," says Tom Lynch, then the acting chief financial officer of Hutton, "didn't want to fight with Fomon. When the Prudential-Bache offer came along, it gave George the position he wanted—CEO—without any conflict."

Fomon, when he heard the news, felt like a lost ball in high weeds. He says he may have offered Ball a large number of stock options, as many as 100,000, to stay on, but he says he did not offer—as some Hutton executives suspected—to make Ball CEO. Ball claims he did. Ball knew, Fomon says, "he could have had the title if he wanted it." Also, says Fomon, "I was not in a bribing mood."

When Pierce heard the news, he was livid. It was unethical, he argued, for Ball to jump ship to a Hutton rival, when he knew everything there was to know about Hutton's retail sales operation. "I felt," Pierce says, "that he had almost a fiduciary responsibility to the employees who looked up to him. I felt just awful."

Pierce tried to talk Ball out of the move, and Ball assured him he would weigh the pros and cons before making a final decision over the weekend.

Miller didn't take the news any better than Fomon and Pierce had.

"Now, Jerry," Ball began, "I want to tell you something, and I want you to accept what I have to say. You and I have worked very closely together. I want you to be the first to know that I'm looking at an offer from another firm."

Miller was astounded. "I can't believe it. You're kidding, right?"

"No, I'm not kidding."

"How," Miller wanted to know, "could you do this? You've accused people who've left of disloyalty."

That was true; Ball frequently did.

"How," Miller demanded to know, "can you resign now?"

"It's an opportunity. I'd be doing what I'm doing here except on a larger scale." Ball's voice disclosed nothing of how he felt.

A sharp exchange followed.

"It's ridiculous," Miller said, "that you would even consider leaving. If it's the CEO title you want, Bob Fomon will probably turn it over to you—if not now, then in the future."

Ball only shrugged.

Years later, at least one top executive at Hutton would say that it was a blessing Ball resigned when he did. "George," says the executive, who asks that he remain anonymous, "was the cause of all our banking problems."

MONDAY, JULY 19

27 3/8

On July 19 the Prudential Insurance Co. jumped the gun. Although Ball had not yet told his colleagues at Hutton that he had accepted the Prudential-Bache post, the rival firm issued a press release formally announcing that Ball had resigned as president of Hutton to head its new subsidiary, Prudential-Bache Securities Inc.

Ball, the release said, would serve as chief executive officer of Prudential Capital and Investment Services Inc., a newly formed holding company, responsible for Prudential's wholly owned subsidiaries, Bache Group Inc., the brokerage operation, and Prucapital, which was involved in investment banking and corporate loans. He would also serve as chief executive of the Bache Group and Bache Halsey Stuart Shields Inc.

Ball, now forty-three years old and a twenty-year Hutton veteran, told Hutton employees that he was attracted by the opportunity to run his own show. "The chance to become a chief executive of a group of major financial services firms and to help shape them is too magnetic to pass up," he said. "It will give me a chance to build something new."

Some Hutton executives immediately assumed that Ball had done Hutton dirty by putting Pierce in charge and then leaving, and the premature press release added fuel to the fire. "No one can prove it," says a former senior executive, "but a lot of us thought Ball went with Pierce because he thought he could eliminate the competition." Ball's version is that he was simply tired of working under what he considered Fomon's arbitrary and freewheeling leadership.

Fomon, who temporarily added Ball's responsibilities as president to his own, was devastated by his protégé's departure. So was the sales force. In the next few months, morale would suffer, and the retail brokerage operation, which had long set the industry standard for productivity, would begin to falter.

A few days later, Scott Pierce offered his resignation to Fomon. If Ball had set up Hutton, Pierce was willing to step aside so an experienced hand could be put at the top of the retail sales force. Fomon, numb, refused Pierce's offer.

Later in the week, Jerry Miller tried to undo George Ball's final act as E.F. Hutton's president. Miller stormed into Scott Pierce's office.

"Can you believe what's happening?" Pierce asked Miller somberly.

"Believe it or not, Scott, it *is* happening."

Pierce shook his head. "I can't believe it. I'm in this new job. I don't know anything about the job."

"Well, I'm in this job that I don't know anything about either. I've got a suggestion. You know more than I do about this job, and I know a hell of a lot more than you do about that job. Why," Miller inquired, "don't we switch jobs?"

Pierce thought for a moment, then rejected the idea. "I'd just as soon stay as not," he said. "I was a bond man," Pierce remembers. "I didn't know anything about equities, which was Jerry's new job."

"Fine," Miller replied and walked out. Soon afterward Miller and Pierce took their case to Fomon.

"The greatest strength of this firm is the retail system," Miller argued. "You now have someone running the retail system who doesn't know anything about it. I do. You've got to do something, Bob." Again Pierce offered to resign.

But Fomon, hurt and angered by Ball's sudden defection, brushed Miller aside. "There have been enough changes around here," he declared. "I don't want any more changes."

"That decision," says one former Hutton executive, "was a terrible error."

"At some point that week," Pierce remembers, "I decided that I'd better learn this job and get going."

The months after Ball resigned proved trying ones for Fomon. He found himself surrounded by people he considered less than stellar. Ball, he felt, had abandoned him. "Bob's divorce," says one senior executive, "was less traumatic for Bob than George's departure."

Scott Pierce says Fomon found it difficult to get back into the firm's day-to-day operations. After a six-year absence from day-to-day management, Pierce says, Fomon "no longer understood parts of the business." Tom Lynch reports that after Ball's resignation, Fomon "lost his cutting edge. He used to love to debate and argue and assert himself. Now, he was much less a fighter. The spark was gone."

Fomon responded to the challenge of daily operational problems by, in part, withdrawing from them. He spent hours, even whole days, working with consultants and visiting galleries to build Hutton's art collection, just as, years later, he would immerse himself in the construction of Hutton's new headquarters building. "Let me tell you," says Tom Lynch, "the last thing Hutton needed was an art collection. That's not what a CEO should be spending a lot of his time on."

Ball's departure would affect the company's bottom line as well. In fiscal year 1982, many of the troubles that would ultimately contribute to the downfall of Hutton began to reveal themselves. For one, when Ball left for Prudential, a number of top retail salespeople went with him.

Also, in the summer, Hutton suffered another key loss. John Shad resigned to become commissioner of the SEC. Shad was, says Fomon, "a great teacher. He taught Fred Joseph the business." When Shad left, a number of rising corporate finance stars—Joseph among them—also departed. (Joseph would later rise to become CEO of Drexel Burnham Lambert.)

But it was not only key defections that hurt Hutton. The company was slow to act in a number of important areas where—as the nation's premier retail brokerage firm—it should have set the pace. For example, when the stock market began its roaring five-year rise in August, Hutton hesitated to expand its over-the-counter stock trading and gather sophisticated marketing data.

Part of the problem was that the energies of Hutton's senior executives were scattered and unfocused. So when opportunity came knocking, no one answered the door.

Moreover, although Hutton was no longer a start-up, it still acted like one. The company operated with what can only be described as a seat-of-the-pants management style. Fomon ruled—and that is the right word—Hutton as if it were his personal fiefdom. "Bob Fomon," says one former account executive, "was born several centuries too late. He would have been a great feudal lord."

While other firms formalized their executive compensation programs, for example, bonuses at Hutton were set by often raucous, one-on-one bargaining sessions with Fomon. The meetings became known as "taffy pulls," because department heads who argued long and loud enough usually got what they wanted. Also, the high living that had characterized Hutton since Fomon came on board continued. In New York City, for example, Hutton kept a number of swank Fifth Avenue apartments at the ready for executives—and their girlfriends.

More serious still, the caliber of people Hutton was now hiring as brokers began to decline. In the past, the firm had made a point of hiring people who were successes in other fields—military officers who'd decided to leave the service, for example, or accountants. "All of a sudden," says one former account executive, "we had a lot of old used-car salesmen. Want to know what kind of guys I'm talking about? If one of them had shown up at my house to take my daughter out, I would have beat the hell out of him."

Hutton was falling victim to its own success, believing that what had made it great would keep it great. "There are few companies," says Robert P. Rittereiser, the man Fomon would later bring aboard to try to save Hutton, "that can play a lead well. They get the lead, and they become fat, dumb, and lazy."

THURSDAY, AUGUST 12

22 ¼

The Dow Jones Industrial Average fell to its low for the year—776.92.

TUESDAY, AUGUST 24

30 ½

The Plaza Hotel is perched like an island at the south end of Central Park, just off Fifth Avenue in Manhattan. Many years ago, E.F. Hutton had maintained a sales office in the Oak Room of the venerable hostelry, where it provided services to its wealthy traveling clients.

The office closed, and the space it occupied became the Oak Bar, one of Bob Fomon's favorite watering holes. One day that summer, one of Hutton's top account executives had joined Fomon for a drink there. The executive was trying to console Fomon, who was mourning the loss of Ball. How could George leave? How could anyone leave Hutton?

Fomon just didn't understand, and his bewilderment was easy to fathom. Fomon had come to E.F. Hutton in 1951; the firm was his first employer—and his last. Now he felt, for the first time since childhood, overwhelmed and dislocated.

In fact, Fomon's personal history—particularly his distant relationship with his father—set the stage for many of the wrong turns he would take with Hutton after Ball's departure.

Fomon spent his childhood in the Midwest. The son of physicians, he was left motherless at the age of four, and he and his brother were sent to live with a maiden aunt in Appleton, Wisconsin. "My father simply could not cope alone," he says.

Fomon attended Catholic boys' schools, then a private Jesuit high school. "It took me twenty years," he says, "to get over the idea that I was going to burn in hell if I wasn't good." After an altercation with the principal, Fomon was denied his diploma, so he never graduated from high school.

Restless, anxious to distance himself from his family, Fomon enrolled at one of the few schools that would accept him without a diploma—the University of Southern California (USC) in Los Angeles. He drifted from one course of study to another, but after five years received his degree in English literature. (He also had enough credits to earn degrees in anthropology and archaeology.)

Then—at his father's prodding—Fomon enrolled in law school. He proved a miserable legal scholar and dropped out before he flunked out. His next stint was as a USC graduate student in English literature. On the side, he taught Latin at a local private school, filled in as a teaching assistant in the English department at USC, and even taught a course in the history of religion for the Anglican church.

But, again, he failed to reach his goal—this time because he never got around to writing his thesis. Finally, his father laid down the law and told him to get a job. At the age of twenty-four, Fomon still didn't know what he wanted to do. One morning he had a brainstorm and decided he would become a stockbroker at a big brokerage house. "It sounded like sort of a romantic kind of life," he remembers. "I'd read all those F. Scott Fitzgerald novels."

So, in 1950, he applied for a job at what would later become Dean Witter Reynolds. He decided against working for the firm when it asked him to write a two-thousand-word essay on why he wanted to enter the securities business and how securities trading was the backbone of the American economy. "As green as I was," Fomon says, "I knew the securities business was not the backbone of the American economy. And so I never wrote it."

Finally, a friend of his father's—an Anglican priest with whom Fomon was living in Los Angeles—introduced him to an executive at E.F. Hutton, and Fomon signed on as a trainee. Fomon's first job at Hutton was as a so-called computer; he kept track, manually, of the brokers' transactions. In time, he was promoted to the interest desk, where he calculated interest charges on margin accounts—again by hand.

Finally, he was allowed to take a stab at being a retail broker. He proved a go-getter in his new position and rose rapidly to become one of Hutton's biggest producers in the United States. After four years Fomon was asked to head his southwestern region's syndicate department, where he was in charge of underwriting new stock issues.

After Fomon completed a few important deals, he was named head of the West Coast corporate finance department. "Actually, Hutton never had a West Coast corporate finance department until I was made head of it," he says. "I never," he adds, "aspired to a national job. I thought I'd be the head of West Coast corporate finance the rest of my life."

MONDAY, DECEMBER 27

38 7/8

The Dow Jones reached its high for the year—1077.55.

FRIDAY, DECEMBER 31

37 1/2

Hutton's fiscal year came to an end. The firm reported revenues of $1.6 billion—up from $1.4 billion. Net income was $81.1 million, or $4.33 a share—up from $78.8 million, or $4.31 a share, in 1981. But earnings still fell below the $82.6 million, or $4.93 a share, they had reached in 1980.

Hutton paid its shareholders a dividend of 64 cents a share, up from 60 7/8 cents a share. Book value was $23.35—up from $19.40.

1983

MONDAY, JANUARY 3

36

The Dow Jones Industrial Average fell to its low for the year—
1027.04.

THURSDAY, JANUARY 6

39 $^5/_8$

"It's been some time since we heard from you." Al Murray, the
prosecutor in Pennsylvania, chided Tom Curnin when the Hutton
attorney telephoned. Curnin ignored Murray's rebuke and got
right down to business, which was to tell Murray that his requests
for Hutton records were way out of line.

"It is impossible," he told Murray, "for Hutton to meet the
government's demands for documents. There are simply too many
of them." Hutton, Curnin said, had already spent $75,000 to
$100,000 copying and forwarding material to Murray. If it supplied
Murray with everything he wanted, the firm could be out as much
as $1 million. "Be reasonable," Curnin urged.

FRIDAY, JANUARY 7

38 ½

The next day, Curnin reiterated his stand in a letter to Murray. "To say that 'It's been some time since we heard from you,'" Curnin wrote, "infers lack of cooperation by Hutton in this investigation, and that is not accurate.

"During the course of our telephone conversation yesterday, I advised you that to require Hutton to assemble the documents requested in your letter of November 26, 1982, would be extremely burdensome and would require months of time and expense."

Curnin—as he had many times before—also tried to convince Murray that many of the documents that the young prosecutor wanted were totally irrelevant to the case.

"While Hutton continues in its desire to cooperate (it has already produced some 30 boxes of documents), the burden and expense an attempt to comply with all your current requests would entail are such that I again urge that we meet to discuss this matter."

Murray, however, stuck to his guns, and a month later Curnin gave in. He buried the young assistant U.S. attorney in mounds of paper—7 million documents, which had to be transported to Scranton from Hutton's Manhattan headquarters in two forty-foot tractor-trailer trucks.

(In the end, Curnin would claim a bittersweet victory. When the case finally wound to a close in 1985, the government was forced to concede that many of the documents Murray requested were, in fact, worthless to the investigation.)

FRIDAY, JANUARY 28

39 ⅜

Bob Fomon is something of a collector. In his automobile period, he owned eighteen cars—among them, two Ferraris, a Mercedes-

Benz, and a Rolls-Royce. His ten horses were all thoroughbreds, and in his California home he kept seven birds.

Fomon is also a collector of people—sometimes the wrong people. If Fomon takes to someone, he will do anything he can to give that person a leg up, even—as in the case of Robert E. Witt—promote him far beyond his capabilities.

By this time, Fomon had become disenchanted with Scott Pierce, whom Ball had placed in charge of Hutton's retail sales force. In conversations with other executives, Fomon would describe Pierce as "a wimp." In fact, Fomon seemed to go out of his way to undermine Pierce's standing with the people who worked for him. One former Hutton retail broker tells this story. "Scottie was right in the middle of a long presentation about the deregulation of the securities industry, comparing it to the deregulation of the airline industry. His presentation was very impressive, very well thought out. Then, right in the middle of it, Fomon said, loud and clear, and with all the top producers in the room, 'That's right, except that everything you're saying is all wrong.' It was typical Fomon."

By early 1983 the pressure on Fomon to replace Scott Pierce as head of retail sales was mounting, and Fomon turned to Witt for help. Witt—a onetime Ripon College football player who had been invited to try out for the Chicago Bears—was a Fomon crony. Joining Hutton as a broker, Witt had worked his way up to the rank of senior vice president. He was managing the Northeast region, which is based in Boston, when the company dispatched him to Houston to head up the South Central region. With money loaned to him by the firm, Witt bought George Bush's house in Houston.

Although Fomon didn't give Witt Pierce's job, he did put him in charge of all operations under Pierce. "That," says one former senior executive, "made bad matters even worse." Witt, the executive points out, was one of Fomon's drinking buddies. Witt clearly worked for Fomon, not for Pierce. "So," the executive continues, "again we had a structure that didn't work." Pierce himself, however, did not resist Witt's coming to New York. "He had some of the attributes I didn't," Pierce says. "He was more of a cheer-leader."

To his credit, Witt did argue for a reduction in the huge commissions Hutton paid its brokers. But no one listened to him. The situation in retail rapidly got worse.

THURSDAY, MARCH 24

47 ¾

At 4:30 P.M. on this rainy Thursday, the audit committee of the E.F. Hutton board convened for one of its rare meetings. The committee didn't even bother to meet in person. Connected by telephone were board members Ed Cazier, Warren Law, Tom Lynch, and Bud Crary, plus two accountants from Hutton's auditors, Arthur Andersen—Joel Miller and John Tesoro.

Crary opened the meeting by asking why the investigation into Hutton's cash management practices hadn't been mentioned in the firm's latest Form 10-K, the document every public company must file yearly with the Securities and Exchange Commission. It wasn't material, Lynch told him. There was no need to raise red flags in either Hutton's annual report or its 10-K.

Hutton's failure to disclose its problems early on brought it much verbal abuse later from congressional investigators. As it turned out, though, the firm couldn't have brought down any more trouble on its corporate head by disclosing than it did by failing to disclose.

THURSDAY, APRIL 14

52 ⅜

Bob Fomon didn't know it, but in April the Justice Department's investigation of E.F. Hutton had begun in earnest. Until then, all but a few key documents in the case had lain in a Scranton office. Al Murray had been swamped with other cases.

That spring, though, Murray once again focused on Hutton. In the months that followed, Murray, with the permission of his superior, David Dart Queen, U.S. attorney general for the Middle District of Pennsylvania, enlisted the help of a team of twenty-five postal inspectors. Murray was handling about two hundred cases at the time, but, with the blessing of Queen, he let them all go so he could work full-time on Hutton.

Using sophisticated computer programs, Murray and his team began to untangle the web of Hutton's check-writing activities.

For Murray, the potential dimensions of the investigation started to grow. He began to regard cash management, as he later told Congress, as "an elitist, esoteric area that needs to be examined, especially since it exposes the banks and the economy to risk." He added, "We really believe that we are working for the good of the economy, for the protection of the banks—whether they recognize it or not."

Now Murray was ready to take the case one step further. He was prepared to call his first witnesses to testify before the grand jury.

TUESDAY, AUGUST 9

44

The chairman of E.F. Hutton had fractured his tibia—the inner and larger of the two bones of the lower leg—in two places. It was widely rumored that he did the damage when he fell out of bed while making love to a young woman. "All I can say," says one former senior executive, "is that he did it in his apartment." (His medical records say only that he suffered the injury "at home.") Fomon has a different story. "I was taking off my pants," he says, "and got stuck in them." He doesn't say whether he was in a hurry, and if so why.

However it happened, the leg break was an important moment for the company—for not-so-obvious reasons. The break was so severe that Fomon had to run Hutton from his bed for two months.

"There was a marked change in Bob from the time he broke his leg," says Tom Rae, Hutton's general counsel. "It just drained the vitality, the spark, from him. It aged him."

WEDNESDAY, AUGUST 10

45 ¾

Inside one of the glazed-white-brick buildings of the New York Hospital and Cornell University Medical College complex, Fomon underwent surgery to repair his fractured leg. In considerable pain, he remained in the hospital until his physician discharged him on August 18.

TUESDAY, NOVEMBER 29

36 ½

The Dow Jones Industrial Average reached its high for the year—1287.20.

THURSDAY, DECEMBER 15

32 ¾

When Scott Pierce had been placed in charge of retail operations, he had gotten only part of George Ball's title—the lesser part. Pierce became president of E.F. Hutton & Co., which was the retail sales arm. Ball remained president of the E.F. Hutton Group, the holding company.

So when Ball bailed out for Prudential, what had been a stable political situation at the top of Hutton—Ball as president and heir apparent to Fomon—became destabilized, and a scramble for the top slot ensued. To quell the turmoil, Fomon named his old pal Tom Lynch to the presidency of the holding company. Lynch had suggested himself as an interim solution, assuring Fomon that when the chairman had settled on his own choice as successor, he could count on Lynch to step aside.

Putting Lynch over Pierce didn't make Pierce any better at his new job, though. Years later, after Shearson had acquired Hutton, Fomon would tell Jerry Miller, who had lobbied hard for the presidency of Hutton, "One of the worst mistakes I ever made was not to give you that job."

"It's too late, Bob," Miller responded, "five years too late, and the firm is gone."

SATURDAY, DECEMBER 31

Market Closed

Hutton's fiscal year ended. The firm reported record revenues of $2.2 billion—up 36 percent from $1.6 billion. Net income came to $110.6 million, or $4.42 a share—up from $81.1 million, or $4.33 a share. Hutton paid its shareholders a dividend of 76 cents a share, up from 64 cents a share the previous year. Book value was $23.42 a share—up slightly from $23.35.

1984

38 ¾

The Dow Jones Industrial Average reached its high for the year—1286.64.

35 ¾

Not only was Al Murray determined to nail E.F. Hutton, but he wanted to put an end to overdrafting by other big corporations as well. So he decided to use the Hutton case as a vehicle to reexamine, as he told Barbara Donnelly of *Institutional Investor*, "the whole corporate euphemism of aggressive cash management."

It didn't take Murray long to convince his boss, David Dart Queen, that he had enough evidence to begin calling witnesses before the grand jury. But to help forestall leaks to the press, he moved the grand jury from Scranton to Harrisburg in early 1984 and set up a makeshift office in the Riverfront Inn. "The room was twenty-nine dollars a night," Murray says. "I was trying to save the government money."

Murray saw that the patterns of Hutton's overdrafts would still appear random and somewhat confusing to a jury. A break in the case came when an accountant on the investigative team uncovered the clearest evidence yet of what Hutton's system was designed to do.

Munley discovered that Hutton had been overdrawing its account at the Northern Central Bank in Williamsport, Pennsylvania, $900,000 day in and day out for the last few months of 1981. Here there were no random patterns. The Northern Central case showed unmistakably how Hutton created float, and it was evidence a jury could understand.

The Northern Central case was important to the prosecutors for another reason. Since the bank was located in the Middle District of Pennsylvania, it would be easier for the government investigators to assemble evidence.

TUESDAY, MARCH 6

29 7/8

Tom Curnin telephoned Al Murray. For more than an hour and a half, the two men debated the Hutton case. The firm's banking practices, Murray argued, were "illegal, fraudulent, and criminal." Now was the time, he said, "for Hutton to admit its guilt."

What, however, did Murray want Hutton to plead guilty to? He refused to say. "I've targeted the company for indictment," he told Curnin, "but I haven't targeted any individuals—at least not yet." Murray was threatening Curnin, and Curnin knew it.

THURSDAY, MARCH 15

29 5/8

Murray's boss knew the rules, and the rules said that Justice Department prosecutors must notify the attorney general if a case they were investigating met certain criteria—for example, if the target of an investigation was a member of Congress or if a case was likely to end up the subject of national headlines.

But not until this Thursday—almost two years after the investigation began—did David Dart Queen notify his superiors in Washington, D.C., of the Hutton case.

In their conversation with Queen, Justice Department officials agreed that the investigation should be kept secret from the public. The last thing the department wanted to do was cause a run on Hutton, which news of an investigation could trigger.

FRIDAY, APRIL 20

Market Closed

Al Murray prepared eleven so-called target letters putting Hutton and Hutton executives on notice that they might face criminal charges. The letters, carrying the signature of David Dart Queen and dated April 20, were virtually identical. "This is to advise you that you are a target of a Federal Grand Jury investigation being conducted in the Middle District of Pennsylvania into possible violations of Federal law."

Murray mailed letters to the E.F. Hutton Group, E.F. Hutton & Co., Michael P. Castellano, the firm's comptroller, Norman Epstein (the head of operations at Hutton), Arthur Jensen (regional vice president for the central region), Thomas Morley (a senior vice president in charge of cash management at Hutton), and William T. Sullivan (the man who had preceded Morley in the cash management job).

Murray opted to hold on to the letters he wrote to George Ball, Tom Lynch, Jerry Miller, and Tom Rae. He would mail these, he decided, only if he were able to develop additional evidence against the men.

MONDAY, APRIL 23

28 ³/₄

Queen and Murray discussed the E.F. Hutton case with Justice Department officials in Washington. It was the first face-to-face meeting between the Pennsylvania prosecutors and department officials in the nation's capital.

The men agreed that Robert Ogren, chief of the department's fraud section, and Peter B. Clark, a fraud-section attorney, would lend a hand during the grand jury phase. They also decided that Ogren and Clark would make periodic visits to Scranton, so that the Justice Department would have a better understanding of the case.

MONDAY, JULY 24

24 ½

The Dow Jones Industrial Average reached its low for the year— 1086.57.

WEDNESDAY, AUGUST 9

33 ⅞

On the twelfth floor of Hutton's world headquarters is the firm's executive dining room. With its unadorned windows, it offers an impressive view of lower Manhattan and the Statue of Liberty. It was there on August 9 that E. Pendleton James joined W. James Lopp II for lunch.

Lopp was then head of E.F. Hutton's corporate finance department, and, as such, was involved in the low-key world of raising capital for companies. James, one-time director of the White House personnel office under Reagan, now headed his own executive search firm in New York, Pendleton James & Associates, Inc.

Lopp was complaining about his boss, Bob Fomon. The chairman was so disorganized, Lopp said. He really needed someone to help him get straightened out. James suggested that Fomon should hire John U. Moorhead as an executive assistant.

"Moorhead," James said, "is a very bright and able guy."

A personable young politico and a graduate of Choate and the University of Vermont, Jay Moorhead, a native of Washington, had signed on with the Republican National Committee in 1977. Two years later George Bush asked him to act as northeastern political director in Bush's 1980 presidential campaign. Moorhead held that post from March 1979 to May 1980.

After Bush's defeat, Moorhead hitched his star to another Republican—Ronald Reagan. When Reagan went to Washington, so did Moorhead. Moorhead first served as executive assistant to Pendleton James in the White House, then went on to become special assistant to the president for private-sector initiatives. In other words, Moorhead was in charge of putting together public and private-sector partnerships to solve domestic problems—convincing a corporation, for example, to allow inner-city kids to use some of its facilities over a weekend.

It was at the White House that Moorhead got to know Peter V. Ueberroth, then the head of the Los Angeles Olympic Organizing Committee and later commissioner of major league baseball and a member of Hutton's board. Ueberroth and Moorhead hit it off immediately, and Moorhead accepted a post with the Olympic committee in 1983.

When James phoned Moorhead, however, the former White House insider was cool to the idea of working on Wall Street.

"How would you like to meet with the chairman of E.F. Hutton?" James said enthusiastically.

"Who's that?" Moorhead asked.

James told him.

"Why?" was Moorhead's unimpressed reply. He wasn't at all

certain that becoming Fomon's executive assistant was something he wanted to do.

TUESDAY, SEPTEMBER 4

31 1/2

On Tuesday, Fomon suffered a transient ischemic attack—known in medical jargon as a TIA. Characterized by numbness in the right hand, arm, and leg, a TIA has the same symptoms as a stroke. However, unlike a stroke—a cerebrovascular accident, or CVA—there's no permanent damage.

Fomon was examined by a neurologist and, within a few weeks, was back, more or less, to normal. The Hutton chairman had a history of vascular problems. In February of 1980, he had experienced a CVA, a stroke. On that occasion, he was hospitalized at New York Hospital and discharged two days later. The stroke, Fomon says, impaired his memory somewhat. Also, it made it difficult for him to write normally. "I kind of trace out the letters," he says.

WEDNESDAY, SEPTEMBER 5

31 3/8

The men around Bob Fomon—among them Tom Lynch and Jim Lopp—had been pressuring Fomon to get some help. Fomon wasn't quite sure what he wanted in an executive assistant. All he knew was that everyone but him on Wall Street had one. He wasn't necessarily opposed to having one himself, he says, just ignorant. "I didn't know about administrative assistants," he says. "I didn't know about personal public relations people. I didn't know that as CEO I was entitled to all these staff people. Also, I was too tight to hire an assistant."

The day after Fomon's TIA, he, James, and Lopp met for lunch at company headquarters. Neither James nor Lopp noticed anything wrong with the Hutton chairman.

At the lunch, James sold Fomon on the idea of Moorhead. "I think highly of Jay," James said. "He's able to juggle complex situations, plus he has a winning personality."

"Well," Fomon replied, "I ought to meet him."

Fomon and Moorhead got together for the first time within a couple of weeks. The chairman, who was still limping and using a cane due to the broken leg he had suffered the previous August, didn't mention to Moorhead Hutton's problems with the Justice Department. The two met three more times before Fomon offered Moorhead a job. It wasn't that Fomon didn't like the young man, he says, it was just taking him awhile to get used to the idea of having an assistant. The plan was for Moorhead to work for Fomon for a year, then to move into a corporate finance job at Hutton.

Moorhead didn't start his new job with Hutton for nearly two months—until early November. After he had been there awhile, he says, he grew fond of Fomon but found him odd. "Bob would never do the easy things, like say hello, thank you, or happy birthday," Moorhead says. "He would do other things—give gifts to people unsolicited."

Personal recognition for kindnesses rendered mattered little to Fomon, according to Moorhead's reading of the man, but celebrity was very important. "He definitely wanted recognition for his artwork. He wanted to be written up in Suzy [the gossip columnist]. He'd hire a socialite to come in and do his [dinner party] guest list for him, so he could have the right people there."

Sometimes, Moorhead recalls, Fomon would treat him like a friend—drop in and talk about the woman Fomon was seeing or invite him to go along to a party. Other times, months would pass between invitations.

"He's a smart man," says Moorhead, "a brilliant businessman. I've heard stories of how he developed corporate finance clients, took over meetings, and made incredibly incisive comments. I unfortunately never saw him that way. I saw him to be what I thought was erratic."

In time, as he worked more closely with Fomon, Moorhead found that the chairman and CEO spent more time on matters relating to the firm's image—advertising, for example—and compensation than any other matter. In fact, some people in the firm believed that those were the only topics that interested him. "Bob," says his friend Fred A. Whittemore, a managing director of Morgan Stanley, "pays attention only to those things he wants to pay attention to."

THURSDAY, NOVEMBER 8

32 ½

Tom Curnin—like any good attorney—had decided to play it safe. He had recommended to all Hutton officers that they take the Fifth Amendment. Fomon refused. In fact, when he appeared before the grand jury in Harrisburg, Pennsylvania, on November 8, Bob Fomon was one Hutton officer to ignore Curnin's advice. (Another was Tom Rae.) "I didn't have anything to hide," Fomon says, "and I was the chairman of the firm. I felt I had to tell the truth, say whatever I knew."

When Fomon walked into the hearing room, Al Murray told him, "Mr. Fomon, I want you to know that you are not a target of this investigation." Fomon breathed a sigh of relief.

FRIDAY, NOVEMBER 9

33 ⅛

Jay Moorhead didn't know it yet, but when he started work on the following Monday, he would play a central role in the Hutton drama. On Friday, he stopped by the firm's headquarters at One Battery Park Plaza to drop off a box of items—pictures, desk accessories, and so on—for his new twelfth-floor office.

"Can I see you for a moment?" Fomon asked Moorhead.

"Of course," Moorhead replied.

"Do you know the attorney general?" Fomon asked, referring to William French Smith. Smith's old law firm—Gibson, Dunn & Crutcher—was under retainer to Hutton in California.

"I don't know him well," Moorhead replied, "but I've met him a couple of times. I've served on committees with his wife. I know who he is and he knows my name."

"Well, there's an investigation going on by the Justice Department of E.F. Hutton," Fomon said. (This was the first Moorhead had heard of it.)

"What is it?" Moorhead asked.

"The investigation is in the Middle District of Pennsylvania, and it has to do with a banking matter," Fomon replied. "We've been having some problems with a lawyer there, and I think I would like to talk to the attorney general about it."

"Do you know the attorney general?" Moorhead wanted to know.

"I've known him socially for years," Fomon responded, "not well, but I know him. I could call him up and get an appointment to see him, but maybe you should call him for me. Do you think you could set up a meeting for me?"

"I don't know," Moorhead replied, "but I can try. I really know his wife a lot better." Moorhead knew Jean Smith from his days in the White House, when she'd chaired an organization called Volunteer, with which his office had been involved. "Why don't I call her?"

"That's perfect," Fomon said. "I know Jean. I'd like her to come, too. Why don't you see if you can set up a lunch with both of them?"

"Okay," Moorhead responded, "I'll call Jean."

"Jay," Fomon said, "if she asks what the lunch is about, tell her it's a social lunch. Say I have to be in Washington on other business anyway, but there is a business matter I would like to discuss."

MONDAY, NOVEMBER 12

33 1/4

Jay Moorhead reported for his first day of work on November 12. His official title was executive assistant to the chairman of the board of the E.F. Hutton Group. The first item on his agenda was the phone call to Jean Smith, whom he reached at the Jefferson Hotel in Washington. She took his call right away.

Smith's husband was a twenty-year friend of President Reagan and a charter member of Reagan's kitchen cabinet. A millionaire, he is low-key, cautious, even-tempered, and comes naturally by his patrician bearing. A Boston Brahmin transplanted to California, he's a direct descendant of Uriah Oakes, fourth president of Harvard College.

"Hi, Jay," Smith's wife said. "How's E.F. Hutton?"

Hutton was fine, he told her, then explained that he and Fomon would be in Washington and would like to have lunch with her and her husband—if possible.

Jean Smith didn't ask Moorhead any questions about Fomon, because she knew the Hutton chairman. And Moorhead said nothing about the Justice Department's investigation. Nor did the invitation to lunch raise questions. Lots of people who came through Washington invited her and her husband to lunch.

"He's very busy," Mrs. Smith said of the attorney general, "but I'll check with him and get back to you."

TUESDAY, NOVEMBER 13

31 3/4

Jean Smith called Jay Moorhead at his office. "Is there anything on the agenda?" she asked about their proposed luncheon meeting.

"Just a social lunch," he replied, volunteering no further information. She simply said that Thursday would be convenient.

Moorhead suggested that the four of them meet at the Jockey Club in the Ritz, at 2100 Massachusetts Avenue.

THURSDAY, NOVEMBER 15

31

Fomon and Moorhead boarded the company's propjet at the private air terminal in Newark, New Jersey. On the short flight to Washington, the conversation turned to the Justice Department's investigation. Fomon confided that he had been called to testify before a grand jury.

With this information in hand, Moorhead started to have second thoughts about the lunch. "Are you sure you want to go through with this meeting?" he asked Fomon.

Fomon assured Moorhead that he did. "If you have a problem with the Justice Department," he said, "you go to the head of the Justice Department. It's just like if you have a problem with General Motors, you go to the CEO of General Motors."

As planned, Fomon and Moorhead met William and Jean Smith at the Jockey Club. A favorite of ambassadors and longtime Washingtonians, the Jockey Club is a not-so-subtle copy of New York's "21" Club. The food is haute French and is less important than the surroundings.

The conversation remained entirely social during the meal— the weather, mutual friends, and so on. But as the attorney general finished his dessert, he said he had to leave; he had a meeting at the White House.

"Before you go," Fomon said, "there is something I'd like to ask you." Then Fomon gave a two- to three-minute description of Hutton's problems with Justice.

"I don't know if you're aware," Fomon said, "but the U.S. attorney in the Middle District of Pennsylvania has been investigating our banking practices for two years. There's a grand jury investigation going on. The grand jury is about to expire. Our lawyers have been trying to extend the grand jury for another couple of months." Fomon went on to explain that the firm was concerned it wouldn't have an opportunity to make its submissions before the grand jury expired. If it had that opportunity, Fomon pointed out, the Justice Department might be less inclined to recommend the indictment of Hutton or anyone at the firm.

"Our lawyers," Fomon said, "have been having problems with your lawyers. Will you look into it?" Fomon didn't go so far as to ask Smith to extend the term of the grand jury, but the message was perfectly clear.

Smith was taken aback. It was apparent from the look on his face that he knew nothing about the Hutton investigation.

As Fomon spoke, Smith looked for a way to put an end to the conversation. "My principal irritation," Smith remembers, "was that lunch would turn out to be a guise to raise a question like this. This was a man who should know better."

"Bob," he said, "I'll look into it." Then he left as quickly as he could. Fomon and Moorhead continued to chat with Mrs. Smith for fifteen to twenty minutes, then the three left.

As soon as Smith returned to his office, he phoned his Justice Department counsel, Tex Lazar, to tell him about the lunch. Smith reported to Lazar that Fomon had "blurted out" what he wanted to say about the case, including, "This is an awful thing Justice is doing to an honest business."

Lazar, Smith said, should inform the appropriate department officials about the lunch, then see to it that Smith was not involved in the case in any way. A few hours later, Lazar phoned two other Justice Department attorneys, Stephen S. Trott and Lowell Jensen. He told them that Smith had been "blind-sided" and the luncheon had been a "setup"—meaning that Fomon had arranged it just to plead his cause with the attorney general.

Trott suggested that Lazar call Fomon or Moorhead to say that they should have contacted him, as head of the criminal division, rather than the attorney general. "We had to set these clowns straight," Trott says. "We had to get them back into proper channels. They should not try to make an end run."

A few days later, Lazar delivered this message. What Fomon and Moorhead didn't know was that, ironically, earlier in the day, the Justice Department had extended the term of the grand jury.

Yet the hoped-for extension ended up doing Hutton more harm than good. "The extension of the grand jury," Moorhead says, "came back to haunt us." For one thing, what came to be known as the smoking-gun memo was unearthed during the extension. "When that memo surfaced," says Moorhead, the Hutton attorneys realized they would have to start negotiating with the Justice Department.

TUESDAY, NOVEMBER 20

31 ¼

Tex Lazar telephoned Jay Moorhead. "You have counsel in Washington," Lazar told Moorhead, "and you should contact the Justice Department through your lawyers."

Then Lazar asked to speak to Bob Fomon. Moorhead gave Lazar Fomon's home number. When he reached the chairman, Lazar repeated the advice he had given Moorhead: "Work through your attorneys." "Okay," Fomon said, "okay."

Later, Fomon confided to Moorhead that he still believed he had been right to meet with the attorney general personally. "I have a right to do so as a citizen," Fomon insisted.

WEDNESDAY, DECEMBER 26

29⅝

It was time for the annual budget review, the first for Jay Moorhead, who had been Fomon's assistant for just a month and a half. He found the process, in his words, "strange."

Managers would come in and present their plans for the next year. Fomon would ask questions, and the managers would respond. Odd, Moorhead thought, that no one ever referred to the budgets from the previous year.

He asked old Hutton hands what was going on. "People told me, 'Jay, this is just an exercise for Bob. People make these plans, and no one has paid any attention to these budgets for years. We don't run this firm on our business plans. They have no basis in reality.'" But that was Fomon's style. He didn't want a systematic review. He wanted to be able to tell people the amount of money they could and couldn't have.

It was also well known around the firm how Fomon helped in the assembling of the firm's annual report to shareholders. "He would take out the pictures of the people he thought were unattractive or not attractive enough," says one former executive. "They may have been good producers, but if they were unattractive . . . they were out."

THURSDAY, DECEMBER 27

28 ⅝

On this cold, gray day in December, Al Murray sat in his office in Scranton and wrote a memo to Peter Clark, the trial attorney in the Justice Department's fraud section in Washington, D.C. The subject was the Hutton investigation.

"We are prepared," the young prosecutor wrote, "to recommend prosecution against the individuals named in the indictment. Happy New Year!"

Murray was in a jubilant mood. For more than two years he had labored to nail the executives responsible for Hutton's massive check scandal. Now he was close to getting what he wanted— the Justice Department's blessing to issue indictments.

As it turned out, his good humor was short-lived.

MONDAY, DECEMBER 31

29 ¼

In the winter of 1984, a change took place within the Justice Department and its bureaucracy that altered the outcome of the Hutton case.

David Dart Queen resigned as U.S. attorney for the Middle District of Pennsylvania to assume a new post with the Treasury Department. And Washington, D.C.–based Stephen S. Trott, assistant attorney general for the United States and chief of the department's criminal division, stepped in to assume control of the Hutton investigation.

Trott, as an undergraduate at Wesleyan University in Middletown, Connecticut, had performed as a member of The Highwaymen, the folk group best known for its 1961 hit, "Michael, Row the Boat Ashore." However, he abandoned his singing career for the law not long afterward. A graduate of Harvard Law School, he rose to the rank of associate attorney general of the United States, making him the number-three man at the Justice Department.

With Queen at the helm, Al Murray had been free to call the shots. But now, in a shift in procedures, he had to run all his decisions by Trott or at least one of Trott's attorneys in the criminal division's fraud section. "This was a tough, complex case," Trott points out, "and we wanted our best players on it. Murray didn't need any help, but three heads are better than one if they're working together."

As the decision-making responsibility in the case shifted to Justice Department officials in Washington, Tom Curnin focused his attentions on them. Curnin hoped he would fare better with the prosecutors in Washington than he had so far with Murray.

Curnin wanted to provide the Justice Department with information on exactly how Hutton's cash management system operated. He also wanted to explain the steps Hutton had taken to halt abuses in the system once those abuses were uncovered. His strategy was to convince the prosecutors that Hutton had acted promptly to correct improprieties once they came to light. "Management," Curnin says, "acted quickly and responsibly."

No one understood Hutton's side of the story as well as Curnin. He had now struggled with the Justice Department over Hutton for almost three years.

The stance Curnin had consistently taken was typical of a Cahill Gordon lawyer. The firm liked to stonewall the opposition— a tactic that usually served its attorneys well in private litigation. But it backfired with the Justice Department.

Curnin—some former Hutton executives claim—appeared contemptuous of Murray and, as time passed, his disdain made the young prosecutor even more determined. (Curnin denies it. "I don't treat people like that. Such an attitude would be against my self-interest and is clearly self-defeating.")

Also, Curnin failed to see that the Hutton case was as much about ethics as about strict legalities, and his misjudgment set in motion a series of events that neither Bob Fomon nor anyone else at Hutton would prove able to control.

When Hutton ended its fiscal year on December 31, Fomon had little to cheer about. The firm reported record revenues of $2.7 billion—up from $2.2 billion. But net income was down again—this time to $52.7 million, or $2.05 a share, from $110.6 million, or $4.42 a share. Hutton's dividend added up to 80 cents a share, up from 76 cents a share. Book value was $24.61 a share— up from $23.42 a share.

1985

FRIDAY, JANUARY 4

27 ¾

The Dow Jones Industrial Average fell to its low for the year—1184.96.

MONDAY, JANUARY 7

28

The threat against Hutton—always very real—showed no signs of disappearing. In the early winter, Tom Curnin decided to make one last attempt to convince the government to either drop its case against his client or pursue the matter as a civil—rather than a criminal—matter. But how? The answer came from the Justice Department itself.

For months, Curnin had been pressing the Justice Department lawyers for a face-to-face meeting. Now, at long last, Assistant Attorney General Stephen Trott said that he would allow Curnin and the other Hutton lawyers to state their case before the department.

January 7 dawned cold and damp.

Curnin arrived at the Department of Justice building on the

corner of Tenth Street and Constitution Avenue in Washington with Thomas J. Kavaler, another Cahill Gordon partner. They were immediately shown to the criminal division's coldly utilitarian conference room. "It's the most perfect government room you ever saw," Trott says. "It's nothing but a table, some chairs, a picture of the president and the attorney general on the walls." It was, he adds, "an icebox, a meat locker."

On one side of the table in this unfriendly space sat Trott; Robert Ogren; Peter Clark; Al Murray; Thomas J. Dagley, the inspector in charge of the U.S. Postal Service investigation; and John A. Holland, a postal inspector. On the other side sat Curnin and Kavaler, representing Hutton, and three attorneys—William C. Hundley of Hundley and Cacheris, a Washington law firm; J. Clayton Undercofler III of Dilworth, Paxson, Kalish & Kaufman, an old-line Philadelphia law firm; and Thomas Fitzpatrick (a former assistant U.S. district attorney in New York)—representing some of the Hutton executives targeted for prosecution.

For nearly three hours the lawyers argued their case. Hutton, they maintained, was guilty of no crime, because the law didn't specifically outlaw the cash management practices in which the firm had been engaged. What was more, the firm had undertaken these activities without criminal intent.

Curnin argued from true conviction.

As far as he was concerned, the cash management system that Hutton had in place was perfectly legitimate. "It was considered so then and is considered so now," he says.

Moreover, he argues, if Hutton deviated from the system, the abuses were neither sanctioned by the company nor widespread. Besides, he says, "the practices themselves should not be considered criminal because the law in this area was not clear."

Although they gave it all they could, the Hutton attorneys were in a no-win situation. The Justice Department was determined to go ahead with its prosecution. The only question was, would the department indict individuals as well as Hutton itself?

For the record, Trott told Curnin and the others that the department wouldn't reach its decision on prosecuting individual executives until after a meeting of the so-called prosecution team—Murray, Clark, Ogren, and Holland. (Trott, as supervisor, didn't take part in these meetings.)

TUESDAY, JANUARY 15

30 ⅝

The following week, Peter Clark and Bob Ogren flew to Harrisburg, Pennsylvania, where they combed through stacks of Hutton documents—some 7 million pieces of paper—stored in a warehouse the Justice Department had rented in Harrisburg.

What Clark and Ogren saw only bolstered their determination to bring the firm to trial. A week later, they officially informed the giant brokerage house that the government was prepared to indict it on criminal charges of scheming to defraud its banks.

Department attorneys worked hard to make sure they had an airtight case, knowing that it might have to hold up all the way to the Supreme Court. "Al [Murray] had this case nailed down," says Stephen Trott. Now, "we were getting ready for first-class war, tying up the loose ends, making sure everything was ready to go. We were," he adds, "making final preparations for battle."

THURSDAY, FEBRUARY 7

40 ¼

Clark and Ogren returned to Harrisburg to complete their review of key documents. By now they were convinced that sufficient evidence existed to indict not only Hutton but some of its employees as well. Al Murray continued to argue his case before the grand jury in Pennsylvania and to collect and review written evidence. If Hutton and the men Trott characterized as the "greeneyeshade money managers" were brought to trial, Murray knew, it was this grand jury that would have to indict them.

In a telephone conversation the next day, Murray told the attorneys representing two Hutton vice presidents—Tom Morley, who headed the firm's cash management operations, and Bill Sullivan, Morley's predecessor—that he had recommended that both men be indicted. Their attorneys wasted no time appealing Murray's decision to his superiors in Washington.

MONDAY, FEBRUARY 18

Market Closed

On February 18, Steven R. Bralove, forty-three years old and manager of Hutton's Connecticut Avenue branch in Washington, D.C., was scheduled to testify before the grand jury in Harrisburg. Now his lawyer asked him to take a look for documents relevant to the case. Bralove, a careful man, found the memo in a file marked "personal."

Although he knew immediately that it would be damaging to Hutton's case, he had no idea of the key role it would play. Bralove turned the memo over to his attorney, who handed it over to Hutton. Hutton, in turn, surrendered the document to the Justice Department, as it was required to do.

The memo, which was later dubbed the "smoking gun" in the case, had been written in April 1982 to Bralove by Perry L. Bacon, first vice president and manager of several other Hutton Washington-area branches. (Bralove, Fomon says, later "blew the whistle on Bacon. There was no love lost between them.")

In the memo, the outspoken Bacon described the illegal activities as firmwide policies. "Our banking activities during the last six months," Bacon wrote, "have been no different than our banking activities off and on during the last five years. Additionally, I believe those activities are encouraged by the firm and are, in fact, identical to what the firm practices on a national basis.

"Specifically, we will from time to time draw down not only deposits plus anticipated deposits, but also bogus deposits. I know of at least a dozen managers at Hutton—managers who along with Bill Sullivan and Tom Morley taught me the system—who do precisely the same thing."

Written in response to Bralove's complaints about Bacon's aggressive cash management tactics, the document greatly strengthened the Justice Department's bargaining position. "When the memo surfaced," a former Hutton executive says, "it was the nail in the coffin."

TUESDAY, MARCH 5

38

After it became known that Steve Bralove had turned over the memo to the Justice Department, other brokers told their colleagues that he should have destroyed it.

"If we had had Watergate people," says Tom Rae, "that memo would have been destroyed in a matter of hours. But," he adds, "we were not Watergate people."

The Bacon memo, everyone knew, tipped the balance in the case. Here was one of the firm's own practically confessing to nearly every charge the government made. And Perry Bacon had written his memo in language any jury could clearly understand.

The appearance of the Bacon memo angered Justice Department investigators—Al Murray among them. They were upset that Hutton and its attorneys had failed to produce it earlier, in response to grand jury subpoenas dating back to 1982. The investigators suspected a cover-up, and, in a March 5 letter to Curnin, Murray accused Hutton of not only withholding evidence but destroying it.

Curnin, not surprisingly, took exception to the department's charge. So did Fomon. "If we had been destroying evidence," Fomon asks, "how would the Bacon memo have ever surfaced?"

What Curnin and Fomon didn't know was that at least one Hutton executive, in conversations with government attorneys, had admitted to destroying documents to avoid turning them over to prosecutors.

In March, Murray asked his superiors at the Justice Department to issue indictments against five men, but Trott authorized only three. (Their identities remain unknown, because federal law prohibits the department from releasing names unless actual indictments are issued. They never were.)

By then, Peter Clark was setting up meetings with Hutton lawyers, interviewing the people targeted for indictment, and preparing draft complaints and injunctions.

WEDNESDAY, MARCH 13

36 ½

With the Bacon memo in the prosecutors' hands, Tom Curnin felt that he had no choice but to plea-bargain. He knew that Murray was no longer in charge, so when he finally decided to negotiate an agreement, it was Peter Clark whom he telephoned. Clark notified Murray of the call, then Clark and Curnin arranged for plea bargaining to begin in Washington. While the discussions were under way there, Murray in Pennsylvania worked out an agreement calling for Hutton to make restitution to its banks. He also continued to put forth evidence before the grand jury.

Murray and his Washington-based superiors were communicating on the Hutton case, but what Curnin didn't know was that they weren't seeing eye to eye. Murray still wanted to take Hutton to court, and, while Trott was sympathetic to Murray's position, he had always doubted that Justice could win the Hutton case. "It was going to be a difficult case to prove," Trott says, "a hard case to sell to a jury."

It was so complicated, he argued, and the law governing overdrafting so gray. Not even the Bacon memo persuaded him otherwise.

Trott reasoned that by letting Hutton plea-bargain, the government could still get what it wanted. "I always believed that a good settlement was in the government's interest, and so did Bob [Ogren] and so did Peter [Clark]," he says. "But," insists Trott, "we were tough as nails. I definitely wanted to punish Hutton. We wanted to settle on our terms, not on theirs."

It was Trott who decided that Hutton would have to plead guilty to 2,000 counts of mail and wire fraud. In addition, the brokerage had to agree to pay back every penny owed the banks, plus interest—an agreement, as it turned out, that was more honored in the breach than in the observance. In addition Hutton had to plead guilty, not nolo contendere. "All the elements were nonnegotiable," says Trott. "We really laid down a bed of coals for them."

Trott and the other prosecutors also thought that the Justice Department should focus its energies not on taking Hutton to court but on halting overdrafting and other questionable cash management practices in which the firm—and countless other big businesses—were engaged.

These practices, the prosecutors believed, endangered the banking system itself. They could easily imagine the scenario. At the end of a business day, some major bank would lack the funds it needed to cover the thousands of payments it had made that day to other banks through one or another of the nation's electronic funds transfer networks. Another bank, counting on receiving money from the first, would be unable to meet its own obligations. Then its default would trigger another, which would lead to still more. The defaults would cascade, and the banking system would collapse.

Keeping the system intact was, in the prosecutors' minds, a more important task than insisting on a jury trial. "If Hutton had failed, a lot of those small banks would have been left out in the cold," says Trott. "We wanted to make sure that this practice was ended." So, because doing so would satisfy all their objectives, they agreed to plea-bargain.

THURSDAY, MARCH 14

38 ¼

But plea bargaining only created a different set of issues for Bob Fomon. He now faced the delicate task of balancing his loyalties to the men around him against his loyalties to the firm. His options—as outlined by Tom Curnin—were these. The firm could plead guilty to mail and wire fraud charges—the lesser charges negotiated with the Justice Department—and its executives would escape indictment. Or Hutton could fight the department, and the firm and three or more of its executives would be brought to trial on charges of scheming to defraud its banks.

Fomon didn't know what to do. In March, he decided to have Curnin run the situation by Hutton's board of directors. "I had been brainwashed by Curnin that [pleading guilty] was the only alternative," he says, "but I still wanted to see how the board felt."

The board was, at this point, made up of twenty-one men and one woman, the actress Dina Merrill. Merrill, the wealthy daughter of Hutton's founder and cereal heiress Marjorie Merriweather Post, had joined the board in 1986. Only four board members were outsiders, people not employed full-time by the company. Merrill was one of them. The others were Warren A. Law, a Harvard Business School professor; Jim Lopp, who had left as head of Hutton's corporate finance division to found Financial Security Assurance, a company that guarantees corporate debt; and Peter Ueberroth, commissioner of baseball and mastermind of the 1984 Los Angeles Olympics.

The remaining seventeen board members were insiders, officers of the company. They all knew the firm had problems, but until the March board meeting they had no idea how serious the problems were. They soon found out.

In the oval-shaped boardroom on the twelfth floor of Hutton's headquarters sat a stone-faced Tom Curnin. He described Hutton's legal difficulties and outlined the choices the board had in confronting them. Fomon let Curnin do all the talking. "I just sat there," he says.

The Justice Department had wanted Hutton to pay huge fines, reported Curnin. But he had been able to negotiate a $2 million fine and $750,000 in expenses. "He made it seem as if Hutton was lucky to get to pay only $2 million," says Tom Lynch.

"We all knew where Curnin came down," says Jerry Miller, who was then part of the capital markets group. "It was either plead guilty or somebody could go to jail."

Tom Rae, however, doesn't feel Curnin presented a one-sided view. Curnin, Rae argues, did what any good attorney would do—present both sides of the case and leave the final decisions up to the client.

"A lot of people were concerned about the continuing publicity," says Rae. "But it was important to Fomon that no one be indicted." In the end, points out the former Hutton general counsel, "it is impossible to predict what a grand jury will do. Grand juries," he adds, "can be pretty much led by government attorneys. A grand jury could indict a ham sandwich."

But Miller and some other board members recoiled at the idea of pleading guilty to a felony when they didn't think Hutton had really done anything wrong. After all, they argued, echoing Curnin's protestations to Justice, the law didn't specifically outlaw the practices the firm had been using.

If Hutton pleaded guilty, Miller maintained—correctly, as it turned out—the brokerage would be "making law," not responding to current law. In fact, Miller insists, "Everybody in the securities business was engaged in trying to get as much of the float as they could. Why should we take a fall for what was a common practice?"

Miller and many of the others felt too that Hutton could have won a jury trial. As he points out, "It wasn't a case of a big megabuck brokerage house against a little old lady. It was a big megabuck brokerage house against a big megabuck bank."

But Curnin presented the flip side. He explained that if the firm didn't plead guilty, at least three people would be indicted. The result, he pointed out, would be a legal battle that would take two or more years to settle. And during that time the firm would be completely vilified by the press.

If Hutton pleaded guilty, Curnin said, the flap would—in his words—go away in a week, especially if Hutton brought in experienced crises managers, as Curnin recommended. In the end Curnin's argument prevailed. "So," says Miller ruefully, "we ended up pleading guilty and being vilified in the press for two years anyhow." Why did Fomon finally side with Curnin? The Hutton chairman, one former senior executive says, "simply didn't want to see his friends fried for something he didn't think they were capable of doing."

The guilty plea, however, held consequences that neither Curnin nor Fomon anticipated. "I really believed that the plea would be the end of the story," Fomon says.

Instead, the plea became big news, and, although Hutton denied it publicly, the scandal badly affected its retail brokerage business. An entire six-broker branch in Connecticut, for example, defected to PaineWebber in December. The assets in Hutton's Cash Reserve fund declined from $5.2 billion to less than $4.0 billion over the next year, a period during which other brokerage houses saw increased deposits in their money-market funds.

Hutton's highly regarded public finance division, however, bore the brunt of the scandal. Several public agencies, such as the Massachusetts Housing Finance Agency, temporarily excluded Hutton from serving as lead manager on deals. And Hutton's ranking in the underwriting of long-term municipal bonds, according to the Public Securities Association, dropped from number two in 1984 to number six by the end of 1985.

"In looking back at the demise of Hutton," says Scott Pierce, then president of Hutton's retail sales arm, "the decision to plead guilty turned out to be a major misjudgment. We thought, well, it happened, admit it, pay our dues, and we could get on with it. In reality, we should have gone to trial. We should have taken our chances. We didn't anticipate the public's reaction to a crime with no criminals. It was a terrible decision."

Indeed, it's hard to imagine that Hutton could have done any worse by a jury than by its own decision to plead guilty. That, however, is wisdom gained in retrospect.

MONDAY, MARCH 25

35 ½

Bob Fomon felt himself very much alone. In the past year he had come to distrust many of the men around him. "There is nothing worse," he says, "than being let down by people you consider friends."

But with the decision to plead guilty, he knew he would need help holding his company together. The sad fact was that, in the cash management scandal, Fomon didn't know whom to believe.

So he asked his ambitious young assistant, Jay Moorhead, to suggest someone from the outside. Moorhead recommended Stuart Spencer, a member of that small and relatively new, but nonetheless powerful, profession of political media consultants.

One of the preeminent Republican strategists in the United States, Spencer had masterminded Ronald Reagan's 1976 presidential campaign and had served as an adviser to George Bush and then Ronald Reagan in the presidential campaign of 1980. He was also the architect of the Reagan reelection campaign in 1984 and would head the campaign of then vice-presidential hopeful J. Danforth Quayle in 1988.

Spencer, Moorhead argued, had the moxie and imagination to concoct a tonic for Hutton's ills. "So set up a meeting," Fomon told his assistant. In his office, a few doors down from the chairman's, Moorhead dialed Spencer's number. Could Spencer meet with the chairman of E.F. Hutton on a confidential basis?

Spencer, a stout man with a facial tic, said he could.

"Spencer," Moorhead remembers, "was the kind of man that Bob Fomon would get along with—tough, a big drinker, a big smoker. He's not a classy guy. Bob is the ultimate classy guy, but Spencer was the kind of man Fomon would respect." And he did. Spencer, Fomon says, was a "diamond in the rough."

At 3:00 P.M. on March 25—a cool, cloudless day in Manhattan—Spencer, Fomon, and Moorhead met in Fomon's office at Hutton headquarters.

"You've got a big problem," Spencer told a dispirited Fomon, "and it's a public relations problem that's not going to go away overnight." In fact, Spencer said gravely, the check scandal could bring down the entire firm if it weren't handled properly.

Fomon was shaken. He wasted no time retaining Spencer and his firm, Spencer-Roberts of Irvine, California. "Put together a plan for us," Fomon instructed Spencer.

"I'm going to be retained only on one condition," Spencer replied, "and that is that you get David Sawyer to work with me, because Sawyer is the best." Fine, Fomon said, and signed up Sawyer and his firm, D. H. Sawyer & Associates, as well.

"Fomon realized he had a tiger by the tail," Jerry Miller says, "and he didn't know what to do with it. He was doing what he could to save Hutton." The Hutton chairman, one former senior executive maintains, was also scrambling to shore up his own reputation. "Fomon," the executive says, "is a very proud man. I think he was concerned about his place in the history of the firm." Of course he was, says Fomon, "that's human nature, isn't it?" But in the view of some senior executives, Fomon's reputation was already beyond saving.

Although best known for their political activities, Sawyer and Spencer had recently shifted their emphasis. Their specialty, crisis management, grew out of their political campaign experience and had been transformed to communications strategies for corporate clients.

Their advice to Hutton came with a hefty price tag—$120,000, payable in four installments ($20,000 at the beginning of the first month they went to work, $40,000 on the final day of the first month, $40,000 on the final day of the second month, and $20,000 on the final day of the third month). Besides this fee, Hutton had to fund all out-of-pocket expenses for travel, meals, telephone, and the like.

WEDNESDAY, APRIL 3

35 ¾

Bob Fomon didn't see much of Stuart Spencer after their initial meeting. Instead, Spencer and Sawyer dispatched Orin Kramer to handle the Hutton crisis on a day-to-day basis. An attorney by training, Kramer had plenty of credentials of his own. From 1981 to 1983 he had served as associate director of the White House Domestic Policy Staff, where he was the senior staff member on financial industry issues.

Some people at the firm thought bringing in Kramer was a mistake. "Bob hired the wrong people," Bob Witt says, "and Orin Kramer was one of them." Witt, along with many other members of the Hutton old guard, believed he knew as much as, if not more than, Kramer. What did Fomon need with high-priced outside advice, Witt wondered, especially when the advice he was getting was dead wrong? But Witt, Fomon says, did not make his feelings known to the chairman.

Kramer's position was that Hutton could escape the glare of the national spotlight only if the firm confessed its sins. Witt was one of those within the firm who believed that Hutton was innocent of any wrongdoing and that it should go toe to toe with its critics. But Kramer soon became invaluable to Fomon. Besides, he was persuasive, and soon Hutton's chairman was marching to his memos. "I had confidence in him," Fomon says. "He grasped all of the elements of the case right away."

On April 3, Kramer drafted one of those memos to Fomon. It took him fourteen pages to outline his thoughts on the check scandal, which by now was known within the firm simply as the F Matter. (The *F* stood for "federal" or "felony," depending on who was asked.) In this document—stamped "strictly confidential"—Kramer warned Fomon that public disclosure of the F Matter would threaten Hutton's most valuable resource, its reputation. Also, it could lead to an erosion of the firm's stature over the long haul.

Even under a best-case scenario, Kramer stressed, the guilty plea and settlement would raise challenges for Hutton with people outside and inside the company.

So what should Fomon do? Hutton first must convince its own employees—particularly the sales force—that it hadn't violated its standards, wrote Kramer. Furthermore, it had to give its brokers the tools they needed to communicate effectively with current and prospective clients.

"The media will explore every negative ramification that is even hypothetically possible and, with the help of Hutton's competitors, will surface underlying questions about the long-term effects on the firm," Kramer wrote. These were serious issues, he said, but he had—as Spencer-Roberts did with its presidential campaigns— immeasurable faith in the power of appearances.

Johnson & Johnson, he reminded Fomon, ultimately enhanced its reputation with its handling of the Tylenol problem, as did CBS in the Westmoreland affair. What mattered, Kramer wrote, was how top management responded—in short, the "spin" Hutton put on the story.

But what was the right way to handle the problem? Hutton, Kramer said, needed a three-pronged attack. It had to formulate a research agenda, an explicit communications strategy, and a detailed and integrated action plan "to reach its key constituencies, internal and external, domestic and international."

Kramer, of course, was at the ready with an appropriate three-phase plan. Phase 1, the research phase, would help Hutton understand better "current constituency attitudes . . . and likely reactions to disclosure of the legal settlement." Kramer's team would first talk to Hutton executives to learn the facts and to hear their views on the risks the firm's reputation faced with its various constituencies. Second, they would gather information from these constituencies.

This outside research would have two components. The first would consist of "in-depth interviews" with representatives of key constituency groups. Hutton's involvement would be disguised. The second component would consist of four focus groups with representatives of Hutton's retail markets. Kennan Research & Consulting, Inc., headed by Ned Kennan, a Ph.D. psychologist, would conduct the groups and prepare a written analysis of the findings for an additional $12,000 fee.

The focus groups, Kramer intoned, would help the team "gain an in-depth understanding of the thought processes among the target audiences, which, in turn, would illuminate consumer communications strategy decisions, including decisions regarding advertising."

Research would be important, said Kramer, because "in the weeks following the public disclosure, the firm will be extremely visible, constituency perceptions . . . will be in flux, and the messages the firm sends to those constituencies during its 'window of visibility' will shape new images of the firm that will be difficult to modify later. The costs of strategic miscalculation are simply too high to risk making decisions without the strongest possible analytical base."

From the information gleaned in phase 1 would come a framework for phase 2, "an integrated, multidimensional action plan," which should be "pro-active and driven by management decision, rather than reactive and driven by events." The plan would include a detailed schedule of events for the time before and after Hutton's guilty plea and specific recommendations and material for the next sixty days.

As examples of effective internal communications, Kramer suggested a detailed, nondefensive letter from Fomon to employees, materials on how to communicate the salient facts to outsiders, and a teleconference connecting top management to E.F. Hutton offices around the country or the world. The teleconference would demonstrate to employees that the firm was eager to address their concerns. After management delivered its prepared remarks, the session could become interactive—a Houston employee, for example, might direct a question to management in New York. Or the New York "set" could include "randomly chosen Hutton employees, who might engage in a question and answer format with top management that would be televised to the regional offices." Not unlike its preparation for presidential debates, the team would run practice sessions and provide media training to prepare top management for "these and other dialogues with relevant constituencies." Finally would come phase 3: implementation.

As for a timetable, Kramer expected to put the plan into action on April 8. At the end of ninety days, he would determine whether there was anything further his firm could do.

Kramer was confident of success, but others were less sanguine. The problem, as Steve Friedman (who the following year would be tapped as general counsel) later observed, was that for such a plan to work, Hutton needed to have built up a lot of personal capital over the years in its relations with the press, analysts, and ratings agencies—all the parties that matter to a brokerage firm.

But Fomon had never put any energy into building bridges to the outside. Public relations simply wasn't his strong suit. Now that a crisis was brewing, the firm had little or no goodwill to fall back on. Without that cushion, Friedman added, the situation was "hopeless."

THURSDAY, APRIL 18

34 3/4

Daniel J. Good, the head of E.F. Hutton's mergers and acquisitions department, was helping Ted Turner raise $5.41 billion to win control of CBS. Turner's potentially lucrative business had come to Hutton via a phone call to Good from the head of corporate finance at Shearson.

Shearson wanted to take on the business itself, but Jim Robinson, the chairman of American Express, Shearson's parent, said no, according to Fomon. "Robinson had made an aborted attempt to take over McGraw-Hill," Fomon says, "and he didn't want to be associated with another hostile takeover." Also, Fomon believes, Robinson's friends at CBS were pressuring him not to help Turner in the battle.

Turner called and arranged a meeting with Hutton's chairman. Although the job had now landed in Good's lap, many mergers experts expected him to be blown away by the giant network. Good had headed Hutton's mergers and acquisitions department for less than a year, and his direct experience as a merger maker was limited. Rather, his long suit was raising operating capital for companies. He'd had an unhappy stint as president and chief operating officer of A. G. Becker Paribas Inc., a job he was forced out of by the firm's French owners before they sold Becker to Merrill Lynch & Co.

The six-person mergers and acquisitions department that Good now headed was, in the view of many in the industry, not well equipped to aid Turner in his quixotic attempt to conquer CBS. In fact, accepting the assignment in light of its relative inexperience in the business turned out to be another serious Hutton blunder, if only because it made the firm appear foolish.

But Hutton needed the money. It stood to pocket more than $50 million in fees if Turner succeeded in his quest. As it turned out, Turner's efforts fizzled and Hutton collected only $5 million, small compensation for its self-inflicted diminution of stature.

WEDNESDAY, MAY 1

32 ½

Late on May 1, Scott Pierce boarded a company plane at the Westchester airport and headed west to Scranton, Pennsylvania.

The next day he was to stand before a federal judge and, on behalf of E.F. Hutton & Co., plead guilty to 2,000 counts of mail and wire fraud. Pierce would also agree that Hutton would pay a $2 million fine, plus an additional $750,000 to defray the costs of the government's investigation. It would also make restitution to the banks it had bilked.

To determine the number of counts to which Hutton would plead guilty, Justice Department prosecutors had worked backward. First, they'd decided that $2 million was an appropriate fine for Hutton's crime. The maximum penalty for mail and wire fraud was then $1,000 a count. So it was a simple matter to determine that Hutton would have to plead guilty to 2,000 counts. When Hutton's attorneys heard that the firm would have to plead to 2,000 counts, they balked. But the Justice Department insisted— plead to 2,000 counts, the prosecutors said, or the deal is off.

How the Justice Department arrived at the number of counts would be lost in the news coverage of the event. Rather, the media eventually jumped on the number of counts as evidence of the enormity of Hutton's crimes.

Early the next day, before Hutton's guilty plea, trading in the firm's stock was halted. Wall Street assumed that a buyout of the big brokerage firm was imminent.

But Wall Street was wrong.

In Scranton, Pierce checked into the Hilton Inn, a hotel set in the historic old Lackawanna railroad station building, then made his way to the hotel restaurant for dinner with Tom Curnin.

It was then that Al Murray decided to introduce himself to the president of E.F. Hutton & Co. The two men would spend tomorrow together in court. Why not get the preliminaries out of the way? Pierce was none too pleased to see the government prosecutor.

"Who do you think you are?" Murray remembers Pierce asking angrily. "And why are you doing this to Hutton?"

Murray says he was not looking for a fight, so he quickly ended the conversation.

Pierce's attitude toward Murray was widely shared among Hutton executives. "Murray," says Fomon, "saw this case as his chance for stardom."

The downfall of E.F. Hutton was, like a Greek tragedy, played out over many scenes. One of these took place on May 2, in U.S. District Court in Scranton. On the bench sat the Honorable William J. Nealon.

At the defense table were Tom Curnin and Thomas J. Kavaler of Cahill Gordon; Thomas Fitzpatrick; William C. Hundley of Hundley and Cacheris; and Thomas I. Vanaskie and J. Clayton Undercofler III of Dilworth, Paxson, Kalish & Kaufman. The government was represented by Al Murray, Bob Ogren, and Peter Clark.

Scott Pierce, as well as Hutton's attorneys, assumed that since the firm had agreed to the guilty plea, the proceedings would be perfunctory. At 9:00 A.M., the Justice Department would summarize the charges against the firm; then Hutton would enter its plea. By 9:30 A.M., they figured, it would all be over. But they were all sadly mistaken.

The judge "made the government go through their whole case," Pierce remembers. The proceedings began at 9:00 A.M., but Pierce wasn't able to plead until noon. It was a scene he is unlikely to forget.

He stood in front of the judge as the courthouse clock began its midday countdown.

"Do you—BOOM—Scott Pierce—BOOM . . ."

"God, it was awful," Pierce remembers.

The timing of the plea also damaged the company further.

Hutton's turboprop was ready to take Pierce and his lawyers back to New York, where they were scheduled to hold a press conference. But the only plane from Scranton to Washington had left at noon, forcing the Justice Department prosecutors—the people most familiar with the case—to drive. They didn't return to the capital until late afternoon.

In New York, Hutton held its press conference. Orin Kramer had prepared a thick stack of documents containing his version of what Hutton had done wrong. Fomon felt, at least, well prepared for the ordeal. A few weeks earlier, he and Pierce had met with David Sawyer—the first and only time Fomon met Sawyer—at Sawyer's midtown office. There, they rehearsed for the press conference. The Sawyer people, playing reporter, peppered the two executives with questions as a video camera ran. Then they critiqued Fomon's and Pierce's responses. "It helped," Fomon says. "It relaxed me."

The real press conference in New York went smoothly for Hutton. "Mr. Fomon and myself and the lawyers sat up there in front of reporters and cameras and said, mea culpa," says Pierce. They confessed, he says, that management didn't have the controls in place to monitor the situation, and that it was the company's fault.

But Hutton was really making something less than full disclosure. Its officers told the press, for instance, that the charges stemmed from the firm's "misuse of the float." That was, of course, only partly true. "Misuse" implied that Hutton was playing with already existing float. If the case had been prosecuted, Hutton would have been charged with *creating* float.

Hutton's press release hewed closer to the facts. It asserted that the practices that led to the guilty plea did "not involve or threaten customer or client funds," and it promised to make full restitution—with interest—to the banks. Finally, the company announced that it had retained a second accounting firm, Arthur Young & Company, to review its cash-management practices and recommend changes.

"This is a sad and difficult day for E.F. Hutton and for me personally," Fomon said in the release. "The practices to which the company pleaded guilty represented violations of our policy and procedures. Nonetheless, the company and its top management assume full responsibility."

In New York it appeared that Kramer's strategy to contain the story had worked. But it didn't look that way in Washington.

Because of their long drive from Scranton, prosecutors couldn't brief Attorney General Edwin Meese III on the case before his 2:00 P.M. press conference, called specifically to announce Hutton's plea. Meese had no idea, for instance, how his department had arrived at the 2,000-count figure.

Why wasn't the press conference postponed? Hutton executives suspected that the White House wanted Meese to announce Hutton's guilty plea to deflect press attention from President Reagan's controversial trip to Bitburg, West Germany, where he had laid a wreath at a cemetery containing the remains of Nazi SS troops. (Meese says the White House wasn't involved in the decision to hold the press conference.)

Whatever the reason, Meese was unprepared for the hostile questions fired at him. How, reporters demanded, could the Reagan administration say it was getting tough on white-collar crime when in this case it had not indicted one individual?

When the prosecutors from Pennsylvania finally arrived in Washington, they, too, held a press conference. It was at this press conference, Pierce recalls, that someone "started talking about hundreds and hundreds of millions of dollars in illegal profits and billions and billions of dollars of illegal loans." Those figures may have been grossly inflated or just plain wrong, but the damage was done. "What had been a story," says Pierce, "but not that big of a story—became a huge story."

In the wake of the plea, "a dozen or so senators," Pierce says, "wrote a letter to the attorney general, demanding to know why he didn't hang everybody at Hutton by their toes."

Ironically, Fomon had a chance to dampen the publicity generated by the guilty plea. Fomon says that a few days before the plea, William P. Clark, onetime national security adviser and interior secretary under President Reagan, had phoned Fomon's assistant, Jay Moorhead, and offered his assistance in trying to get Meese's press conference canceled. (Clark, then a lawyer practicing in California, had, like many Washington insiders, offered his assistance to Hutton in hopes of pocketing a hefty fee.) Fomon turned it down flat. "I didn't think it would be a big deal," Fomon says, "but it turned out that it was."

For some reason, Hutton's stock dropped only three points that day, but Fomon knew that something bad was happening. Imperceptibly at first, Hutton had entered a spin. Its future was at stake, and no one—not Spencer, not Kramer, not Fomon—would be able to do anything to halt the accelerating spiral.

Meanwhile, in response to the criticism they soon received from Congress, Justice Department officials defended their decision to plea-bargain with Hutton on several grounds.

First, they said, they needed an injunction to stop Hutton's abusive practices. Assistant Attorney General Steve Trott wrote in a statement submitted later to Congress: "Murray, Clark, and Ogren viewed [the plea bargaining] as absolutely essential to obtain an injunction that barred the full range of Hutton's overdraft practices, including the use of the drawdown sheet and its multiplier. Hutton had made clear to us its intent to continue its drawdown practices involving the use of the multiplier without disclosure to its banks. Hutton further indicated that it was computerizing the process to make it more efficient and uniform throughout the firm's operations."

Second, the injunction would "send a message" to other businesses engaged in similar activities. In his testimony before Congress, Al Murray reiterated his view that such practices "threatened the financial health of the country."

Hutton, says Steve Trott, was trying to tell Justice that there was absolutely nothing wrong with their cash management practices. That notion, Trott says, was "absolute bullshit."

FRIDAY, MAY 3

31 ½

Under the glare of national publicity, Bob Fomon was being forced to come up with answers—and fast. He met with Curnin again a few days after Hutton entered its guilty plea. With the heat on, Fomon was in no mood for small talk.

"I've got to know who's responsible for this," he told Curnin. It took Curnin several days to come up with a list. Among the names on it, Fomon says, were those of Tom Morley, Perry Bacon, George Ball, and Jerry Miller. But the evidence Curnin had against these men, Fomon says, was "thin."

To give himself more time to prepare a statement for stockholders, Fomon decided to postpone the company's annual shareholders' meeting for two weeks—from May 3 to May 17. At the same time, criticism from Congress and the media of the Justice Department's decision to allow Hutton to plead guilty continued to grow. Congress would soon undertake its own investigation.

Meanwhile, in Batavia, where the check scandal began, Keene Bolton, president of the Genesee Country Bank, learned of Hutton's plea in the *Rochester Democrat & Chronicle*. That's the end of it, he thought. But, he mused, blame should have been laid at the feet of some individuals.

THURSDAY, MAY 16

31 ⅞

His decision to appoint former U.S. Attorney General Griffin B. Bell to perform an independent investigation of Hutton's check scandal was not something that Bob Fomon just slipped into. For days he had mulled over the idea of hiring an outsider to help him uncover the truth. He had considered conducting his own inquiry but soon nixed that idea. The people involved were too protective of one another, he told himself, and he would never figure out who—if anyone—was guilty. What was worse, he realized, an internal investigation would lack credibility. "A whitewash, a cover-up," the Democrats in Congress would charge.

What he needed, he concluded, was a credible outsider, a straight arrow who would dig deep and come up with answers. He needed someone who would appeal to Hutton's critics in the House and Senate, someone who would erase the blot on Hutton's reputation—and his own. "Fomon," says one former senior executive, "desperately wanted to get his name off this problem. He didn't want to go down in history as the chairman of Hutton who presided when the firm experienced all these problems."

So Fomon—at the suggestion of Terry Adamson, a Georgia attorney employed by Hutton—turned to Griffin Bell. A country boy who made good, Bell had been named to the Fifth Circuit U.S. Court of Appeals after he had helped run John F. Kennedy's Georgia campaign in 1960.

In 1976, Jimmy Carter appointed Bell U.S. attorney general. Once confirmed, Bell confronted the entire range of unresolved Watergate-era issues—from Central Intelligence Agency reform to alleged Federal Bureau of Investigation crimes. All involved sticky questions of public confidence. As his first act, Bell symbolically— and literally—flung open the chain-locked doors of the Justice Department's Pennsylvania Avenue entrance for the first time in eight years and began to hack away at the department's problems.

Tall and gaunt, Bell—who likes to be called "Judge"—was often praised for his candor. His homespun humor and accessibility made him a natural for the media. Howard Cosell even interviewed him at halftime on "Monday Night Football."

On May 16, a warm, overcast day in Manhattan, Fomon phoned Bell at the law firm of King & Spalding in Atlanta, where the sixty-seven-year-old attorney had served as a partner since he resigned as attorney general in 1979.

Would Bell undertake an independent investigation of Hutton's check scandal and ascertain who was guilty? Bell said that he would. The two men agreed to the terms of the assignment, and Fomon promised to abide by Bell's findings—regardless of what they were. "If he told me I had to go," Hutton's chairman remembers, "then I was prepared to go."

Fomon might have thought twice about his decision to hire the former attorney general if he had known what he was getting into. By the time Bell was through, he and his staff of fourteen attorneys would have interviewed more than 378 past and present Hutton employees—including 300 people at the branch level, 38 at the regional level, and more than 40 at the company's New York headquarters. They would also have spoken to employees at more than sixty-three banks, plus various regulators, accountants, and cash management experts. And they would have reviewed 11,000 "nonfinancial" documents—40,000 pages of memoranda, correspondence, and notes—as well as thousands of financial documents.

As with so much else connected with the check scandal, Bell would not come cheap. King & Spalding would charge Hutton a hefty $3 million for the services of Bell and his team of attorneys— $1 million more than the fine Hutton paid the government.

In the end, the national press would greet the Bell report—like the Justice Department's decision not to indict individual executives—with icy skepticism. In fact, the report would do more harm than good. Fomon had hired Bell thinking that his investigation would put an end to the scandal. In reality, it would only raise more questions about Hutton's cash management abuses.

Meanwhile, at Hutton headquarters, Fomon decided that a head had to roll. He picked Tom Morley, the man in charge of Hutton's cash management operations. "Everyone was afraid to fire Bacon," Moorhead says, "because of his mouth. He would come back and implicate Fomon and Ball, and they were worried about that."

Fomon called Morley and asked him to come to his office. An hour later, Morley left. Moorhead, Kramer, Jerry Miller, and several other Hutton executives were waiting to learn the outcome from Fomon. "What happened? Is it all over?" Moorhead asked. No, Fomon reported. Morley said that he was only following directions that had been given to him by someone else—his predecessor.

So Fomon hadn't fired him, after all. The Hutton chairman's inability to take decisive action was indicative of the management weakness that had permeated the firm for years. Hutton's guilty plea that day only brought evidence of this weakness into public view.

"Tom Morley was a very nice man," says Scott Pierce. "He wasn't a crook by any means. He wasn't encouraging people to overdraft. But from my point of view he was the man on watch and he should have called it to our attention. I thought it was a bad decision not to fire him."

FRIDAY, MAY 17

31 ⅝

If Cahill Gordon had had its way—some former Hutton executives argue—the firm's postplea public relations strategy would have been entirely different. The big Wall Street law firm, these executives say, had wanted Hutton to "circle the wagons." In its view, the brokerage giant should issue a short press release citing mere technical violations by a few low-level employees, then have no further comment.

The strategy that Hutton ultimately followed was to "let it all hang out," in the words of a former Hutton vice president. The Cahill Gordon strategy might have dampened the public's interest, but the tack Hutton took almost guaranteed that the story wouldn't go away.

The morning of May 17 was no exception. Hutton employees and shareholders woke to yet another story about the firm and the scandal, this time on page 1 of the *New York Times* business section. Two weeks after the guilty plea, Hutton was still front-page news.

That same day, at 10:00 A.M., Hutton's stockholders gathered in the auditorium of the Chase Manhattan Bank at One New York Plaza in lower Manhattan for their annual meeting. Bob Fomon knew he had some explaining to do, which was why he'd postponed the meeting. He needed time to think, he had told himself. Now he got down to business.

"The company and its senior management—myself included—assume responsibility for what occurred," Fomon began, reading from the text prepared for him by Orin Kramer, which later in the day would be released to the press. "We assume responsibility, because we stand accountable for activities undertaken in the firm's name and because the company is responsible for failing to have imposed what in retrospect were needed controls in internal cash [management] procedures."

Then Fomon sought to defuse what he thought could be an explosive issue—customer protection. The practices in question, he assured his audience, did not involve customer or client funds. What was more, he declared, Hutton's commitment to its customers and clients had in no way been breached. Rather, the injured parties were some of the approximately four hundred commercial banks where the company had maintained checking accounts from 1980 to 1982.

Fomon would turn out to be only half right. Documents that Hutton would later submit to Congress would prompt regulators to question whether the firm was playing fast and loose with some of the most important customer safeguards on the books. Although the documents would not prove conclusive—and some of Hutton's actions would be ruled legal—they suggest that Hutton thought customer protection stood in the way of sound cash management. For example, a March 7, 1980, Arthur Andersen & Co. memo made available to congressional investigators said that Hutton used customers' securities as collateral to cover uncollected funds at several banks.

In his speech, Fomon also gave a stirring defense of Hutton's wait-and-see attitude toward managers and executives who might be culpable. "Much has been debated about individual punishment," he said calmly. "Many, including some of our own employees, feel that even though the government has stated 'this was a corporate problem' and 'the employees involved did not think they were doing anything wrong,' that there must be a purge.

"I have wrestled with the personnel problem for two weeks now," he said coolly, while the stockholders and members of the press watched attentively. "If any of our clients had been injured, if we had breached any of our fiduciary responsibilities, if we had violated any securities laws, the decision would be easy. The people involved would be gone. But these things did not happen.

"If the motive behind these actions had been personal gain rather than mistakenly thinking they were acting in the firm's best interest, they would be gone. But that was not their motive. After three years of investigation, the Justice Department concluded that no individuals should be indicted because of the difficulty in proving 'criminal intent.' "

So, Fomon said, everyone should have an opportunity to be heard, and he promised that Hutton's own inquiry would be fair and objective. "I realize, by not acting hastily on this one question," he went on, "I run the risk of prolonging the debate, of keeping our name in the media, and of possibly doing further damage to our image. But to act and perhaps ruin people's careers and lives without a fair hearing is not the American way or my way."

And, on an issue of keen concern to shareholders—the bottom line—he reassured them that neither the $2 million fine Hutton paid nor the restitution program would adversely affect the company's present or future financial health.

"In developing a long-term response to this unpleasant episode," Fomon continued, "your company has had one central objective—to prove to the public, to our clients, to our employees, and to you, our shareholders, that the confidence that has been entrusted in us was not misplaced."

Then Fomon announced the Bell investigation. "I feel that taking this action is the only way to credibly deal with the situation," he said. "Any allegations of cover-up must be put to rest. E.F. Hutton's name must continue to be associated with the highest standards of corporate conduct."

The chairman ended his fifteen-minute speech on an upbeat note. "Painful as this experience has been," he let shareholders know, "I believe that you can continue to take pride in your company. To the extent that we have erred, we are acknowledging our failings, compensating those who might have suffered, and ensuring that such events will never be repeated.

"This has been a humbling and difficult experience—for me, for senior management, for the company, and its loyal employees. We have faced many challenges in the past, but nobody ever questioned our integrity. But we have learned from our experience, and our hope in the coming weeks is that we will demonstrate that we are stronger for it."

TUESDAY, MAY 21

32 5/8

The forces pushing against Bob Fomon were unbalanced. On one side were Hutton's brokers, so sure of themselves and of the firm's rightful place in the vanguard of Wall Street's retail sales organizations, urging Fomon to get on with business as usual. On the other side was the real power—the newspaper and television reporters and the state and federal regulators, all clamoring for answers.

So Fomon could not, as Hutton's sales force wished, put the scandal behind him. On May 21 Congressman Peter W. Rodino, Jr., Democrat from New Jersey and longtime chairman of the House Judiciary Committee, took aim at the big brokerage firm.

In a letter to Scott Pierce, the president of Hutton's retail sales arm, Rodino, who had led the drive to impeach Richard Nixon in 1974, invited Pierce to appear before his committee's Subcommittee on Crime. The subcommittee—headed by Congressman William J. Hughes, also a New Jersey Democrat—was initiating hearings on white-collar crime in America.

Hutton wasn't the only company to receive an invitation to testify. Rodino also wrote the Bank of Boston, which, at the time, was embroiled in a scandal of its own, an accusation that it was laundering money for organized crime. In fact, it was the Hutton story—coupled with allegations against the Bank of Boston—that had sparked the hearings in the first place.

At Hutton's headquarters, there was some uneasiness about the hearings. But it quickly dissipated—courtesy of Jay Moorhead. Moorhead phoned an old friend at the Bank of Boston. Did the bank plan to send anyone to testify? he asked. The bank did not.

Moorhead reported his conversation to Fomon, Pierce, and Orin Kramer, who shared the news with Tom Curnin and the other attorneys representing Hutton. The decision was made quickly. Hutton—like the Bank of Boston—would decline the invitation to testify.

MONDAY, MAY 27

Market Closed

Just weeks after Hutton pleaded guilty, it found itself in trouble with a different set of regulators.

In a separate case, North Carolina and Pennsylvania securities officials alleged that Hutton had sold units of Silver Screen II, a limited partnership created to finance feature-length motion pictures by Walt Disney Productions, without getting approval for the units in those states. Also, North Carolina officials charged that some Hutton brokers might have leaked nonpublic information about the units. And in Boston officials announced that they were investigating whether sales of Silver Screen II in Massachusetts were authorized.

In April, Cahill Gordon had assured the brokerage that Hutton had the green light to sell the limited partnership units in all fifty states. Cahill Gordon was in the wrong, and it accepted responsibility, blaming the error on mixed signals at the law firm. "This time," a Cahill Gordon attorney told a reporter for the *Wall Street Journal*, Hutton "is getting a bum rap."

Hutton customers had bought Silver Screen II units in minimum offerings of $5,000 and, in certain states, in denominations of $2,000 for IRAs. It was a popular investment: All $150 million worth of units were sold in a few weeks. If the investigations went against Hutton, the brokerage would be forced to return the amount that customers in those states had invested, plus interest.

TUESDAY, MAY 28

32 ¼

In his Manhattan office, Bob Fomon wrote a brief letter to Griffin Bell, outlining the terms of the former attorney general's employment and promising to direct Hutton employees to cooperate with the investigation. Meanwhile in Washington, Judiciary Committee Chairman Rodino and Crime Subcommittee Chairman Hughes were mulling over Hutton's decision not to accept their invitation to testify. They decided not to take no for an answer. Hughes wrote Scott Pierce again, this time informing him that the subject of the subcommittee's inquiry had been narrowed—to Hutton alone.

Also, this letter—forwarded by fax machine—contained a threat. If Hutton didn't respond by noon that day, the subcommittee would issue a subpoena. The letter didn't arrive until 1:00 P.M.

Jay Moorhead wasted no time calling Patton, Boggs & Blow, Hutton's Washington lobbyists. They, in turn, called Hughes to let him know that Fomon would appear before the subcommittee.

Unfortunately, Hughes's staff had already issued a press release that accused Hutton of refusing to cooperate with the subcommittee and announcing that a subpoena had been issued. The newspapers played up the story the next morning.

By this time E.F. Hutton was no longer either prosperous or harmonious. With executives suspicious of one another, all semblance of camaraderie had disappeared. The firm was losing brokers, and it was losing business, although it never admitted either loss publicly.

In time, a few of the senior executives at Hutton took aim at Fomon, lobbying with the board for his ouster. Only Pierce mustered the nerve to speak to Fomon face-to-face. Pierce had always had doubts about the way Hutton was handling the check scandal, and on several occasions he made his reservations known to Fomon. But in this one conversation, he called on Fomon to resign.

"It would take a lot of pressure off us from the regulators and the media," Pierce argued, "if you would fall on the sword." Fomon, says Pierce, brushed him aside and said he thought he would stay to see the thing through. Pierce didn't push the matter, even though he remained convinced that Fomon's ability to govern Hutton was deteriorating steadily. Fomon claims not to recall the conversation.

"A normal firm," says Kendrick R. Wilson III, a managing director at Salomon Brothers who would later join Hutton as head of corporate finance, "would have fired the chairman. Not Hutton."

The answer to his problems, Fomon thought, was to bring fresh blood into the firm. What he was looking for was a strong new number-two man, not a successor. "I wasn't looking ahead far enough to be looking for a successor," he says now. (Rumors later flew that the board had directed Fomon to bring in someone new. But Fomon vigorously denies it. "I never had a single conversation with a single board member or with the board as a group [on this subject]," he maintains.)

The man Fomon found was Robert P. Rittereiser, the knowledgeable and impatient chief administrative officer of Merrill Lynch & Co., the nation's largest securities firm. Rittereiser,

Fomon thought, was the quintessential self-made man. He had joined Merrill Lynch in 1958, the year before he and his wife married, and he had been there ever since, rising from the humble post of margin clerk. Fomon liked Rittereiser immediately.

At the time Rittereiser, forty-six years old, was one of three executives in line to succeed William A. Schreyer as president of Merrill Lynch. (The others were Daniel Tully, head of Merrill Lynch's retail activities, and Jerome Kenney, head of the firm's capital markets division. Tully ultimately got the job.)

In one of their first conversations, Rittereiser told Fomon that he was—for all practical purposes—second in command at the rival brokerage. And he backed up this assertion with an anecdote about Schreyer's recent hospital stay. To hear Rittereiser tell it, Schreyer had turned to Rittereiser before he underwent heart surgery and said, "You're responsible for the firm while I'm gone."

Later, Fomon says he learned that if Schreyer had put Rittereiser in charge, Schreyer had told no one else at Merrill Lynch. "I bought the whole story," Fomon remembers. "Here was a guy who had been given all this responsibility at Merrill Lynch, so I thought that he must have some talent."

(Before Schreyer went into the hospital, Rittereiser counters, he gave Rittereiser a letter that stated clearly that he was in charge. However, Rittereiser adds, Schreyer told him not to show the letter to anyone. "In other words," says Rittereiser, "Schreyer was telling me, 'You protect my interests, but I'm not going to be brave enough to tell people that you're in charge.' He didn't want to create political problems for himself. It was one of the things that led me to lose my respect for [Merrill Lynch].")

Rittereiser also boasted to Fomon that he had single-handedly executed Merrill Lynch's acquisition of A. G. Becker, an old-line Wall Street firm with retail and investment-banking operations. "To listen to his oral résumé," Fomon says, "Rittereiser had everything."

In one conversation after another, Fomon says, Rittereiser told him, "all I want to do is help you." Rittereiser, Fomon counters, never once asked Fomon to specify salary. "But," Fomon adds, "I did tell him it wouldn't be a step backward for him." (Indeed it wasn't. Rittereiser signed on for $1 million a year, about 30 percent more than he was making at Merrill.)

Nor did Rittereiser ask what his title would be, although Fomon named him chief operating officer of the E.F. Hutton Group. All Rittereiser cared about, Fomon decided, was saving Hutton. "Here was a guy who had complete faith in me. He didn't talk about money. He didn't talk about title, about position, which are the first things most people talk about. That impressed me."

Rittereiser argues that he discussed both compensation and title with the Hutton chairman before he signed on. Fomon, he says, outlined a minimum salary of $1 million a year, plus bonuses for performance. And Fomon further told the Merrill Lynch executive that he would come on board as president of the parent group. Fomon's feeling, says Rittereiser, "was that the title alone would ease my entry into Hutton in terms of the acceptance of the company."

In any case, Fomon offered Rittereiser the job, and Rittereiser accepted. "I feel I am ready to lead my own firm," he told friends at the time. "It was the right time to move on." Rittereiser was the first outsider in recent memory to be recruited for a top spot at Hutton.

Fomon spoke to no one at Hutton about his decision. "If I had," he says, "they would have been opposed to bringing him in, because he was an outsider. You know, everyone thinks that lightning might strike them, that they might get the job."

Nor did he speak to anyone at Merrill Lynch. "On the Street," Fomon says, "you don't do that sort of thing." A year or so later, at a party, Fomon would complain to William Schreyer about Rittereiser. "Well," Schreyer would respond, "you hired the guy."

The decision to hire Rittereiser was not something that Fomon now likes to recall. He labels it "the biggest mistake" of his career.

Fomon was right about one thing. Rittereiser was indeed self-made, influenced by a mother and a father whose dissimilarities extended far beyond their different ethnic backgrounds—his German, hers Irish.

Rittereiser grew up on East Eighty-fourth Street, in the German Yorkville section of Manhattan. "My father," he says, "was a guy who was right out of Damon Runyon. He was the youngest of thirteen children and grew up in New York City." When his own children came along, Rittereiser's dad worked several jobs—including driving a truck and managing small parking lots—to support the family.

But he was no Puritan. "My father," Rittereiser says, "was the kind of guy who could come home on a Friday and quite possibly have gambled some of his salary away. It was his imagination, risk-taking, and survival skills that helped prepare me for business. My mother went to work when she was fourteen years old, dropped out of school to work for the New York Telephone Company. She believed in doing everything straight, right, and no cutting corners. This lady was a leadership training school from the time we were little.

"She taught us to be self-reliant in every way. . . . She was constantly telling us to reach high, have high standards. We should always think beyond Eighty-fourth Street, was the way she put it."

Mrs. Rittereiser died of cancer at age fifty-two, but in the months between her diagnosis and her death, says her son, she took the high-school equivalency test and received her diploma. "That was the kind of determination and standards," says Rittereiser, "you can't help but have rub off on you."

MONDAY, JUNE 17

33 ¼

Bob Fomon had thought that pleading guilty to 2,000 counts of mail and wire fraud would allow Hutton to get back to business as usual. Now he realized that he was wrong. Orin Kramer, the public relations adviser, was insisting that someone would have to be sacrificed on the altar of public opinion. But who? Sitting behind his elegant antique Regency desk in his corner office, Fomon scribbled the names of potential sacrificial lambs on a yellow legal pad. Again, as in May, Fomon zeroed in on Tom Morley, the man responsible for Hutton's cash management operations. After all, Morley wasn't part of Fomon's inner circle. In fact, until the check scandal had broken, Fomon hardly knew the man.

"You can't fire Morley," Norman Epstein, Hutton's chief of operations, protested. "He didn't do anything wrong, and he's got seven kids." Fomon backed off, but Kramer kept up the pressure. Fire someone, he urged. It was all getting to be too much for the already agitated chairman.

"I'll fire anybody you want me to fire," Fomon snapped at Kramer one day. "Just tell me who. I can't figure out who did it, and that's the truth." Kramer, the seasoned politico, only shook his head. "I knew Fomon was telling the truth," he recalls, but he also knew the momentum of the scandal had to be stopped.

That evening, Fomon had dinner with Sanford I. Weill, who, having resigned as president of American Express, was casting about for something else to do. Fomon says his only intention was to pick Weill's brain. That wasn't, apparently, what Weill thought.

"We hadn't seen each other for a while," Fomon remembers, "and I thought we should catch up. Sandy didn't come out and say it, but it was obvious what he thought the purpose of the dinner was. He thought I was sizing him up for CEO. I wasn't. I thought it would have been disloyal to Rittereiser to bring Sandy in."

WEDNESDAY, JUNE 19

33 ½

At the corner of Independence Avenue and First Street, S.E., in Washington, D.C., stands the Sam Rayburn House Office Building. Built in 1965, it is resplendent in oversized columns, pediments, cornucopias, and other marble ostentations. In Room 2237, at 10:10 A.M. on June 19, the Honorable William J. Hughes gaveled the ten-member House Judiciary Committee Subcommittee on Crime to order.

The hearings that were about to begin would prove enormously damaging to Hutton, not so much because of what they uncovered—Steve Trott, for one, would characterize them as a "cockamamie witch hunt"—but because of the widespread negative publicity they generated. Newspapers nationwide, as well as the television newscasts, covered the testimony daily. And each day's events were broadcast live to an incredulous middle America via the Cable News Network.

The Hutton story, it seemed, would never be relegated to a media back burner—Fomon's fondest wish. That first day of hearings saw an ashen-faced Bob Fomon seated at the witness table. Next to him were Hutton Vice Chairman Tom Lynch and two of the firm's vice presidents, Tom Morley and Mike Castellano. Only Lynch looked calm. Although the subcommittee had set out to explore white-collar crime in America, the inquiry had turned into a pointed investigation of E.F. Hutton alone.

The subcommittee's ranking Republican, Bill McCollum, was the first to draw blood. McCollum, a straight-arrow conservative, had come to Congress from Florida's fifth congressional district in 1980, when he defeated the not-too-bright incumbent, Richard Kelly, who had been videotaped stuffing Abscam money into his pockets.

"I would like to inquire," McCollum began formally, "as to the role in the corporation that each of the individuals here today plays." McCollum was trying to determine who at the top of Hutton was responsible for overseeing the firm's cash management operations. It was a question, he knew, that Justice Department prosecutors had been unable to answer after three years of investigating the firm.

Fomon attempted to provide the answer. During the period under review, Fomon said matter-of-factly, Lynch was chief financial officer, Castellano was comptroller, and Morley was in charge of money mobilization. As comptroller, Fomon explained, Castellano was responsible for the company accounts. But he wasn't charged with observing what went on in the money mobilization area. Neither was Lynch, as chief financial officer, responsible for overseeing the cash management or money mobilization areas.

Cash management was part of Hutton's operations department, headed by Norman Epstein. But since the guilty plea, Fomon said, he had moved money mobilization and cash management into a different department under different management.

McCollum was far from satisfied with Fomon's explanation. "Let me ask you," the congressman went on, "if you have a board of directors. Do you have a holding company? Can you give us some idea of the overall umbrella of E.F. Hutton?"

"We have a holding company," Fomon said. The E.F. Hutton Group, he explained, was the holding company that owned E.F. Hutton & Co., the firm's retail sales arm. It was E.F. Hutton & Co. that had pleaded guilty to the 2,000 counts of mail and wire fraud.

"Now, Mr. Lynch," McCollum said, shifting his gaze, "today you are the president of the holding company, and you were the chief financial officer of the subsidiary before—"

"Well, this is rather complicated," Fomon began, then thought better of interrupting.

Lynch quickly reviewed his role in the company. He had become vice chairman of the board of the holding company earlier that month. He had previously been president of the holding company from December 15, 1983. And during the period in question, he had been executive vice president.

"Of the holding company?" the congressman asked.

"Of the holding company and of the broker-dealer," Lynch responded.

"And you were chief financial officer in that capacity?"

"Yes."

"Now," McCollum asked calmly, turning to Fomon again, "the brokerage subsidiary is the one that the public most readily identifies as E.F. Hutton?"

Fomon nodded.

"And it is this company that all of the testimony will be about?"

Fomon nodded again.

"In terms of the two individuals in the middle level of management we keep hearing about who were pinpointed as being primarily responsible for all of this, where did they fit into the subsidiary? What level of management are we talking about relative to the four of you gentlemen?"

"I am glad you asked me that," Fomon declared, "because I don't know who they are."

"Okay," the congressman said, his tone becoming dry, "if you don't know who they are, you don't know where they fit in."

"That is correct," Hutton's chairman responded.

"But it is your understanding that they were somewhere down the road?"

"I don't know who they are," Fomon reiterated. "I have no idea whom Justice is talking about when they talk about two middle-level individuals."

McCollum paused, then asked, "When did the activities of this nature come to your attention at your level of management? When did all of this first get to your desk, Mr. Fomon?"

"In February 1982," responded Fomon.

"And how did it get to you? Who brought it to your attention?"

"Our general counsel came to my office accompanied by outside counsel and told me that we had a problem with our banking activities, and I said do whatever is necessary to cure it. It was about the time of the Genesee Country Bank problem in Batavia, New York."

Fomon was only half right. On February 10, 1982, the New York State Banking Commission had summoned Hutton to appear at its offices. Three Hutton executives—Senior Vice President and Deputy General Counsel Loren Schechter and Senior Vice Presidents Tom Morley and Bob Ross—had been dispatched to the meeting, after which Schechter had broken the news to Tom Lynch. Then the two men had informed Fomon of the investigation.

Soon afterward, Fomon had decided to initiate an in-house probe and call for a temporary halt to Hutton's aggressive cash management practices. He had also hired Arthur Young & Co.'s cash management specialists to help straighten out the mess. But Fomon provided McCollum with none of these details. He felt no need to.

"Did you have a board meeting to discuss the check scandal?" McCollum wanted to know.

"No, I did not," Fomon responded.

The next questioner was Democrat Edward F. Feighan, who had been sent to Congress in 1982 by the voters of Ohio's nineteenth congressional district, which is reputed to have the largest concentration of bowling alleys in the country. Feighan, a former state legislator, county commissioner, and candidate for mayor of Cleveland in 1977, usually voted along liberal lines and had little patience for what he perceived as the shenanigans of corporate America.

Feighan tried again to have Fomon describe Hutton's organizational structure. "One of the problems that we face in identifying how the problems developed at Hutton and why they were not— at least in the judgment of some people—addressed on a more timely basis," he said, "is not having a full understanding of the organizational structure of your company. . . . As part of our subpoena," he continued, "we had asked for an organizational chart. It is my understanding that was not submitted. Am I to understand that one does not exist?"

Fomon was flustered. "I am sorry it was not submitted, because I have given several to Griffin Bell, and if I would give them to him, there is certainly no reason why I wouldn't give them to you."

"So we can anticipate receiving—"

"Absolutely," Fomon interjected.

Hutton's organizational chart—or lack of one—would become a major issue in the hearings. It took weeks for the subcommittee to get its hands on a chart. And even then, it would be one prepared on June 21—two days after Fomon promised to deliver a copy of the chart that had been, ostensibly, provided to Bell.

The fact was, Hutton had never had an organizational chart until it was forced to produce one for Bell. Its lack of that traditional management tool speaks volumes about the way the firm was run. More than eighty years after its founding and with 17,000 employees, Hutton still operated as if it were an entrepreneurial enterprise.

"Let me just ask," continued Feighan, "who are the individuals that you would identify in the corporate center offices having direct responsibility for cash management?"

"Well," Fomon waffled, "cash management is a very broad term, and Mr. Morley is in charge of cash management."

"Am I to assume," Feighan said, his tone becoming stern, "that beyond Mr. Morley there is no one that you would identify in the corporate center offices who has direct responsibility for cash management?"

"I think that's one of the things that caused all of our problems," Fomon began. "We did not have anybody specifically accountable for the cash concentration system.

"Tom Morley taught the approved cash concentration system. He taught it to regional officers. He taught it to branch officers. They violated those practices.

"Now, if you would ask me why they violated them, there could be a number of reasons. These occurrences took place in a very-high-interest-rate environment."

"Every corporation in America," Feighan interjected, "was looking for ways to increase interest profit and reduce interest cost. Some of your personnel became too aggressive, and you are familiar with the results." The congressman stopped there.

Again, Hughes pressed Fomon on the issue of the organizational chart, and, again, Fomon promised to make a copy available to the subcommittee as soon as possible.

THURSDAY, JUNE 20

33 3/8

The House subcommittee released to the press a November 1981 memo addressed to George Ball, then president of the E.F. Hutton Group, and three of his top aides. Obtained through a subpoena, the eleven-page memo, written by Linda Curtiss, an assistant vice president in Hutton's treasury department, had been circulated to senior marketing and financial officers and suggested that Ball not only knew about the overdrafts, but encouraged them.

"The rapidly changing nature of our business," Curtiss wrote, "demands that our managers have the right tools with which to evaluate opportunities and to plan for the future. Interest profits contributed over 70 percent of the net profit for the retail firm in 1981. Therefore, understanding and managing the components of interest profitability is essential to the profitability of the firm."

At Hutton's headquarters, after the memo leaked, Orin Kramer turned to Bob Fomon. Did Fomon think Ball knew what his branch managers were up to?

"Are you kidding? Of course he knew," a grinning Fomon insisted. "Look at the way he ran the place. He would have known, and he would have loved it."

Whatever Ball's culpability, Steve Trott, in any case, didn't think the Justice Department had enough rope with which to hang him. "We work by evidence and proof in the Justice Department," says Trott, "not on the basis of surmise. We could never prove that Ball was guilty."

Early on July 1 Bob Rittereiser took the elevator to the twelfth floor of One Battery Park Plaza. He pulled on the handle of the glass door that led to the executive offices. It didn't budge; it was locked tight. Rittereiser glanced at his watch.

Odd, he thought, 7:30 A.M. and Hutton's executive offices were empty. By this time, Merrill Lynch's senior management would have been hard at work. Senior executives at Hutton, Rittereiser soon learned, took their cue from Bob Fomon. Since the chairman didn't report for work before 9:30 A.M., neither did they.

Rittereiser's office was across from Fomon's, and it was decorated to Fomon's taste—with elegant wing chairs and paintings of English hunting scenes. The office's previous tenants had been powerful men in the firm. George Ball had worked there when he was president of Hutton. So had Tom Lynch.

Thus, it was not unreasonable for people to assume—as they did—that Rittereiser was next in line to Fomon and would, in fact, succeed him. Still, Rittereiser had no plans to redecorate and make the office his own, at least not yet. "It's not the way to go," he told himself, "not now, not under these conditions."

When word went out that Fomon had named Rittereiser president of the E.F. Hutton group, the firm's stock jumped $1.50 a share to $33.25. Merrill Lynch's stock price, on the other hand, dropped 12.5 cents a share to $31.875. This ostensible vote of confidence by the financial markets delighted Fomon, who retained the titles of chairman and chief executive officer.

But if investors saw Rittereiser as the man to cleanse Hutton of the check scandal's taint, reaction to the news inside the firm was mixed. In the minds of some senior Hutton executives, Rittereiser was nothing more than an administrator, a paper shuffler.

To Pierce, Rittereiser's appointment spelled the end of his own ambitions to succeed Fomon. Nonetheless, he welcomed the new man to the team. Indeed, he claims to have been happy to have him on board. Fomon, Pierce says, was growing increasingly arbitrary. "I needed someone to help me control him. Also, we had to have somebody with credibility. I knew that Bob [Rittereiser] didn't know anything about cash management, but the public didn't know that."

Rittereiser's mandate was to polish Hutton's reputation and reshape operations. Specifically, in his new post, Rittereiser was responsible for strategic planning, finance, human resources, and data resources policy. In the role of strategic planner, the new Hutton executive was in charge of assessing where the company was and where it was going. "I was," he says, "de facto chief operating officer."

Under the reorganization plan Fomon had crafted in the wake of the check scandal, Rittereiser became part of a new office of the chairman. That group included—in addition to Fomon—Tom Lynch, whom Rittereiser succeeded as president of the holding company, and Pierce, president of E.F. Hutton & Co., the firm's brokerage subsidiary.

Hutton insiders speculated that Lynch, who was kicked upstairs by being named vice chairman of the parent firm, was taking the fall for the check scandal. In reality, Lynch had volunteered to give up the title of president of the holding company to make way for Rittereiser.

Fomon announced the new organizational plan with appropriate fanfare. Hutton's "recent experience, painful as it has been," he said in a press release, "has also given us a mandate to consider far-reaching changes in our entire top management approach." The office of the chairman, he went on to explain, simply institutionalized what Hutton had been trying to achieve informally all along. It would function as a core management group, responsible for all key strategic and operating decisions.

In another move designed to shore up Hutton's reputation, Fomon announced that Paul Hines, who had been executive vice president for planning, control, and executive development, would assume authority for all of Hutton's treasury functions, as well as continuing in his position as chairman of the Hutton Insurance Group.

From now on, Fomon said, all treasury functions would be subject to periodic review by the audit committee of the Hutton Group's board. In making the change, Fomon acknowledged that "in part, our recent problems were symptomatic of a structural weakness," the fact that cash concentration and control functions were not integrated. "This reorganization will remedy that weakness," Fomon said.

What Fomon didn't say—and what insiders at Hutton knew—was that the audit committee was something of a joke, meeting only once or twice a year, as Griffin Bell would discover in his investigation. Nor would the appointment of Hines do much to mend the cracks in Hutton's foundation.

Fomon also announced that Richard S. Locke, executive vice president in charge of the public finance division, would take charge of the corporate finance division, which had been under the direction of Jim Lopp. The move resulted in the merger of the two departments into a single new investment banking group. Fomon saw "synergies between these related disciplines," and generally had kind things to say about Lopp, who was leaving, Fomon said, to become the chief executive of a new venture, which would be announced shortly. (Lopp, a longtime Fomon crony, remained on the board, where he continued to do Fomon's bidding.)

Finally, Fomon announced that William Dunn would be promoted to division head in charge of fixed-income trading and sales. Although Fomon had high hopes for him, the tough-talking Dunn would prove a disaster to Hutton's bottom line. In one month alone in 1986, the fixed-income trading department, under his leadership, would rack up a loss of $60 million. Fomon says he continually warned Dunn to be more cautious, but the new chief ignored the chairman's admonitions. He persisted in trading as he saw fit, and fixed-income trading continued to absorb enormous losses.

FRIDAY, JULY 12

31 ³⁄₈

Early July 12, Rittereiser—on his way to Newark Airport for a flight to a National Association of Securities Dealers meeting in Washington, D.C.—unfolded his *Wall Street Journal.* The headline on the front page read:

BATTERED BROKER: E.F. HUTTON

APPEARS HEADED FOR LONG SIEGE IN BANK-DRAFT SCHEME

WITH JUSTICE AGENCY POISED TO

REOPEN INVESTIGATION, MANAGEMENT MAY SUFFER

IS CHIEF'S CREDIBILITY INJURED?

"Turn around," Rittereiser told his driver, "and take me back to the city." At Hutton's headquarters, Rittereiser waited—his trip now canceled—for Fomon to arrive.

"I know you told me to stay out of the F Matter," Rittereiser said, "but I'm not staying out of it. It's out of control."

One reason the *Journal* article took so negative a tone, Rittereiser believes, is that Fomon had refused to talk to the reporter.

MONDAY, JULY 15

32

On Saturday, more than sixty of Hutton's most productive brokers and branch managers—twenty-five of them alone generated about $50 million in annual revenues for the company—had gathered in New York from around the country for a meeting of the Directors' Advisory Council, a group made up of Hutton's biggest producers. Members would first confer among themselves at the Parker Meridien Hotel on West Fifty-seventh Street. Then they were slated to meet with Fomon, Rittereiser, and Bob Witt. Witt and Fomon had asked Rittereiser to come to the meeting as observer. The new Hutton executive, however, was totally unprepared for the events that unfolded.

It wasn't an ordinary meeting. The leaders of the group had decided that Fomon and Witt, the national head of the retail sales force, had to go. Rittereiser knew nothing of this agenda when he arrived for a 5:00 P.M. meeting with the retail superstars. As he looked around the room, he sensed a brawl was developing. "It had the appearance," he says, "of a kangaroo court."

Wary, he took his place on the dais with Fomon and Witt. Fomon was giving a progress report on the check scandal when several brokers stood up and demanded that heads roll.

"It would hurt us," Fomon said, "to fire one person this week, and another person the next week, although the press would love it."

"But how," one broker demanded, "are you going to stop the publicity, the congressional subcommittee? We have to stop the publicity now."

"You have to understand," Fomon began, "that to the congressmen, this is show biz, a road to stardom. I don't know what to do about stopping it."

Another broker painted a doomsday scenario. He worried, he said, that the states, by pulling the firm's licenses to operate, would force Hutton to close its doors altogether. Already Connecticut's attorney general had taken on Hutton, using the scandal as a stepping-stone to the governor's mansion.

Fomon, as well as the brokers, knew a distinct possibility existed that Hutton could lose its license in Connecticut. "This is not going to be across the board," Fomon stated defiantly. "We will not be shut down."

Then one broker rose and began a speech that Rittereiser believes was leading to a demand for the resignations of Fomon and Witt.

The speaker had just said "And therefore, we—" when Fomon interrupted him. "I know what you're going to say. You're going to say that I should fire Bob Witt, and you're wrong."

What the brokers were going to ask for was both heads—Witt's and Fomon's. But Fomon's impassioned defense of Witt disarmed them. They never got to their demands.

It appeared to his audience that Fomon had begun to pace the floor, as he always did. But instead of spinning about, he kept right on going, out the door and into the street. The brokers didn't know it, but Fomon was on his way to meet with Warren Christopher, a Washington insider best known for his efforts to free the American hostages from Iran. He wanted to hire Christopher to help put the pieces back together.

When it became apparent that Fomon was not coming back, the group erupted. "It reached a new level of violence and profanity," Rittereiser says.

For the next fifty minutes Rittereiser took questions and got, in return, a primer on the depth of the management deficiencies at Hutton. To alleviate the brokers' concerns, he suggested that the council elect representatives to meet with him the next day as part of a new communications task force. "I got them to caucus right then," Rittereiser claims, and by channeling their anger into a task force, he blunted the drive to oust Fomon. "The fact was, these people felt they were being treated with absolute disrespect. All they wanted," says Rittereiser, "was to know more about the business and to feel that management was in command."

"I don't know if Rittereiser realized at that time that he had to get Fomon out," says one former senior executive. "But it was at that meeting that he knew he had to get somebody out, whether it was Witt or Pierce—but somebody." Rittereiser, in fact, wasn't thinking about ousting anyone in particular. He just knew, he says, "that some changes had to be made."

Eventually, Rittereiser would get them all—but not soon

enough, critics would claim. "Some people," Rittereiser says, "believe that meeting was my downfall. They say that I should have let them run amuck and chase Fomon and everyone else out of there."

Bob Fomon paced back and forth across the Pirelli rubber floor of his elegant office. Here he was trying to be helpful to the congressmen who were investigating Hutton, and all he was getting was grief. What was worse, on July 19 he would be back before them.

"This time," Fomon announced defiantly, "if they give me a hard time, I'll say, 'Listen, I don't have to be here. Either you guys show me some respect or I'm leaving.' "

Orin Kramer, the damage-control expert, and Jay Moorhead, Fomon's executive assistant, were seated around Fomon's Kortan steel coffee table. They glanced sideways at each other.

"Bob," Kramer said in a tone that became increasingly animated, "think of it as method acting. Think about those congressmen sitting up there thinking that they're more important than you. That's how you've got to think about it. That's how you've got to behave—as if those congressmen are more important than you."

Fomon got the point. "Jay," he said, turning to Moorhead, "is that really true? A congressman, more important than me?"

Moorhead nodded, and Fomon groaned in disbelief.

Nonetheless, before his next appearance in Washington, Fomon managed to swallow some of his pride.

At 10:00 A.M. on July 19 the House Subcommittee on Crime reconvened, this time in Room 2141 of the Rayburn Building—the same room where, in 1974, the House Judiciary Committee had met to consider impeachment proceedings against President Richard Nixon.

At the front of the hearing room sat Fomon, fidgeting. At his side was Warren Minor Christopher, the man who, in the 1970s, had turned down the job of Watergate special prosecutor, saying he hadn't been promised enough freedom. Fomon—at the urging of his aides—had turned to Christopher for help after Hutton's disastrous first appearance before the subcommittee.

A host of Washington insiders had offered Fomon their services. Among them was former Vice President Walter Mondale, in private practice since his 1984 defeat by Ronald Reagan. But Fomon had opted for Christopher, a discreet, hardworking, skilled negotiator who slipped easily through the Capitol's halls of power. Fomon was counting on him to extricate Hutton from the mire into which it was sinking.

As it turned out, Hutton was already in too deep for anyone, even one of Christopher's stature, to help. Christopher had advised Fomon to cooperate fully with the committee, simply to tell the truth and give the congressmen what they wanted.

Up to now, Fomon—oblivious to the lessons of the past— had treated the committee members just as Tom Curnin had treated the officials from the Justice Department. That is, he had stonewalled. Justice, however, just didn't "go away," as Curnin had hoped, and the congressional subcommittee wasn't likely to, either.

Now, Fomon would try another tack.

"When I appeared on June nineteenth," Fomon began, reading from a statement drafted for him by Kramer, "I pledged on behalf of E.F. Hutton to cooperate fully with your investigation. I am here today to say that we have kept that pledge."

He assured the subcommittee members that all the documents they had requested would be available by the end of the day. And he reminded them that he had made available to their staff investigators all fifteen of the Hutton employees with whom they had asked to speak. "Our employees made every possible effort to respond to the committee's investigation," Fomon said, "and I pledge that we will continue to work with your committee and your staff."

He went on to say, "We come before this committee as a company that has paid a heavy price for our past behavior. We were prosecuted in accordance with the law and have suffered a painful and lengthy public penalty. That, in turn, makes us a company with two abiding missions.

"One is to learn how this could have happened in the first place, and who was responsible." He then mentioned the ongoing independent investigation by Judge Bell, which, although he didn't know it at the time, would turn out to be more of a problem than a solution.

"But," he continued, "we also must not and will not neglect our second mission, which is to get on with the job of serving our customers, our shareholders, and the public."

Hughes, apparently unmoved by Fomon's eloquence, wasted no time getting back to the topic raised in the first hearing— Hutton's organizational structure. He acknowledged that the subcommittee had finally received the organizational chart it had requested, but he thought that chart might be somewhat different from the one produced for Griffin Bell. And he wanted Fomon to say definitively whether the two charts were the same.

This time, Fomon decided to be frank. Maybe they weren't, he conceded, and explained that both charts were reconstructions, because no official chart had actually existed during the time the cash management problem had surfaced.

Hughes then recognized Congressman Bruce A. Morrison from Connecticut's third district, home to Yale University. A liberal Democrat, Morrison is best known today as the man who argued that George Bush should be impeached for his role in the Iran-contra affair.

Morrison reminded Fomon that at the first hearing Hutton's chairman had admitted that the firm's banking activities were known to employees "way down the chain" but were not controlled, understood, or monitored by Hutton's senior executives.

But since that last hearing, he said accusingly, Hutton executives had been quoted extensively in the *Wall Street Journal* and the *New York Times* telling quite a different story. He then read from the *Times,* quoting Fomon as saying that "the Justice Department's description that only two middle-level management employees were involved seems incredible to me. I cannot believe the whole thing was orchestrated by such a few middle-level managers."

So, Morrison wanted to know, what had happened since the first hearing to give rise to this different interpretation?

"Well," Fomon responded, "from the beginning, I never believed that two forty-thousand-dollar-a-year employees—which is the way the Justice Department characterized them—could have devised such a scheme." But the media, he complained, seemed to have leaped to the conclusion that if it hadn't been two $40,000-a-year employees, it had to have been top management. "You must understand," he told the subcommittee, "that there is a huge range of employees between top management and two forty-thousand-dollar people."

The ball was back in Morrison's court.

In the *Times,* the congressman pointed out, Fomon had said that if he had it to do all over again, the company would not take full responsibility. Fomon, the newspaper reported, claimed that he would have pleaded guilty on behalf of Hutton while allowing the individuals involved to stand trial. Why did he now hold that view, Morrison wanted to know.

Fomon again tried to explain his position. He had expected, he said, that by entering the guilty plea, he could avoid dragging the matter out. But had he known then that the scandal would go on, "that the case would become a major public issue, [and] that it would continue to divert us from our business . . . perhaps I would have preferred going through [a] trial and let[ting] those individuals who the Justice Department chose to indict stand on their own."

Morrison reworded and repeated his question, and Fomon reiterated his answer.

The day began damp and drizzly, but by 9:30, when Congressman Hughes gaveled the Subcommittee on Crime to order, the skies had cleared.

Hughes's face showed nothing of what he was thinking. Before him sat Perry L. Bacon, a Hutton first vice president, branch manager of the firm's Alexandria, Virginia, and Washington, D.C., offices, and author of the smoking-gun memo.

Seated at the witness table with him were his attorneys, John J. Tigue, Jr., and Gerald Hibey. A white-faced Bacon began by reading a prepared statement.

"Between the latter part of 1981 and early 1982, [my] branches utilized a procedure for increasing profits on the interest derived from our bank accounts.

"I understood Hutton's system for the utilization of funds was a mechanism that competed with the banks' practice of withholding availability of checks in order to have free use of those funds for a period of time. These money mobilization principles were set forth and explained to me in various conversations, memoranda, and meetings."

Bacon, of course, was trying to underscore the fact that Hutton's cash management practices were just that—company-approved practices taught by the firm itself. They weren't something he had made up.

"Further," Bacon said, "I was encouraged orally and in writing by my regional supervisor to be aggressive in applying these money mobilization principles." Again, Bacon was trying to shift the blame from himself to others in the firm.

"I always understood that any negative balance that might have been caused by our drawdown practices would be covered by the company, and, therefore, I believed that our drawdowns were a logical implementation of the Hutton system as it was taught to me by our money mobilizers."

Bacon was referring to Tom Morley and Bill Sullivan, the two men who, at different times, had headed up Hutton's cash management operations.

"For these reasons," Bacon said, not looking at Hughes, "it never occurred to me that what we were doing was wrong by any standard, to say nothing of the criminal law."

Next, he turned to the question of the memo. "I wish to comment on a document, which I authorized, which has been the subject of media attention and comment. In April 1982, I wrote a memorandum out of anger, in response to what I considered an unwarranted attack on me by my associate. In that memorandum, I pointed out that drawing down was part of a system the banks knew well and participated in themselves and cited, as an example, public reports of banks holding checks for a period of time before honoring them, and thereby enjoying the use of the funds interest free.

"On the other hand, I specifically stated in the memorandum my belief that 'our objective is not to steal money from the banks.'

"In order to understand my intent in writing about the system," Bacon said, his tone becoming more animated, "and my endorsement of a method that gave Hutton, rather than the banks, the benefit of the float, one must consider that statement of the objective.

"The entire context of this memorandum reflects my personal feelings at the time, which, in turn, influenced my less than precise verbiage on issues of overriding importance. It was never my intent, and I so expressed it, to cheat the banks. . . .

"In conclusion, it is an understatement that I am chastened by this affair. The embarrassment my colleagues and I have experienced is great." Bacon then thanked the committee.

Bacon had done just what the congressional committee had hoped. The legislators wanted the branch manager to pass the buck up the chain of command, and he had obliged. But Bacon wasn't as innocent as he painted himself. The worst offender in the check-writing scheme, his Alexandria office had raked in an astounding 300 percent more in interest profits than in profits from selling stocks and bonds.

Hughes now wasted no time getting to the point. He referred to Hutton's policy, to which George Ball had previously testified, of paying branch managers 10 percent of the interest profits their offices generated. He asked if Bacon was also compensated in that way. Bacon conceded that he was.

Then Hughes reviewed and characterized much of the testimony taken earlier. Hutton's upper and middle management, Hughes said, had suggested that it was branch managers like Bacon who had devised certain parts of the cash management scheme. They say, Hughes said in a tone of rising indignation, "that you were off the reservation; that this was not company policy; that, in fact, you were responsible for the aggressive overdrafting practices. What do you have to say to that?"

Bacon's face flushed. "I don't believe that characterization of the branch manager's role in this affair is an accurate or fair one," he said simply.

"Tell us," Hughes demanded, "who specifically told you to engage in aggressive overdrafting?" The hearing was running late, but Hughes was keeping the pot boiling.

"No one did."

"Well, then, whose idea was it?"

"I identified in my statement that I believed that our particular drawdown practices in our branch were the logical extension of the system we were taught."

"By whom?" the congressman demanded again.

"By a combination of conversations and memoranda and branch managers' meetings. We had a branch managers' meeting in New York in the middle of June 1981."

Hughes shifted his focus. "You knew that the more interest profit you generated, the more salary you would draw?"

"Yes."

"So you knew that if you had a successful money-market policy in place that you would generate more remuneration for your services?" Hughes asked with calculated toughness.

"That is correct."

"How did you decide how much to draw down on a given day?"

"Beginning in the middle of 1981," Bacon replied, "we were encouraged to become aggressive with our cash management practices. Beginning in the middle of 1981, we developed our own formula that enhanced the firm's basic drawdown system."

Hughes kept pressing. "Who determined that particular formula?"

"I did," Bacon conceded.

"What was the formula?"

"The formula was a system whereby we would begin to over-draft by small amounts and increase those drawdowns. If a bank objected and felt they were not getting proper use of the funds, we would stop doing it," Bacon said, not realizing he'd waded into dangerous waters. "In fact, in the most notable instance, that of Alexandria, as our drawdowns increased, the bank would call me up and thank me for the increased deposits."

"Of course," Hughes interjected bluntly, "they didn't realize what was happening, did they?"

"They were fully aware of where the deposits were coming from."

"You think," the congressman asked tartly, "that the banks were fully aware?"

"Yes, I do," Bacon said softly.

Hughes provided Bacon with a copy of a sheet listing deposits to and withdrawals from Hutton's account at the United Virginia Bank in Alexandria and asked him to look at it.

Before the branch manager had a chance to comment, however, Hughes recessed the subcommittee for ten minutes to attend to a vote in progress on the House floor. But Bacon was far from off the hook. When Hughes came back, he returned immediately to his previous line of questioning.

"At that time, was there any relationship whatsoever between the amount of moneys that had been deposited by customers and the amount you were drawing down?"

"It would appear from this sheet that there was not," Bacon said meekly.

"When was the system changed—that is, the formula changed, where you [no longer] linked what customers deposited with you and the drawdowns?"

Still, Bacon resisted.

"I don't believe we did it in the manner in which you suggest. I believe that we consistently increased our drawdowns over a very lengthy period of time, and, in the instance of United Virginia Bank, they were aware where the deposit checks were coming from.

"I spoke with the branch manager," Bacon said firmly. "He believed the account was a profitable one for them, and I have no reason to believe he was incorrect."

Hughes looked annoyed. "You know that is not the case today, don't you, because obviously, there is a claim directed at E.F. Hutton by United Virginia Bank."

"I am not aware of any specific claim," Bacon protested. "I know we received a letter from them that I have not seen." So far as he knew, Bacon concluded, United Virginia Bank had never been unhappy with its arrangement with Hutton.

"That is because," said Hughes, showing real annoyance, "they didn't know what was going on, did they?"

FRIDAY, AUGUST 23

35 3/8

The audit committee of Hutton's board convened for one of its rare meetings on August 23. This one was called by Judge Bell, who asked Bob Rittereiser to sit in.

"I can't find any minutes of audit committee meetings. Did you have any meetings?" Bell asked. "Not many" was the response.

The audit committee, Rittereiser says, narrowly missed getting called on the carpet by Bell. In fact, in Rittereiser's mind at least, the committee *should* have been called to task because of its lack of oversight.

Rittereiser maintains—as do some other former Hutton executives—that the situation at Hutton wouldn't have gotten as far out of control as it did if the audit committee of the board had taken an active role in the financial management of the company.

FRIDAY, AUGUST 30

36 7/8

"Mr. Fomon," reads the notation in his medical record, "awoke on Friday, August 30, with clumsiness of the right hand and face and was noted to have slurred speech."

Fomon, in fact, had suffered another transient ischemic attack, or TIA, his fourth. Again, his doctors didn't think it was necessary to admit him to the hospital, and, within a few weeks, his symptoms had disappeared.

One day in August, Griffin Bell had pulled Scott Pierce aside. "You know," Bell said, "it would be in Tom Lynch's best interest if he resigned now."

"It was a casual sort of remark," Pierce remembers, "but one that had a pretty serious message. He knew that I would go in and see Tom and relay that message."

A few days later, Pierce, ashen faced, had burst into Lynch's office. Lynch had known at once that something was up. "We've got a loose cannon here," Pierce had said, trying to soften the blow to Lynch. "We can't control this guy." Pierce was referring to Bell.

"If Bell has his way," Pierce had warned, "you'll all be out."

Lynch had tried to dismiss what Pierce said, but, of course, he couldn't. In his mind, he had re-created his meetings with Bell.

"None of the people who were involved in the check mess reported to me," Lynch had said soberly to the former attorney general.

"But you're the chief financial officer," Bell had insisted.

"Look," Lynch had said with conviction, "it's not even an official title. There is no chief financial officer in the bylaws of the company. It's just that when somebody has to sign as the chief financial officer, I do it."

"The accounting department doesn't report to me," he had continued. "The comptroller doesn't report to me. The money manager doesn't report to me. The internal audit manager doesn't report to me. The branches don't report to me. None of these people report to me."

"Well," Bell had drawled, "this is a very strange situation. It shouldn't be this way."

"I agree with you. It's a strange organization."

"Well, there should be a separate financial organization."

Lynch had only been able to agree. Then he had offered to give up the title of chief financial officer, as long as he could remain vice chairman and a member of the board of directors. Bell, who had been given a broad mandate by Fomon, had agreed to the deal.

Although Lynch didn't know it, by August, Rittereiser had decided that both Lynch and Tom Rae had to go—regardless of the outcome of the Bell report.

"The firm," Rittereiser says, "didn't have a grip on its day-to-day management processes at all, and Lynch and Rae were in charge of those processes."

At 10:00 P.M., on September 3, the telephone rang at Lynch's house in Madison, New Jersey. It was Tom Curnin from Cahill Gordon. The Bell report would be released the next day, Curnin told Lynch, and it would announce Lynch's resignation.

Even though he'd been warned by Pierce, Lynch was flabbergasted. So was Curnin.

In his initial conversations with Bell—and later in writing—Lynch had agreed to relinquish responsibility for the firm's financial management. But he had done so with the understanding that he would remain vice chairman of E.F. Hutton and a member of the firm's board of directors. "I had the same understanding," Curnin told Lynch.

"Something else," Curnin said. "I don't see how I can represent you at the board tomorrow. It would be a conflict of interest."

Lynch, feeling numb, hung up. In June, he had raised the question of whether it was proper for Curnin and Cahill Gordon to represent both Hutton and most of its executives. The attorneys had assured him that it was. Yet now, when he needed them, they were abandoning him. Again and again in his mind that night, Lynch went over the same hopeless ground.

He didn't know that Cahill Gordon was backing away from representing Hutton officials, as well as Hutton itself, because of Griffin Bell. Bell had called the Cahill attorneys on the carpet in August and told them that representing both Hutton executives and the firm was a clear conflict of interest. The law firm should clean up its act, Bell had advised sternly. Unfortunately for Lynch, Curnin had waited until the night before the report was issued to do anything about the situation.

36 ⅜

The pressures were building. At 9:00 A.M. the Hutton board convened on the twelfth floor of the firm's headquarters.

A few minutes before the meeting began, Bob Rittereiser cornered Bob Fomon. What, Rittereiser wanted to know, did Fomon plan to do at the meeting? Did he intend to endorse or reject the findings of the Bell report? Fomon said he would argue in favor of accepting the report.

Rittereiser was relieved. But he had another question for Fomon. Had the chairman prepared a resolution for the board to adopt? No, Fomon said, he had not.

Rittereiser raced back to his office, where he dictated and his secretary typed up a resolution recommending that the board accept Bell's findings.

The board had little time to prepare a response to Bell's report. The former attorney general had scheduled a press conference for noon, and the report was coming in piecemeal on Hutton's fax machine. Copies were made, and the board was given an hour and a half to read and digest it.

In his 183-page report, Bell blasted Hutton for its inadequate internal financial controls. And he charged that it was the firm's "loose management structure" that was to blame for the massive overdrafting. "Overdrafting became tantamount to a loose cannon," Bell wrote, and this cannon was "fired at will" by some Hutton employees.

In assigning blame, Bell asserted that Tom Lynch, as chief financial officer, "should have been aware of potential abuses."

"Lynch," Bell wrote, "has agreed to relinquish all corporate officer titles, duties and responsibilities." Bell left open the question of whether Lynch would remain on the board.

Bell also took aim at Tom Morley, Hutton's chief cash manager. Although he stopped short of recommending that Morley be fired, he did say, "We think Morley should be removed from any responsibility connected with money management or banking."

Tom Rae came under fire as well. The general counsel, said Bell, "bears responsibility" for "incompetence" and "failure to systematically search executive files." The incompetence stemmed from the company's failure to turn over several documents subpoenaed by federal prosecutors.

The report, however, absolved Bob Fomon and George Ball, then the head of Hutton's retail sales arm, of all blame.

Bell conceded that Lynch and other senior managers hadn't actually participated in the check kiting. But he recommended management changes that he thought would prevent the kiting from recurring. For example, Hutton should reshape its board of directors to give outside directors majority control.

Bell also called for thirty-day suspensions for three regional managers and recommended a formal sanction for Ernest Dippel, a regional sales manager in the Midwest. Dippel, Bell said, "knew or should have known that branch managers within his region were excessively overdrafting their accounts." In this middle layer of Hutton's organization, Richard G. Genin, a headquarters official who supervised regional operations managers, also was cited for a reprimand.

Lower down the chain, Bell and his team of investigators concluded, six out of three hundred branch managers had "participated in patterns of intentional overdrafting" that "were so excessive and egregious as to warrant sanctions. The conduct of the managers in these six branches was such [that] no responsible person could have believed that [his or her] conduct was proper."

Bell identified the six managers as: Perry Bacon; Anthony Read of the Baltimore branch; John Pierce of the St. Louis and the

Bethesda, Maryland, offices; William Shaw of the Fresno, California, branch; Robert Clark of the Hartford, Connecticut, office; and John Holland (no relation to Postal Inspector John Holland) of the Wilkes-Barre, Pennsylvania, branch. Bell suggested fines of $25,000 to $50,000 for each man, with the exact amount of each fine left up to the audit committee of Hutton's board. As it turned out, the board would never impose these fines.

The Bell report had made for sobering reading. One by one, board members—some annoyed, some frustrated, all concerned—made their way back to the boardroom.

The meeting reconvened with an emotional appeal from Tom Lynch. He had done nothing wrong, he argued, so why single him out now, at the end of his career? Why should he retire in disgrace? John Latshaw, an executive vice president and managing director, and Peter M. Detwiler, another vice chairman, jumped to Lynch's defense. So did the chairman—despite his earlier statement to Rittereiser.

"Fomon," Scott Pierce remembers, "was under a great deal of pressure. Lynch was a very good friend of his, so when it came down to nut-crunching time, Bob was all for telling the judge to go jump."

Rittereiser and Pierce were the first to speak in support of the Bell report's recommendations. "I can't make a decision whether the judge is right or wrong," Pierce began. "But we can't even entertain the idea of doing anything other than what Bell recommended. Otherwise," he continued, "we will lose all credibility with the media, the public, and the regulatory bodies that are waiting for this report."

Dick Locke sided with Pierce and Rittereiser. "Look," Rittereiser said, "we've got to go along with Bell. We told him that we would do whatever he said, and he says this is what we have to do."

Then Tom Rae made a soldierlike speech. "I don't agree with the results," he said, "but I am prepared to do what I have to do for the good of the firm."

Lynch first urged that the Bell report's conclusions be toned down. Then, knowing now that the situation was hopeless, he followed Rae's lead. "If this is the way it is going to be, I'll voluntarily give up the titles." Secretly, however, Lynch hoped he could at least hold on to his board seat. (He would not.)

At that point, Edward C. Cazier, Jr., a Los Angeles attorney who had served on Hutton's board since 1983, confirmed the practical wisdom of these concessions by Rae and Lynch. If the board doesn't go along with the Bell recommendations, he said, "all the independent directors will resign."

That ended the discussion.

Someone suggested that the board write Lynch a letter of appreciation for all he had done for the company. "Ultimately," Lynch says, "I got this glorious document signed by all the members of the board. But the damage had already been done."

Across the table, Scott Pierce noticed with alarm that Fomon was slumping slightly in his chair. "I was afraid he was having a stroke," Pierce remembers. Pierce asked a man who worked for Fomon to drive him home. Hutton's chairman had not yet fully recovered from the TIA he had suffered less than a week earlier.

Neither Lynch nor Rae actually left Hutton until April of 1986; both stayed on until their replacements were up to speed.

THURSDAY, SEPTEMBER 5

36 5/8

Press reaction to the Bell report was skeptical at best. The article published by *Business Week* was typical. "When Hutton hired Bell to investigate its cash-management practices," the magazine wrote, "it was like coming to the last chapter of a whodunit.

"You could almost picture the crafty investigator assembling the suspects, carefully analyzing one clue after another, and finally impaling the guilty with sheer logic. This mystery, however, has a denouement that would never have passed muster with Agatha Christie."

In a confidential memo to Bob Fomon written on September 16, Rittereiser, for the first time, revealed that he had developed serious doubts about the capabilities of many senior Hutton executives. The memo indicated that he had already decided that he would have to go outside the firm to find people capable of helping him turn Hutton around. "It is important," he wrote to Fomon, "that I be given a free hand and some time to effect the type of changes I envision. I need your support. . . ." The memo went on to outline ambitious plans. "We need to (1) revisit our strategy and then to articulate it; (2) alter reporting relationships or assign people to fit the strategy; (3) improve short- and intermediate-term operating results; (4) develop a management approach based on teamwork, communication, and business planning and develop our people accordingly." He would, he said, bring on an entirely new administrative management team. He signed the memo "Ritt."

One predictable effect of Rittereiser's decision to bring in new blood was to create an us-versus-them polarity between the old guard and the new, which destroyed what was left of Hutton's culture. "We believed that we were the best firm on the Street," says a longtime Hutton executive. "Bob Rittereiser comes in and says, 'You guys don't know how to run this place, and I'm going to bring in a bunch of folks who have never done it before, and we'll show you how to run it.' Well, they blew it."

In the fifteen years since Bob Fomon had taken Hutton's helm, the firm had grown enormously in size and complexity. It had required one kind of leader in earlier, entrepreneurial days, but now it demanded someone with different talents. Fomon had been unable to make the transition, and lately he had become increasingly withdrawn. Friends and colleagues say that he worried that his power was slipping away, as indeed it was.

Some people on Wall Street regarded Fomon almost as a pathetic figure. "He had a serious leg break in 1984," Scott Pierce remembers, "which really affected his performance. He ran the firm from his bed, and he was in pain for a long time afterwards. In fact, I don't think he has ever fully recovered."

Still, as far as Hutton's board was concerned, Fomon was the man in charge. At 10:00 A.M. on September 17, the board convened again—for the last time with its then current membership—at the Park Lane Hotel. Fomon opened by proposing—in line with Bell's recommendation—that most of the insiders resign from the board. Only he, Rittereiser, and Pierce would remain.

Just before the meeting, Fomon had called Jerry Miller into his office and told him what he planned to do. "Don't get upset," Fomon said, promising to put Miller "right back on the group board in two or three months." Fomon then told Miller that he had to make a clean sweep to get some of the old-timers to go along with the housecleaning.

But Miller wasn't happy with the deal. "There were a group of us very upset about what was going on—both with the firm and what they were doing as a result of the Bell report. What [Fomon] should have done was get enough outside directors and left enough inside directors who knew what they were doing on the board. He didn't want to do it, because he was afraid some of the old-timers would want to stay on and he wouldn't have a majority of outside directors." Miller wouldn't promise Fomon not to speak up.

When the meeting started, he did more than just speak up. Miller pointed out that they were trying to operate a major corporation with a board that had very little experience in the financial services business. As far as he was concerned, two of the inside directors—Fomon and Pierce—didn't know how to run a brokerage firm, either.

After the meeting the board adjourned for luncheon. Rittereiser then pulled Miller aside and said that he didn't understand why Miller was so upset. "He made some comment about there having to be some changes made around here," Miller recalls.

Board member Peter Ueberroth, too, was surprised at Miller's tone. After the meeting he approached Miller, Norm Epstein, Dick Locke, and Tom Styles, Hutton's head of research, who were also eating lunch at a nearby table.

Ueberroth walked over to the table. "Can I join the clique?"

"As long as you understand that this is the clique that runs the firm," Miller replied.

"I understand that, sort of," Ueberroth said, "but I don't understand why all of you are so upset about this."

Miller explained to him that very few people on the board had any knowledge of the financial services business, and that someone had to run the firm.

"I didn't know it was this big a deal. Why don't we talk about it?" Ueberroth suggested.

But they never did. Ueberroth apparently forgot about the problem.

Miller is still dismayed. "For some reason, which I don't understand to this day, I guess the outside directors thought we would just accept whatever Fomon wanted to do. . . . A whole bunch of us disagreed with what he did. We were very afraid— with good reason, I might add, considering what happened a year or so later—that the group which ran the business would not have a lot of knowledge of the business and would make bad decisions." Subsequent events did prove Miller's fears well grounded.

After lunch, Miller and the others returned to Hutton's head-quarters. Rittereiser again pulled Miller aside. "I have had it with the way the retail system is being run," he told Miller. "I'm going to put you back in retail if you want to take the job."

Miller was delighted. Within a few weeks he and Rittereiser talked again. The retail side of the firm was suffering from terrible morale, Rittereiser said. It had to be repaired. Likewise, he went on, the capital markets side of the firm had pretty much been destroyed. Rittereiser said that he would put Miller in charge of retail. "I'll leave you alone to run retail," he said. "while I try to figure out what to do with capital markets."

THURSDAY, OCTOBER 3

34 ⅛

The Hughes Subcommittee on Crime reconvened on October 3. The first witness was Abraham Briloff, professor of accounting at the City College of New York. Testifying as an expert witness, Briloff was to tell the legislators whether, in his opinion, Arthur Andersen—the accounting firm employed by Hutton—had acted properly and in the best interest of Hutton shareholders. Had the accounting firm alerted shareholders, as it should have, to Hutton's difficulties with regulators? In other words, the subcommittee wanted to know, how could Hutton have been writing all those overdrafts without its auditors noticing and com-plaining?

Hughes first directed Briloff's attention to a note in Hutton's 1984 10-K statement, the filing every public firm has to make with the Securities and Exchange Commission. The note pointed out that Hutton and its subsidiaries were defendants in legal ac-tions and that claimants were seeking damages for "indeterminate amounts." Even so, Hutton's management concluded, "these ac-tions will not result in any material, adverse effect on the con-solidated financial position of the company."

"In your opinion," Hughes pressed, "was this disclosure adequate, given that it was a little more than a month before Hutton pleaded guilty to two thousand counts of mail and wire fraud, that, obviously, at this time, Andersen was on notice of the ongoing grand jury investigation, and, in fact, had been subpoenaed?"

The professor smiled. "Mr. Chairman," Briloff said, looking pleased with himself, "this disclosure was very much like a bikini bathing suit. What it revealed was interesting, what it concealed was vital." A wave of laughter swept across the audience.

THURSDAY, OCTOBER 31

35 ⅛

At 10:25 A.M., Congressman Hughes once again rapped the House Subcommittee on Crime meeting to order. That day's star witness was former E.F. Hutton president George Ball. After he was sworn in, Ball was given permission by Congressman Hughes to read a short opening statement.

Ball first reviewed his career with Hutton, noting that he had become president of the firm in 1977, after serving as its national retail sales manager for the preceding seven years. As president, he pointed out, his chief responsibility was the management of the retail sales function. "In other words," he said pointedly, "I was not the firm's chief operating officer. I reported directly to Robert Fomon, who was chairman and chief executive officer."

Ball then noted that others reporting directly to Mr. Fomon included the chief financial officer, the head of operations, the company's general counsel, and the heads of the corporate finance, public finance, and trading departments.

"I mention this," Ball said, "to underscore the diffuse nature of Hutton's management structure." He hastened to add, however, that the structure did "not mean to suggest that I was a minor figure in the company. To the contrary, the retail sales force which reported to me consisted of over four thousand account executives and generated revenues of over one billion dollars a year at the time I left Hutton in 1982.

"During my tenure," he continued, "my knowledge of the drawdown [overdrafting] system was rudimentary. I was not aware of any improprieties in the conduct of that system until February 1982. At that juncture, Mr. Fomon informed me that a problem had been brought to his attention by counsel, that he, Mr. Fomon, had told them to remedy the situation."

Even after that time, Ball stressed, he was not included in meetings at which drawdown system problems or modifications were discussed. Ball made it as plain as he could. "In other words," he said, "I had no knowledge of, nor responsibility for, the deficiencies in Hutton's control mechanisms that resulted in the abuse of its cash management system."

Ball was aware, he testified, that Hutton had a cash management system in place that was designed to bring money from branches to headquarters as quickly as possible and to minimize loss of interest on the float to banks. And he also knew that the system used overdrafting against uncleared check deposits to reduce the loss of float. However, he went on, "I was not aware of the procedures or specific methods used to reach that result. I was certainly not aware that some regions and branches were abusing the system in order to generate additional interest income by excessive overdrafting."

Ball then tried to defuse the impact of his damaging memo. "As you well know," he said, "I was a prolific memo and note writer and consistently encouraged employees to achieve excellence in their work. . . . However, one should not mistake a search for improvement for willingness to cut corners. Exhorting branches to increase their interest profits or stock sales or cost-effectiveness was in no way a call for sharp practices.

"To the contrary," Ball protested, "on several occasions in the course of reviewing the financial results of the branches, I sent memoranda to my colleagues asking questions about branch profit

margins and interest income that appeared unusually high."
Moreover, Ball pointed out, those memos went to branches that
were exonerated from any responsibility for abusive practices by
Bell's report, as well as branches that "were engaged in wrongful
actions."

"At no time did I receive a reply indicating any impropriety,"
he concluded.

After he finished making his formal statement, Ball turned to
Hughes, who returned to one of his favorite topics, Hutton's organizational structure. "As president of E.F. Hutton," Hughes
began, "who did you report to?"

"I reported to Mr. Fomon, the chairman and chief executive,"
Ball replied.

"And who reported to you, both directly and indirectly?"
Hughes pressed on.

Ball ticked them off: the nine or ten regional vice presidents
of E.F. Hutton; the director of the retail marketing organization;
at various times some of the marketing departments that supported the retail area—the tax shelter department, the municipal
bond liaison department, and so forth; Hutton's director of research; and, after Hutton acquired it, the head of the E.F. Hutton
Life Insurance Co.

Hughes leaned forward. "And would you describe in a little
more detail for us—you did touch upon it—your responsibilities
as president of the brokerage firm?"

"My responsibilities as president of E.F. Hutton," Ball said
firmly, "were to see that the branch network generated revenues,
was cost-effective, and that it was properly supported by product
and idea flows that would be of benefit to it."

"And would it be correct to say that part of your job was to see
that your various regions maximized their profits?" Hughes asked,
cutting to the heart of the matter.

"Yes," Ball conceded. "One of my tasks was to see that the
results of Hutton were optimized. And I would differentiate just
a bit from maximize in that sense: In a very slow market, one

cannot maximize profits, one can only optimize them relative to the environment that exists within the investment world."

Hughes reiterated his point. "But one of your primary functions was to see that E.F. Hutton was profitable?"

Ball admitted that was certainly the case. "As with any corporate executive, I was not only responsible but should have been responsible for seeing that Hutton's profits were as high as possible within every proper and legitimate means," he maintained. "And here, of course," he said emphatically, "I'm underscoring 'proper and legitimate' as opposed to things that would be done in a corner-cutting or underhanded way."

Ball ended his testimony on a high-minded note. "I do think," he said earnestly, "if I could just add, Mr. Chairman, that given the frailties of mankind and leaving the money management wrongdoings aside for the moment, that the firm did both a fine job of operating profitably and in a way that was honorable and good."

FRIDAY, DECEMBER 6

35 ¾

The House Subcommittee on Crime—after a five-week break—was back in session in Room 2141 of the Rayburn Building. Congressman Bill Hughes glanced around the room, which, as in the past, was crowded with newspaper and television reporters.

The subcommittee had called Assistant U.S. Attorney Albert R. Murray, Jr., and U.S. Postal Inspector John Holland to testify, and both men were sitting at the witness table. Murray, dressed in a dark three-piece suit, was the first called.

Murray asked if he might make a statement before the legislators began their questioning. Told to proceed, he rose, then spoke with deliberation and in language that suggested the apocalyptic terms in which he viewed Hutton's crime.

"If I might just start from the beginning. . . . Basically, John

Holland and I and a team of postal inspectors for two years . . . worked in anonymity. In March 1984, we joined forces with the Department of Justice to try to fight what we believed were two evils.

"We were fighting Hutton," the prosecutor said in his grave, judicious way. "And we were fighting the cash management system in this country."

Murray excused himself if he appeared to be waving the flag, but, he explained, the deeper the investigators got into the case, the more convinced they became that they had discovered not just an isolated violation but systemic abuse that threatened the financial health of the nation.

There were clearly understood and well-enforced laws that governed the individual consumer's relationship with the country's banking institutions, Murray pointed out. But, he said, it had become apparent that those laws broke down, or didn't exist, when it came to governing the cash management practices of large institutions.

What they had discovered, he said, were "novel and new issues involving financial cash management that nobody really knew about. We found the law was basically nebulous and undefined. We found that the guidelines in cash management were nebulous at best. . . . We believed a double standard existed in the country between how the banking industry deals with corporate America and . . . with the individual."

Murray knew, because Hughes had told him earlier, that the subcommittee chairman believed that individual Hutton executives should have been brought to trial. So in his testimony the assistant U.S. attorney attempted to explain and defend his differing view.

"We don't play favorites," he said. "We didn't play any favorites for these big, high corporate muckety-mucks." He wanted to prosecute, he said, only when he thought he could prove actual guilt. And in the Hutton case, he wasn't even sure individual, malicious guilt was involved. "There is no individual—I know in my heart—

there is no individual of E.F. Hutton walking around saying, 'I got away with a crime.' "

Even the corporation, he explained, didn't seem to understand that what it was doing in its cash management practices constituted fraudulent behavior. But by prosecuting the corporation instead of the individuals, Murray had hoped to bring the abuses dramatically to the attention of Congress. "I wanted to rectify a problem," he said, "and hoped that Congress would do what it should, which is reform the banking system."

At this point, Bill McCollum, the Florida Republican, took over the questioning. "I would like to know," he said abruptly to Murray, "who made the decision not to go forward with an attempt to indict and bring charges against individuals?"

"I did," Murray replied. "I made the decision. I felt it was in the best interest of the country to accept the plea agreement." (In reality, decisions in the case were not made by Murray but by Justice Department officials in Washington.)

McCollum, an attorney, pressed harder. "Were you in any way pressured into making that decision, or—"

Murray interrupted, "Let me just—"

"Or," McCollum demanded, "was it totally on your own?"

Murray looked hard at the congressman. "Let me just tell you something," he said. "Nobody pressures me, tells me what to do, tries to influence me, or causes me to give up my morals, ethics, or principles. The only person is God above and my dad right back there. He is the only person who tells me what to do. My loyalty is to the people of this country. I know that sounds corny. I know it does, but that is where my loyalty is."

The still photographers scrambled to snap Murray's picture. McCollum paused, then leaned forward. "Let me ask, then, the bottom-line question. Why did you decide not to prosecute individuals?"

Over and over, Murray had reviewed the events of the past three years.

"One," he said, "we believed, ultimately, that the plea agreement was one that served the people, that there were possibly two or three individuals who might have been responsible for that conduct. . . .

"But what you have to do is look at the corporation that was acting collectively . . . [and] the banks were, in a way, equally—I don't want to say—culpable. Many of the banks knowingly approved this conduct and participated in the actual practices. The fact of the matter is that [in] a trial of this case, my so-called victims become, in fact, possibly coconspirators and defendants.

"I had a very difficult time in the grand jury," he went on. "It was like pulling teeth from the bankers, because there is an interwoven business relationship between corporate America and the banks. Nobody wants to accuse Hutton of committing a crime. Nobody wants to say that these practices might be fraudulent, because, in fact, many of the banks in this country are doing the same thing. They are teaching it."

"All you are telling us," McCollum said, "[is that] you would have had a great deal of difficulty in proving a case against individuals and that is one of the reasons why you did not prosecute?"

"That is right," Murray shot back, "because the individuals, other than Mr. Morley and one other person, thought they were acting in accordance with industry practice, in accordance with what the other corporations are doing, in accordance with the services that the banks are providing them. And the reason why banks in this country provide that service is because they make money off the float."

But why plea-bargain? McCollum wanted to know.

Murray explained that, by plea bargaining, prosecutors had been able to dictate their own definition of what, specifically, in the Hutton cash management practice had been illegal. "If we had gone to trial, we would never be able to do that, and we would have had chaos."

"You are saying," McCollum asked, again trying to sum up Murray's remarks, "the practices you were able to stop by this plea agreement, instead of trying individuals, [are] something that would have been going on to this day if you hadn't accepted a plea agreement?"

"That is correct," Murray said. "Individual prosecution is important. It has always been my policy. [But] this was a novel issue. I was not going to jeopardize the health of . . . the banking industry for purposes of trying to indict one individual."

"I think my time is up," said McCollum, leaning back in his chair. "Thank you very much, Mr. Chairman."

WEDNESDAY, DECEMBER 11

36 ¼

The House Subcommittee on Crime reconvened, this time in Room 2237 of the Rayburn Building. At 10:30 A.M., Bill Hughes gaveled the session to order.

Among those scheduled to testify that day were Stephen Trott, assistant attorney general for the criminal division of the Department of Justice; Department of Justice Fraud Section Chief Robert Ogren; Department of Justice Fraud Section trial attorney Peter Clark; Bob Fomon; and Jay Moorhead. The primary topic of debate: Did Fomon—at his 1984 lunch with former U.S. Attorney General William French Smith—attempt a political fix?

The exchange between Fomon and Congressman Romano L. Mazzoli, from Kentucky's third congressional district, was especially heated. Mazzoli, a conservative Democrat, is a thin man with bushy eyebrows, large ears, a small mouth, and slightly droopy eyelids. Born in Louisville in 1932, he earned his undergraduate degree from the University of Notre Dame and a law degree from the University of Louisville. He narrowly won his seat in 1970, beating a Republican incumbent who had been mayor of Louisville.

"I must remark on what appears to be a total lack of contrition on the basis of what has happened over the last several months,"

148

he began, addressing Fomon. "It would appear that you find this whole thing so exasperating and so trying that you can barely show the patience to answer our questions."

"Well," Fomon replied, "that's not true. I mean, I don't think contrition is something that you show through great displays of emotion."

"I was just curious," the congressman went on. "You rank yourself in a position where if you want to get something done, you call the top person. You don't waste time with the underlings, the lackeys. You go right to the top. If you have a problem with GM, you call the head of GM. My question is this: When you called Mr. [William French] Smith, you called his wife first. Was there some reason you did not call the attorney general? Why did you use this gentleman?" Mazzoli pointed at Moorhead.

"I don't know," Fomon responded.

"I think you do know," Mazzoli persisted. He went on to point out that Moorhead had Republican party connections, that he had worked in the White House.

"I don't know," Fomon said again, interrupting.

"Let me pursue that for a second," Mazzoli continued. "I find it remarkable. I am sure that Mr. Moorhead is a man of real talent. . . . Mr. Moorhead, do you feel put upon in, you know, calling to arrange a lunch? I mean, as an [executive] assistant, you are paid, I am sure, very well. Do you do that sort of thing every day? Do you call once a day to make Mr. Fomon's luncheon arrangements, or do you call often, or never? What is it?

"And don't feel offended, because this is what my friends back home, unsophisticated as they are, would [call] a fix, an attempted fix that didn't work out. And you were being used as a fixer in an attempt to try to influence in a nonjudicial way—"

"You know," Fomon interrupted yet again, "I resent that word *fix*."

"Well, then, what would you say, Mr. Fomon, in all respect? What was that thing meant to do? To influence a pending investigation? I don't know what else it could have been."

Mazzoli then tried to ask whether Fomon thought he could influence the investigation by applying pressure from the top down, although the wording of his question was confused and its meaning obscure.

"I don't understand your question," said Fomon.

"I think you do," Mazzoli said. "I think that you realize—"

"Don't tell me what I understand, when I say I don't," Fomon shot back angrily.

"Well, you are trying—"

Fomon interrupted again. "Please repeat the question."

"You are trying to put me in my place," Mazzoli said, assuming a hurt air. He tried to ask again whether Fomon thought that by exerting pressure at the top with Attorney General Smith, he could have an influence that would trickle down to the investigators. "I know of no other conclusion," he said.

Fomon's response wasn't arrogant, only typical. If he had wanted Moorhead to help him exert influence at the top, he said, he wouldn't start with the attorney general. "I would go to the president of the United States."

FRIDAY, DECEMBER 13

35 ½

As president of the E.F. Hutton Group, Bob Rittereiser's first important mission was to undertake a sweeping reorganization of the firm and its management practices. But how would he do it? By mid-December he settled on what he thought was a winning formula. Rittereiser would divide Hutton into two parts—a retail brokerage services arm and an institutional and capital markets arm. (This structure was exactly the same as Merrill Lynch's. That Rittereiser would take such a step was the retail system's worst nightmare when Rittereiser came on board.)

He would oust Scott Pierce, whom he thought ineffectual as president of E.F. Hutton & Co., the firm's retail sales company, and give himself that additional title. Then he would promote Jerry Miller, a twenty-three-year veteran of Hutton, to senior executive vice president in charge of individual investment services, which included retail brokerage services, marketing, and asset management. Miller would replace Bob Witt, a man who, in Rittereiser's words, "had responsibilities far in excess of his abilities." Miller, of course, had known for some months that he was about to be elevated to this position. Finally, Rittereiser would promote Dick Locke to senior executive vice president in charge of institutional and capital markets.

Before all these shifts could occur, though, he had to break the news to the executives involved. Pierce was first on the list. Pierce was never the most popular person around Hutton, and even Bob Fomon no longer felt at ease with him. "Scottie," says one former Hutton vice president, "got on Bob's nerves, but it wasn't Bob. Scottie got on everybody's nerves from time to time." Pierce could be sanctimonious and self-righteous. "I'm the only clean person here," he liked to tell his colleagues.

Pierce, Rittereiser said, was to be "promoted" to vice chairman of the E.F. Hutton Group and given responsibility for strategic planning, human resources, and executive development—"all euphemisms for being put in the bleachers," Pierce says today. He was taken aback. He assumed that Rittereiser had sought and received Fomon's blessing for the move. Fomon later told Pierce that he had not. Rittereiser remembers events differently. "Fomon seemed to relish the change I was making with Pierce," he says.

Publicly, Hutton would put the best face possible on the change in Pierce's duties. In the firm's annual report Fomon wrote, Pierce's "appointment reflects our recognition of the increasing importance of our strategic positioning and resource development and allocation decisions."

For a long time Bob Witt had known little about Rittereiser's planned reorganization, because Rittereiser hadn't told him about it. What he knew, he had heard through the grapevine. Nonetheless, Witt resolved to confront Rittereiser. He decided to make his move in late December, when the two flew west for a meeting with Hutton account executives.

The plane climbed swiftly and settled into its course for Los Angeles. Witt peered down at the great gray city of New York and finally turned to Rittereiser. He had heard, he said tentatively, that the new president planned to divide the retail group into east and west divisions. Rittereiser said he hadn't made up his mind yet on what to do with retail. The two men spent the next five hours discussing possible reorganizations for the retail sales arm. At no time in the conversation, Witt says bitterly today, did Rittereiser hint that he'd already settled on an organization or that he had plans to demote Witt.

For his part, Rittereiser was not prepared to tell Witt what he was planning. "The problem at Hutton," he says, "was that no sooner would I confide my plans to an executive than I'd read my comments in the next issue of *Securities Week*." But he adds, "In the five hours, I made a lot of statements that were at the heart of what I was considering."

After his demotion—a demotion Fomon approved—Witt confided to his friend and mentor that he planned to resign. The volatile chairman said he understood. After all, the two men conceded, Hutton was no longer the old Hutton they remembered. But Witt, Fomon said, was naive about corporate life. Then he recited for Witt one of his favorite stories.

"A father told his six-year-old son to get on the mantel," Fomon began. " 'Son, I'm going to teach you a lesson about business that you won't ever forget all through your life,' the father said. 'Get up on the mantel, jump off, and I'll catch you.'

"So the boy, who, of course, loves his father, gets up on the mantel and jumps." At this point in his recitation, Fomon began to grin. "And the father steps away. The kid crashes to the ground. He lays there crying and his father says, 'Remember, you can't even trust your father in business.' " That's a lesson, said Fomon to Witt, that you've yet to learn.

MONDAY, DECEMBER 16

35 ⅜

The Dow Jones Industrial Average reached its high for the year—1553.10.

Along with everything else on his busy agenda, Rittereiser was working hard to shore up Hutton's increasingly precarious capital position. "I was buried in survival activities," he says.

On December 16, Hutton's CEO flew to Minneapolis to call on a banker. They shook hands in his office, and Rittereiser sat down to begin discussions. "Well," the banker began, "if you're in Minneapolis on December 16 when it's four below zero, you must really need money." Rittereiser just laughed nervously.

TUESDAY, DECEMBER 31

34 ⅞

Hutton still looked strong financially. It ended its fiscal year having earned $43.7 million on total revenues of $3.1 billion—compared to earnings of $52.7 million on revenues of $2.7 billion in 1984. It would be the last time the firm would post a profit before being forced to sell itself off in an embarrassing public auction.

Hutton paid stockholders a dividend of 82 cents—up 2 cents from the previous year. Its book value increased from $24.61 a share in 1984 to $26.48 in 1985. But its earnings per share declined by 20 percent—from $2.05 to $1.63.

1986

For a battered E.F. Hutton, 1986 was a turning point. The year would bring with it both the seeds of destruction and the hope of salvation.

Bob Rittereiser would start the year off by putting into effect the reorganization plan he had mapped out the previous month. On January 14, a frigid, snowy day in Manhattan, he announced the changes.

Rittereiser's master plan—which was dictated in part by the Bell report—was to streamline operations and boost managerial accountability. In the long term, he hoped to rebuild several key areas, particularly a corporate finance department weakened by the check scandal.

In the near term, though, his focus was on creating more central control—as the Bell report had suggested. That's why he wanted to adopt at Hutton the structure he had grown familiar with at Merrill Lynch—that is, he wanted to divide Hutton into two parts: a retail brokerage services arm and an institutional and capital markets arm.

Another Rittereiser innovation was the creation of a management committee to review corporate policies regularly. The com-

mittee would consist of Hutton's most senior executives—
Rittereiser, Bob Fomon, Dick Locke, Jerry Miller, Scott Pierce,
and Norman Epstein, as well as the firm's incoming chief financial
officer and general counsel. Eventually, Rittereiser would hire for
the committee new experts in various areas.

In time he did put together a team of people who were very
qualified in their fields. "The problem," says one former senior
executive, "was that not all their expertise was in the brokerage
business." A former senior vice president had a harsher judgment.
"Bob Rittereiser," he says, "brought in a bunch of people who
didn't know the foggiest thing about the brokerage business and
who didn't even like the firm they were working for. The new
hires' personalities would also be an unusual mix and would often
clash."

Wall Street and the business press reacted favorably to the
news of Hutton's reorganization. The new plan received positive
coverage on page 1 of the *New York Times* business section, for
example.

WEDNESDAY, JANUARY 22

37 ⅝

The Dow Jones Industrial Average fell to its low for the year—
1502.29.

TUESDAY, FEBRUARY 11

38 ½

Most executives fall into one of three categories—autocrats, who
tell subordinates what to do and expect them to do it; participative
managers, who involve subordinates in decisions but retain final
authority; and democratic leaders, who try to do what their subordinates want them to do. Bob Fomon believed in participa-

tive, Bob Rittereiser in democratic management, which is why Rittereiser set up a committee of senior managers to run the firm.

On this snowy day in February, the new management committee met for the first time. It would thereafter meet on company business every Tuesday morning at 9:00 until, finally, there was no company.

MONDAY, MARCH 3

39 ⅞

On his management team, Rittereiser says, he wanted strong-willed men who would always tell him what they honestly thought. He disdained what he called the "flagpole" style of management. That, he explains, is when the person at the top of the pole wants to look down and see only smiling faces. The problem is that the people the next level down—the ones who are looking up at the people who are smiling at the chief executive—"see only assholes."

While he was at Merrill Lynch, Rittereiser had been impressed by Edward J. Lill, who had made a name for himself as partner in charge of the financial services industry practice group at Deloitte Haskins & Sells, the Big Eight accounting firm. Since Merrill Lynch was a client of Deloitte, Bob Rittereiser knew Lill's work and style.

On March 3 Rittereiser named Lill—an imposing man of six feet, three inches—executive vice president and chief financial officer of Hutton. As was his practice, Rittereiser hadn't consulted with many other Hutton executives on the hire, although he did talk to Norm Epstein, Fomon, and Tom Lynch before he made the offer to Lill. Rittereiser typically suspended management democracy when it came to picking his senior managers.

Lill himself had been reluctant to make the move when Rittereiser had first approached him in December. He was, after all, very comfortably situated. But Rittereiser had made the new position seem quite a challenge.

He told Lill he wanted a financial officer he could rely on, one who combined treasury knowledge with accounting know-how. And because of Hutton's earlier legal problems, Rittereiser explained, he needed someone with a lot of credibility in financial circles. Lill, according to Rittereiser, had that. At no point, says Lill, did Rittereiser try to "gild the lily. He said, 'Let me tell you. We either make it together or we don't. This is not a sure thing.' "

Rittereiser was particularly eager to sign Lill on because he wanted somebody who could be productive quickly. In the new CEO's view, Lill was that man. "[Lill] was particularly qualified to come in here," says Rittereiser, "since he knew the unique aspects of brokerage accounting inside out."

The idea of a second career at age fifty-three began to appeal to Lill. He'd been at Deloitte for thirty-three years, perhaps too long, he began thinking. Moreover, two years previously, his son had been killed in an auto accident. "When something like that happens to you," Lill says, "one of the things you think about is a new start." So after talking the offer over with his wife, Lill decided to sign on. Doing so didn't entail much financial sacrifice. His employment contract called for a base salary of at least $300,000 a year and an annual bonus of at least $300,000 for three years.

The job did have some constraints, however. Lill knew, for example, that it wasn't his responsibility to make operating decisions. He could—and would—voice his opinion as financial officer, to Jerry Miller and later Mark Kessenich, who became head of capital markets. But he accepted the fact that those two ran their divisions, and their views carried more weight than his.

He also was well aware that his first task was to cut costs. But it didn't take him long to realize that that task was hopeless. Seventy cents out of every dollar went directly into people's pockets—that is, as salary and bonuses. "I could play with the other thirty cents all day long," Lill says now, "and it wouldn't help Hutton."

Hutton veterans had a mixed response to the new CFO. Miller, for example, liked Lill. He was well respected in the industry and knew accounting methodology inside out. But key members of the retail division doubted that Lill knew that much about the brokerage business. And they thought that when it came to making decisions about the direction the firm should take or how it should solve its problems, Lill was too easily swayed by other people's opinions.

Fomon, with hindsight, is particularly harsh on Lill. "I wasn't smart enough at the time to know that if you have a successful career as an accountant, that doesn't necessarily qualify you to be chief financial officer of a brokerage firm." Lill, Fomon says bluntly, "was a bum choice."

MONDAY, MARCH 17

38 ⅛

Bob Fomon spent the first few months of 1986 extinguishing the brush fires that had raged on months after Hutton's precedent-setting guilty plea in May of 1985. Unfortunately, he no longer was operating at peak capacity. The 1980s had taken their toll on the sixty-one-year-old chairman. His stroke and other serious ailments, including the compound leg fracture, had seriously undermined his physical and emotional well-being.

"It was incredible how much he'd aged," remembers Tom Rae, who, despite the announcement of his retirement by the Bell report, continued as corporate counsel. What was worse, Fomon's personal proclivities, which in the past had not interfered with his role as chairman and CEO, now began to prove a source of embarrassment to the firm. Fomon, like his predecessors, had always been something of a playboy, and as he aged the pace of his philandering only accelerated.

Fomon had been married for five years to Sharon Kay Ritchie— Miss America of 1956. During their marriage, which, according to Ritchie, "was not a happy one," the Hutton chairman had continued to see other women. After his divorce from Ritchie had become final in 1980, Fomon had turned increasingly to the party circuits of Manhattan's Upper East Side, the Hamptons, and Palm Beach.

Fomon preferred the company of very young women, and he made no effort to disguise his predilection. In fact, he went out of his way to flaunt it. On his frequent evenings out, Fomon often invited other Hutton executives to join him.

An investment banker acquaintance says that if Fomon had "had as much interest in his company as he did in his libido or his own bank account, all three would be in better shape today."

Lonely and with few real friends, Fomon was also fast developing a reputation for heavy drinking. "I've never once seen the man sober," says a Wall Street banker who, like Fomon, belongs to New York's prestigious Brook Club—known properly as "The Brook." Eventually Fomon's drinking became a source of concern within the firm because he sometimes became abusive on Hutton outings and at the office.

But to the world outside Fomon still looked firmly in control. And he made sincere efforts during the first half of 1986 to plead Hutton's case, particularly to the congressional committee that was wrapping up its investigation of the check scandal. Managing the scandal had always been a public relations matter. Unfortunately, when it came to managing public perceptions, Hutton was proving extraordinarily inept.

On a sunny March 17, Fomon renewed his public relations campaign by writing a six-page letter to Congressman Bill Hughes, chairman of the House Subcommittee on Crime. Designed to bring the congressman up to date on Hutton's actions since the hearings—and intended by Fomon to become part of the official hearing report—the missive was a mix of half truths and omissions.

"Hutton's rehabilitation began as soon as senior management learned of the abuses in the company's cash concentration system [in late 1981] and long before the filing of federal charges," maintained Fomon. Even though they did not believe the problems were widespread or illegal, he said, these senior executives "recognized that they were improper and in contravention of established company policy and acted immediately to halt them."

Fomon then pointed out that all branches received written instructions prohibiting any deviations from the company's established check-writing procedures. "The language used," said Fomon, "left no doubt that departures from the company's lawful system would not be tolerated.

"The effectiveness of management's immediate remedial action," Fomon triumphantly continued, "is conclusively demonstrated by the fact—undisputed in the record before this subcommittee or anywhere else—that all abusive practices stopped in early 1982." Of course, in reality this "fact" was far from undisputed.

Hutton executives had been grilled the previous fall by members of the subcommittee about abusive cash management practices that had continued long *after* the period covered by Hutton's guilty plea. Moreover, prosecutors had told the subcommittee that they had agreed to plea-bargain because they were concerned that Hutton was continuing to create huge amounts of float. Also, many banks complained about Hutton's overdrafting well beyond the date of the plea.

Fomon knew as well that Hutton had agreed to a restitution program for its banks that covered ten months *beyond* the date mandated by the plea agreement—that is, until December 1982. Why, Hughes might have asked, was there a need to extend the time if the practices that required restitution had stopped in February 1982?

Undeterred by the facts, Fomon continued his spirited defense of his embattled firm. "Hutton did more than merely halt the improper practices in 1982," he went on. The firm also explained in detail its cash concentration system to its banks and instituted— as the plea agreement required—a massive restitution program. Through this program, Fomon said, "Hutton has insured that each and every bank harmed by improper drawdown activity will be fully repaid with interest."

Fomon then went on to quote Stephen Trott, the assistant attorney general in charge of the criminal division of the Justice Department, who declared that Hutton's plan was "the most comprehensive program of restitution ever developed in a federal criminal case." "In terms of curing the harm done by the improper banking practices," Fomon said, "the restitution program offers a *complete* remedy." Here again, Fomon strayed from the facts. Despite his—and Trott's—claim to the contrary, he knew that the restitution program, because of the way it was written, ensured that many banks would be unable to claim a single cent and that many more would be forced to claim far less than the amounts to which they were entitled.

Fomon then detailed for Hughes the treasury control procedures and policies he had instituted in May of 1985 and pointed to the sophistication of the $30 million computerized system Hutton had installed. In addition, he assured the congressman, both Hutton's internal and outside auditors had been instructed to develop special procedures that would detect any future questionable practices.

Finally, he pointed out, Hutton was "studying" the implementation of a system of regional disbursement banks, which would provide customers around the country with checks drawn on the closest regional bank. If it implemented the system, Fomon said, Hutton would be the first brokerage firm in the country to provide regional disbursement checks. Of course, Fomon failed to point out that Hutton had been *ordered*, through a consent decree filed with the New York State Supreme Court, to stop its practice of remote disbursement. He also neglected to mention that the Federal Reserve had issued a statement disapproving remote disbursement almost eight years previously.

Hutton, Fomon went on, had also taken steps to educate its employees about the practices that had led to past abuse and had instituted new procedures and policies to prevent future violations. It had, in fact, not only issued clear instructions on how Hutton's banking was to be conducted in the future but also given seminars in eighteen cities to inform employees about the illegal activities and the steps the firm had taken since the plea to prevent future problems. If that weren't enough, Fomon said, the company had engaged the services of the Ethics Resource Center, which would help Hutton develop a written code of ethics for employees.

Finally, Fomon reminded Hughes, Hutton had gone far beyond the steps required by the guilty plea. Determined to find out what had gone wrong and who was responsible for the conduct that had led to the plea, Fomon had retained the services of Griffin Bell to conduct an independent investigation. The Bell report had recommended that a number of Hutton top managers be disciplined, and Hutton had implemented those recommendations. In several instances, Fomon said, Hutton had gone even further than Judge Bell had suggested, "even though none of the affected employees was found guilty of any intentional criminal conduct."

The testimony of Perry Bacon had been particularly damaging, Fomon reminded Hughes. And Bell had recommended actions against six branch managers, including Bacon. As a result, Fomon said, the brokerage had immediately obtained Bacon's resignation. Four other branch managers also gave up their posts, were fined $25,000 each, and received official reprimands. In each of these cases, including Bacon's, Fomon pointed out, Judge Bell had recommended only a fine and the reprimand.

While Fomon made much of the fact that the firm had not only followed Judge Bell's recommendations but gone well beyond them, his descriptions of the actions Hutton took against various officers and employees were, at best, misleading. Fomon neglected to mention, for instance, that Bacon never paid his fine. But Hutton did pay Bacon approximately $630,000 when he tendered his resignation. The firm also agreed to help the former branch manager establish a new business and promised not to sue him. In return, Bacon said he would cooperate with the company in any investigation of its wrongdoing.

Fomon was also eager to assure Hughes that the consequences

of the guilty plea "reached into the highest ranks of Hutton's management." Thomas Lynch, he reported, formerly the company's de facto principal financial officer and vice chairman, had resigned from all corporate positions. And Tom Rae, the company's general counsel, had taken early retirement, not been booted out, as the report had recommended.

Here again, Fomon left out a few critical details. Lynch, for example, continued as a senior consultant to Hutton, earning a hefty $250,000 a year. Rae received $293,333 in retirement pay— an amount equal to one year's compensation—and agreed to serve Hutton as an "independent consultant" at a *minimum* annual compensation of $62,500 a year for six years. According to the agreement, he would receive $250 an hour with additional compensation for all hours over the first 250 each calendar year. (Still, Rae says, his deal wasn't as good as it sounds. His retirement benefits for twenty years of service amounted to only about $22,000 a year. "Hutton had a lousy retirement plan," he says.)

Fomon concluded his letter by stating Hutton's commitment to "far-reaching changes in its basic structure of corporate governance." He pointed out that the firm, following Judge Bell's recommendation, would hire a majority of outside directors and set up a separate audit committee for E.F. Hutton & Co. in addition to the audit committee of the Hutton Group.

Finally, he assured Hughes, Hutton had devoted enormous resources to its internal reforms and to full cooperation with the subcommittee. "We have done this," he wrapped up, "to assure that all abuses come to light and that they never recur."

Hughes may have been reassured by Fomon's glowing report of remedial action, but if so, his reassurance was short-lived.

WEDNESDAY, APRIL 2

41

Stephen J. Friedman was optimistic when he decided to join the management team. Like most of the men Bob Rittereiser hired, Friedman knew nothing of the special kind of warfare he would soon be waging to save the giant brokerage firm.

A respected securities attorney and partner in the Wall Street firm of Debevoise & Plimpton, Friedman joined Hutton as executive vice president and general counsel. He had previously served as clerk to a Supreme Court justice. In addition, he had taught at Columbia Law School, and served—along with Rittereiser—as a director of the Chicago Board of Options Exchange. During part of the Carter administration, Friedman had been deputy assistant secretary of the treasury, and in 1980 he was appointed to the SEC.

"Ritt is no dummy," says a banker who knows him well. "At the time, he needed somebody who was squeaky clean, and that's what he got when he hired Friedman."

From his days on the SEC, Friedman, of course, knew John S.R. Shad, commission chairman, who had lost out to Fomon in the race for Hutton CEO in 1970.

Friedman was intelligent, controlled, and hard-driving, a graduate of Harvard Law School. Like the best of corporate counsels, he was a good listener. He shared with Rittereiser a devotion to his family, and in a cynical decade, he still had heroes he looked up to—men such as Dean Acheson, President Truman's former secretary of state, and John McCloy, onetime head of what would later be known as the National Security Council. By all the evidence, Friedman was a straight arrow.

For years Friedman had pondered moving to a large financial institution, although he leaned more toward banks than brokerages. But when Bob Rittereiser had called him in the fall of 1985 and asked if he'd be interested in coming to Hutton, Friedman had been receptive. In the months that followed, he and Rittereiser had met several times, often at 800 Fifth Avenue, where Hutton kept one of several luxury apartments. Eventually, Friedman had lunched with both Rittereiser and Fomon.

It took Friedman five months to decide to join Hutton, and as with the other newcomers to the executive suite, his decision involved no financial sacrifice. Like Ed Lill's, his employment contract specified a base salary of at least $300,000 a year and a minimum annual bonus of $300,000 for the next three years. If he needed to bail out, a $2.5 million golden parachute would prevent serious personal injury.

Friedman reported for work on April 2. His first unexpected revelation was to learn that Bob Rittereiser played as large a role in the company as he did, given Fomon's retention of the chairman and CEO titles. Fomon was a puzzle to him. "He's a very complex person," Friedman says. "He can be mean and vindictive or nice and generous. I don't know him well enough to understand him. In fact, I don't know anyone who understands him."

The more Friedman saw of Fomon, the stranger he found the chairman: funny, smart, clever, and charming—in short, thoroughly likable at times, says Friedman, but at other times embarrassingly mean and cruel. Insecure, too. One day just after Friedman arrived, he and Rittereiser were talking in Rittereiser's office. The door sprang open and in barged Fomon. Saying nothing, he walked around the room a couple of times, smoked a cigarette, and walked out. Friedman learned that this was normal behavior for Fomon. "He wanted to know what was going on," says Friedman. "He was getting nervous and anxious about what Bob was doing."

Fomon says he doesn't recall the incident.

The chairman might have been nervous about Friedman as well if he'd known the extent of the lawyer's ambitions. One former senior executive came to believe that Friedman had his eye on the top job. "I don't know how interested [Friedman was] in running the legal department in a brokerage house," the executive says. "He really had bigger ideas and said that in an industry publication right after he came on board."

Before he actually got into the job, Friedman says, he didn't understand the nature of the company's problems. The first thing to hit him was the mess Tom Rae had left in the legal department. Rae, though a good enforcement lawyer, had not been a manager.

Any retail brokerage normally generates six or seven hundred phone calls a day to the legal department; Hutton's lawyers had to field both those calls and a huge volume of litigation problems and customer complaints. And they also had to handle the investigations by Congress and the Securities and Exchange Commission as well as state proceedings. The department had been overwhelmed.

Friedman took command of about fifty-five lawyers, some very good and some mediocre. Standards were low, and the working conditions, he says, were "just vile. There was no library, and the file room looked like a wastepaper basket. . . . They couldn't do their work."

He began to streamline operations, and he also added new people, which, predictably, upset the Hutton old guard. "The last thing we needed," says one former vice president, "was more lawyers." But the new people did create some improvements. For example, one of them thought they should create a special group just to handle customer complaints. A great idea, decided Friedman. When they did, the time required to deal with most complaints dropped from three or four months to just twelve working days.

Friedman also hadn't known the extent of Hutton's larger management shortcomings. "What I didn't understand when I joined Hutton," he says, "was how much of a problem Bob Fomon was. That came as a great surprise to me."

Fomon, he learned, routinely abused the chain of command and ignored the normal checks and balances built into the system. He fixated on details. "Bob had a set of old friends, [although] some of them were young, particularly in the corporate finance area. These people," Friedman says, "would come to Bob and he would pour holy water on their deals. Then they would go back with approval from the highest level, bypassing the head of corporate finance, all the committees, and all the others. That's the way Bob ran the whole company.

"Plan? Forget plan. There was no concept of what they were trying to accomplish. There never was because Bob Fomon was basically a problem solver rather than a manager." For instance, Fomon took it upon himself to insist that an adequate number of urinals be installed on the floor housing Jerry Miller's retail department in the new building. "That is not," the lawyer observes, "what a CEO does."

"Friedman," says Fomon, tit for tat, "is the kind of guy who has an opinion on every subject. This guy built up a staff [of attorneys] you wouldn't believe."

FRIDAY, APRIL 4

39 ½

The Honorable William J. Hughes, member of Congress, Democrat from New Jersey, began the day as he always did—with a copy of the *Washington Post.* As he thumbed through the paper, a headline buried on page 9 of Section C caught his eye—"Hutton Paid Bacon $600,000 Severance."

Bacon was a name Hughes knew well. In fact, it was Bacon who had written what was later dubbed the smoking-gun memo. In the memo, Hughes recalled, Bacon defended Hutton's overdrafts on the grounds that they were "encouraged by the firm" and were, "in fact, identical to what the firm" practiced nationwide.

In his letters to Hughes, of course, Bob Fomon had never disclosed that the firm had made severance payments to any employee involved in the check scandal. In fact, he had stated that

Hutton had dealt harshly with these employees—Bacon in particular.

Now Hughes learned about the sizable payoff only because a *Post* reporter had dug up an affidavit, which was part of a lawsuit filed in Superior Court in Washington, D.C., by Bacon's estranged wife, Susan, accusing Bacon of adultery and asking for a legal separation.

MONDAY, APRIL 7

38 ⅝

It was a warm day, almost too warm for this time of year. Bill Hughes arrived early at his office. There was a long letter he wanted to write to Bob Fomon in response to Fomon's of March 17.

"I was disturbed to read in last Friday's *Washington Post*," Hughes began, "that Hutton has paid Mr. Bacon a $600,000 'separation and bonus compensation' in connection with his resignation, and disappointed that I learned this information in this manner, rather than directly from you. If the information is true, the subcommittee has a number of questions that it wants answered."

Hughes then asked Fomon for copies of all written agreements with Bacon, a summary of all oral agreements, and an explanation of how Bacon had satisfied the fine of $25,000 to $50,000 recommended by Griffin Bell. Hughes also wanted a complete report on the status of all other Hutton employees who had been cited by Bell and who had subsequently left the company.

In addition, Hughes demanded a full account of the actions Hutton had taken with regard to every other Hutton employee who had been cited by Bell but had remained with the company. Also, he wanted to know who at Hutton had approved the severance actions.

"You stated," Hughes concluded, "that the purpose of your letter was to supplement your testimony and 'bring events up-to-date.' We, too, are anxious to be brought up to date. The subcommittee will not close its investigation of the Hutton case until these key questions and other outstanding requests are satisfied."

FRIDAY, APRIL 11

38 ⅞

In his response to Congressman Hughes, Fomon tried to justify the large severance payments the firm had made to Perry Bacon. Hutton, Fomon argued with some justice, made payments to all employees who are terminated, and Bacon's case was no different from the rest. Moreover, he added, the firm was concerned about lawsuits for wrongful discharge. So it executed severance agreements in which the company—in exchange for financial compensation—secured the terminated employee's promise not to sue Hutton.

Again, it was Fomon's omissions that were telling. He failed to point out that these arrangements were in sharp contrast to the severance policies outlined in Hutton's own "Branch Office Procedures Manual." According to the manual, all employees, with the exception of account executives, who were terminated for reasons other than cause, were entitled to severance pay—up to a maximum of two weeks' pay. Moreover, the manual said, employees who resigned voluntarily were not eligible for severance pay. Under these provisions, Bacon, who had been terminated for cause, was entitled to no severance pay.

Fomon pointed out that Hutton had good reason to fear lawsuits. He referred to the resignation agreement offered to John Pierce, a former branch manager from St. Louis, Missouri, and currently an account executive in Sarasota, Florida. Instead of accepting the company's proposal, Fomon said, Pierce had brought a $20 million suit against E.F. Hutton and Judge Bell in the U.S. District Court for the District of Columbia for defamation and breach of privacy.

By contrast, Fomon pointed out, Bacon had agreed to resign. A letter of reprimand stating that he was "responsible for enacting and supervising a sophisticated scheme of overdrafting the Alexandria branch bank account" and that "no reasonable person could have believed this conduct was proper" was placed in his personnel file. Fomon also said that Bacon was not required to pay the fine recommended by Bell because, as Bell had said in his press conference, "If they want to leave Hutton, they won't have to pay the fines."

"As you know," Fomon wrote, "the fine was recommended with the expectation that Mr. Bacon would continue as an employee of the company. Instead, he lost his job over these events and his future is uncertain. . . . The severance arrangements do not in any way affect Mr. Bacon's cooperation with investigations into the conduct that led to Hutton's plea. In fact, the company's release of Mr. Bacon is conditioned upon Mr. Bacon providing his best efforts to cooperate with the company in any litigation now pending or which may later arise in which the company requires or desires his cooperation as a witness or otherwise."

Hughes was less than pleased with Fomon's response. In fact, he was getting increasingly angry, a mood which did not bode well for the report that his subcommittee would issue in December.

FRIDAY, MAY 2

38 ⅛

By most accounts, Bob Fomon's business decisions were becoming increasingly erratic. For example, when he was informed that the Hutton bond-trading department had lost $60 million in April, he called the firm's management committee together for a special session. Despite Bob Rittereiser's absence, Fomon announced that Bill Dunn, head of the bond-trading department, had to go.

Giving Dunn the boot wasn't an entirely unreasonable action

for Fomon to take. Dunn's performance, according to Scott Pierce, had been inexcusable. "You could have thrown darts," says Pierce, "and done a better job than he did." The trading losses had eaten up several months' profits earned by other Hutton departments.

What was unreasonable, however, was Fomon's next move. He turned to Norman Epstein, head of operations, and asked him to take over the department. A startled Epstein, who knew nothing about bond trading, couldn't believe what he had heard. "No fucking way, Bob," Epstein said.

It was still possible for managers to point out Fomon's own lapses to him; he had no delusions of infallibility. At a later management meeting, for instance, Fomon was insisting that another employee, a man in retail sales, should be fired. Jerry Miller agreed. "Not only should we *fire* the man," Miller said in response to Fomon, "but we should *fire* the guy who *hired* him."

"That's right," Fomon said. "I'm all for it."

Miller then looked at Fomon and said, "Bob, turn around." Fomon didn't know what Miller was getting at.

"Why?" Fomon asked.

"Just turn around, Bob," Miller said. Fomon turned around and found himself facing a mirror.

"Now, Bob," Miller said, "you're looking at the guy who hired that guy."

Fomon laughed.

"Bob was not arrogant in the sense of failing to recognize his own failings," says Steve Friedman, who recalls the incident. "He knew himself well."

About the same time, when Orin Kramer, Hutton's outside damage-control expert, asked Fomon to outline his strategy for the firm for the annual report, Fomon replied, "Beats the shit out of me."

From Scott Pierce's vantage point, Hutton appeared to be in much better shape by the late spring of 1986. The brokerage's capital position was stronger, and Hutton employees had remained remarkably loyal.

Despite the fears of many executives, few brokers had actually abandoned ship and the majority of Hutton's individual clients had stayed with them. Further, most of the institutional accounts, which had shut the brokerage off after the guilty plea, had returned.

In spite of Pierce's generally optimistic outlook, he knew that Hutton had been particularly hard hit in the public finance area, and that business was still weak. Politicians feared that their constituents would skewer them for doing business with Hutton. Likewise, revenues from corporate finance were way down. Few companies, it seemed, wanted to do business with a corporation that was an admitted felon.

Moreover, one of Hutton's biggest problems—the growing rift between Fomon and Rittereiser—just hadn't surfaced yet. Fomon still insisted on being a part of every Hutton decision. He had a habit of barging in on closed-door meetings between Rittereiser and other executives—as he had done when Steve Friedman and Rittereiser were meeting in early April.

But Fomon and Rittereiser didn't go head to head until later in their conflict, according to Friedman. What happened instead, he says, was that Rittereiser started to fill up the management spaces Fomon left, and that made Fomon uncomfortable. "He didn't want to fill those vacuums, but he didn't want anybody else to fill them either."

As the year wore on, the acrimony between Fomon and Rittereiser became openly bitter. In some people's eyes, it became a class struggle—Rittereiser the streetwise kid versus the patrician Fomon. The groundwork for Fomon's ouster began to take shape.

TUESDAY, JUNE 10

35 ¼

To the outside world, E.F. Hutton looked like a plum ripe for the plucking. The check scandal—by weakening the firm's reputation and calling into question the competence of its management— had turned beleaguered Hutton into a takeover target. A merger might breathe new life into the company, or so some on Wall Street said.

In years past, Hutton had acquired a reputation for gobbling up smaller brokerage houses. In 1949, it had swallowed the Clement Curtis Co. of San Francisco; in 1954, Ullman & Latshaw of Kansas City; and in 1962, Beer & Co. of Atlanta, Memphis, and New Orleans. In the seventies, Hutton had continued to grow by acquisition, bagging dozens of regional brokerages. It had also snared the fourteen largest and most successful offices of duPont Walston when that prestigious Wall Street firm had gone belly up. Only briefly had Hutton itself been considered a merger partner by another firm—Morgan Stanley in the mid 1970s—and then not seriously.

Now Hutton the hunter had become Hutton the hunted.

On June 10, Bob Fomon and Bob Rittereiser met with representatives of what Hutton described in its Securities and Exchange Commission filings as a "major U.S. manufacturing firm" for preliminary discussion of a possible merger. The manufacturer, it turned out, was Chrysler Corp., the company Hutton had taken public in 1923.

Chrysler had some interest in expanding into the then booming financial services business, and it thought Hutton might be a good vehicle to ride in on. The auto giant ultimately decided, however, not to make an offer for Hutton, or any other brokerage company for that matter. Instead, Chrysler used its capital to purchase American Motors.

But while it was considering a Hutton purchase, Chrysler

and—more important in the long run—its outside adviser, Shearson Lehman Brothers, got a good look at Hutton's confidential financial data. Hutton had turned over all this information before calling in its own outside investment banker, Salomon Brothers. "Very dumb," says Ken Wilson, then a managing director at Salomon Brothers.

"Ritt," says Wilson, "was very inexperienced in these kinds of matters." But in Rittereiser's defense, says Wilson, "he had seen how screwed up things were at Hutton and [doing] this deal looked like good high ground." Fomon, too, was eager to merge.

In a conversation soon after Chrysler backed out, Rittereiser and Fomon agreed not to pursue any potential mergers. Rittereiser was convinced that Hutton wasn't ready for merger talks. For one, it didn't have enough information to give a potential buyer. "We didn't even have a business plan," says Rittereiser. "We decided that we should repair the company and manage it before going through this kind of a process [again]."

TUESDAY, JULY 15

32 7/8

Bob Rittereiser had hired Steve Friedman to help him mop up the mess at E.F. Hutton, and, day by day, Friedman found more and more messes to attend to.

George Aubin was the latest. By now, Hutton was a vulnerable and troubled company, and Aubin and his commodities-trading scam made it more vulnerable yet.

In a lawsuit filed July 15 in U.S. District Court for the Southern District of Texas, Hutton accused Aubin, a forty-two-year-old Houston resident, of defrauding the company through schemes dating as far back as 1980. Aubin's scams all had a common thread. He and his associates would open trading accounts, then issue checks they knew would bounce to cover their losses.

In 1983 Aubin opened thirty-nine margin accounts with Hutton. Trading in the accounts was fast and furious. When Aubin suffered big losses in September 1984, he covered himself by getting Hutton to prepay him for securities he sold, then repurchasing the same securities with the money he'd received from Hutton. In other words, although a brokerage normally has five to seven days to pay a customer, Aubin demanded that Hutton pay him the day after each sale. Then he delayed paying Hutton for his purchases until after the settlement date. By playing the float among his many accounts, Aubin could buy stock and maintain futures positions even though he had negative balances.

Finally, Hutton caught on to Aubin's game and refused to execute any more orders for him. Then the brokerage ordered the Texan to pay up what he owed—a total of $46,430,686.28. In early 1985, Aubin responded by issuing twenty-eight checks to cover the amount of his debt. They bounced.

Still, Aubin persevered. In a meeting with Hutton senior managers, he brought along his buddy John Haralson, who assured the executives that he wanted "to make good Aubin's debt." Haralson proposed to do so by selling two savings and loans—Mercury and Milam—that he owned. They would fetch, he said, about $100 million. After studying the S&Ls' financials, Hutton entered into an agreement with Haralson that allowed Aubin to continue trading. Aubin made the most of it. Over the next few months, he withdrew more than $40 million in equity from his Hutton accounts.

Alas, in the middle of March, the Federal Home Loan Bank Board, citing numerous illegalities in Mercury's and Milam's business practices, placed the S&Ls—which not surprisingly turned out to be owned by Aubin, not Haralson—into conservatorship. Hutton was left holding the bag.

Now the brokerage was suing Aubin and his associates for more than $48 million, plus accrued interest, plus triple damages. But the real damage had been done. The $48 million hit to the firm's bottom line would turn out to be greater than Hutton's entire 1985 earnings of $43.60 million.

Moreover, the incident was acutely embarrassing to the firm. "Here we were," says Scott Pierce, "being accused of kiting checks. Yet, at the same time, someone was kiting checks on us—to the tune of forty-eight million dollars."

The Aubin fiasco was especially worrisome for one other reason. It involved one of Hutton's biggest and most consistent revenue producers, Don Sanders of Houston. Sanders generated $2 million to $3 million in commissions every year for Hutton. He was prominent in the community, a part owner of the Houston Astros, and a member of the board of the University of Houston. Sanders also served as a member of the board of E.F. Hutton & Co., the retail sales arm, and as a member of the firm's influential Directors' Advisory Council, a group made up of Hutton's top brokers. DAC members collectively accounted for more than $50 million annually in revenues to the firm, so when members of this group spoke, Hutton listened.

FRIDAY, JULY 25

34 7/8

Two qualities set Mark F. Kessenich, Jr., apart from the other men Bob Rittereiser hired. One was his arrogance, the other his abrasiveness. A former U.S. Marine, Kessenich came to Hutton from mammoth Citicorp, where he had been executive vice president for investment banking. His reputation on Wall Street as a securities trader was solid, which was why Rittereiser wanted him and was willing to pay so much to get him.

Kessenich's employment contract called for him to receive a minimum of $4.7 million over three years, and he got paid regardless of how well—or how poorly—he performed. He would also receive bonuses based on performance. He joined Hutton on July 25 as executive vice president and managing director of capital markets. There, he would be in charge of trading fixed-income instruments—bonds, certificates of deposit, and so forth. His mission was to help build an institutional business to balance the earnings from retail. However, Hutton's capital markets group—unlike those of other big brokerage houses—was drowning in red ink.

Before he joined the firm, Kessenich went to Fomon's Fifth Avenue apartment for drinks and a talk. "I'm not interested in how much money you can make [for the firm]," Fomon told him bluntly, "I'm interested in your not losing money."

In fact, Fomon had proposed to Rittereiser a year earlier that Hutton get out of the fixed-income business altogether. Rittereiser did not take the suggestion seriously. "I thought the statement was thrown out more for the shock value than for anything else," he says. In any case, Rittereiser said a firm no. "If you're going to do that, you better understand what you're doing," he said to Fomon. "You can't be in the securities business without being in the fixed-income business." So Fomon backed off.

Now the forty-eight-year-old Kessenich was charged with turning the tide. Was he up to the job? Rittereiser thought so at the time—and so, it seems, did Bob Fomon. Shortly after Kessenich came to Hutton, a senior executive from Citicorp telephoned Fomon. If Hutton hired anyone else from Citicorp, the executive said, Citicorp would stop doing business with the firm. "I figured if the guy was that angry," Fomon remembers, "then we must have picked off somebody pretty good."

As the year wore on, Rittereiser, Fomon, and the other members of Hutton's senior management team would learn otherwise. The huge trading losses that Kessenich and his group would pile up would ultimately contribute to the downfall of the firm.

But it wasn't all Kessenich's fault. For months, not one senior executive at Hutton ever stepped in to stem the trading losses. "I don't blame Mark Kessenich," says then operations head Norm Epstein. "Somebody should have sat him down and told him, 'Man, if you lose any more money, I'm going to kill you.' "

The next six weeks were not easy ones for Hutton. In early August, the firm's public relations problems grew more acute. In an embarrassing interview published in *M*, the upscale men's magazine, Fomon revealed, if not all, quite enough about himself to generate consternation throughout the firm. Fomon confessed to *M* that he preferred young women because they were "decorative." Most older women, he pointed out, have emotional problems. "Basically," he allowed, "I'm very shallow when it comes to women. . . . I don't want every dinner conversation to be about what people think of Muammar Qaddafi."

Accompanying the interview was a picture of the grinning Fomon holding his teddy bear, Ralph (a gift from a girlfriend), and flanked by two nubile members of Southampton's partygoing set. The article caused an uproar, and not only at Hutton headquarters. "His daughter was furious with him," according to one former senior executive. "The implication [of the article] was that Bob had no use for women except in bed. Bob," the executive adds, "has never been known for his emotional maturity."

M titled its profile "Robert Fomon, Without Apologies," and Hutton's battle-scarred boss made none once the article was published. "Every older man likes young girls," he told anyone who cared to listen. "I'm just honest enough to admit it."

His colleagues didn't see it that way, though. A few days after *M* published its profile, Norm Epstein charged into Fomon's office waving a copy of the offending issue. "What are you, crazy?" Epstein demanded to know. Fomon only shrugged.

"We were all bullshit," remembers Epstein. "It was fine for Fomon to be in the spotlight as long as the publicity was favorable. But that article made him—and the firm—look foolish." Executives couldn't help comparing *M*'s portrait of Fomon to *Manhattan, Inc.*'s glowing profile of Rittereiser, published just the previous month. Entitled "Hutton's Hidden Asset—Robert Rittereiser Is the New Man on a Hot Seat," the piece hailed Rittereiser as the firm's savior.

As for Rittereiser, he had more pressing matters on his mind than Fomon's foolish public self-revelations. In late August, Fomon pulled Rittereiser aside and asked him if he could talk with top executives at Transamerica Corp., the giant insurance and financial services company in San Francisco. Rittereiser didn't know it yet, but Transamerica was interested in acquiring an even larger stake—perhaps a controlling one—in Hutton.

For years, Transamerica had bought and sold Hutton stock, strictly as an investment. The company had always kept its holdings at less than 5 percent (the amount at which the Securities and Exchange Commission requires shareholders to report their purchases).

Occasionally, when then Transamerica chairman and CEO John R. Beckett came to New York, he would stop by Hutton's offices for lunch and to see how his investment was doing.

And he would tell Fomon that if Hutton was ever interested in talking about a merger, $7.2 billion-a-year Transamerica was interested in listening. But "nothing ever developed," says Fomon. Beckett retired as chairman in 1983 and was succeeded as chairman and chief executive officer by James R. Harvey, whom Fomon had known socially in Los Angeles. Harvey, a pleasant-looking man with a large nose and receding hairline, was named chief executive officer of Transamerica in 1981 and chairman in 1983. He had earned a bachelor's degree in engineering from Princeton University and an MBA, then served as a management consultant with the public accounting firm, Touche Ross & Co., before casting his lot with Transamerica in 1965.

What did Harvey see in Hutton? For one, as Transamerica announced in its 1986 annual report, "we made a vital strategic decision to concentrate on insurance and financial services." Specifically, Harvey envisioned Hutton's huge retail sales force hawking Transamerica's insurance products. "Hutton was—and still is to this day—the one firm that has done the most effective job of selling insurance," says Fred Whittemore of Morgan Stanley, Transamerica's investment banker.

The insurance products Hutton sold were those of its life insurance subsidiary. "If you go to Merrill Lynch, it has brokers who sell insurance and brokers who sell stocks. Hutton's brokers sell both products, and they'll go—like all brokers will—for the product with the highest commission rate," Whittemore says.

Fomon's interest in pursuing discussions with Transamerica surprised Rittereiser. "I thought we weren't going to sell the firm," he told Fomon. "I thought we were going to give ourselves time to clean up the place. We have our work cut out for us just getting this place cleaned up."

"I'm still CEO," Fomon, annoyed, retorted, "and I don't think we should turn these people off."

At the time, Rittereiser didn't know why Fomon was so interested in pursuing a marriage with Transamerica, but he had his suspicions. "I was bringing in a new management team," Rittereiser remembers, "and I think part of his thinking was that this was his last chance to have some impact on the future direction of the company."

SUNDAY, SEPTEMBER 7

Market Closed

Flushing Meadow Park—across from Shea Stadium in New York—is a swamp turned oasis. The site of the magnificent 1939 World's Fair, it houses the United States Tennis Association's National Tennis Center and is home to the U.S. Open and Davis Cup tennis championships.

On September 7, after the close of the 1986 U.S. Open finals, Bob Rittereiser and his wife, Pat, a pleasant, down-to-earth woman with short-cropped hair and an open face, drove from Flushing Meadow to the Carlyle Hotel at 35 East Seventy-sixth Street in Manhattan.

There they met for dinner with Bob Fomon, Jim Harvey, Transamerica President Frank C. Herringer, and Fred Whittemore. As discreet as a Swiss bank, the Carlyle is a favorite of old-money gentry and millionaire CEOs. The dinner, which was arranged by Whittemore, lasted four hours.

Despite their social contacts, Jim Harvey wasn't impressed with Bob Fomon. At the age of sixty-one, the check scandal still hanging over his head, his health increasingly fragile, Fomon was, in Harvey's opinion, clearly on his way out.

But Fomon wasn't impressed with Harvey, either. He, like a number of others on Wall Street, regarded the man as indecisive. "You got the feeling," says an investment banker who knows Harvey well, "that once he'd tied his shoes in the morning, he'd made most of his decisions."

Harvey "loved Rittereiser" though. "They wanted him to run Hutton for them," Whittemore remembers. And that night, Rittereiser and Harvey arranged to meet in San Francisco, where Rittereiser would be a week later on business.

Fomon and Whittemore continued the discussion as they left the restaurant. Would Fomon entertain an offer in the $45-a-share range?

Fomon said he would not. "You know forty-five dollars is nowhere near the mark," he said to his friend. Whittemore, says Fomon, "had had the idea that we were talking to Chrysler in the forty-five dollar range. We weren't. There were never any discussions with Chrysler on price."

In San Francisco, Rittereiser and Harvey chatted privately for about three hours. Before they parted, Rittereiser agreed to allow Transamerica and its investment banker, Morgan Stanley, to take a closer look at Hutton.

The offer Transamerica was prepared to make for Hutton called for a tax-free exchange of stock between the two companies. "It was a good deal for stockholders," Whittemore insists, "even though it didn't necessarily put a lot of cash in people's pockets." "We believe they never really did make a formal offer," says Rittereiser.

The question of whether Transamerica ever actually made an offer is still being investigated by the SEC. Hutton didn't disclose the terms of the proposed agreement publicly and maintained that it wasn't required to because no offer was ever formally made.

The value of the offer Transamerica had in mind is still a matter of debate, too. Some Hutton insiders argue that the firm was worth as much as $47 a share, others as little as $39 a share.

In any event, the deal fell through over the next few months. For his part, Fomon now says he never even considered the potential offer seriously. In fact, he argues, he went to the dinner meeting only out of politeness to his friend Whittemore. Fomon and Whittemore went way back. After John Shad resigned as head of Hutton's corporate finance department in 1972, Fomon offered Whittemore the job. Whittemore, however, decided to stay on at Morgan Stanley.

"Morgan Stanley could see a nice merger fee out there for themselves," Fomon says. "I never took Transamerica seriously, because I didn't think they could afford to buy Hutton."

Besides, Fomon maintains, from a personal point of view he was interested only in a cash purchase. He didn't want to own Transamerica stock.

Fomon also claims that he was so unimpressed with Transamerica's proposed offer that he never even brought it up with the board, despite the fact that board member Peter Ueberroth also served on Transamerica's board. "I never thought it was important enough," Fomon says.

Rittereiser sees it differently. "His behavior at the time," Rittereiser maintains, "indicated to me that he took the matter very seriously. If Bob wasn't interested, we would not have been doing preliminary work to put these guys in a position to make a judgment about Hutton."

A week or so later, Rittereiser and Norm Epstein, Hutton's longtime head of operations, met for breakfast. Rittereiser complained how difficult he found running Hutton with Fomon still around.

Epstein expressed his view, which was that Fomon had to go— and the sooner the better. In fact, Epstein offered to bring up the matter himself with Hutton's board. "No, no," Rittereiser replied. "I'll do it my way."

MONDAY, SEPTEMBER 22

41 7/8

When he was a young man, Peter Anthony Cohen showed no signs of great ambition. Born in Manhattan in 1946, the son of upper-middle-class parents, he drifted through school. Only with his father's prodding did he manage to pull up his grades at Ohio State and go on to earn his MBA at Columbia.

Cohen thought he would assume a comfortable post in the family business. His parents, Florence and Sidney Cohen, were the owners and founders of Andover Togs of New York, one of the country's largest manufacturers of children's clothing. At an early age, he and his brother William began working for their father on Saturdays—Peter assembling cardboard boxes and William running the label machine. Peter learned something in this early work experience. William earned more than he did, because, his father said, William was performing skilled labor. Peter decided he'd never perform manual labor again.

Cohen could make decisions about what kind of work he would or wouldn't do, but he couldn't do anything about his height— just five feet, six inches tall. His parents, however, regaled him with stories of short men who had achieved great success— Fiorello La Guardia was one—and he took that lesson to heart as well.

In 1969, instead of joining the family business, Cohen began a Wall Street career by signing on as a securities analyst with Reynolds & Co., the predecessor of giant Dean Witter Reynolds. Two years later, on January 3, 1971, he jumped to Hayden Stone, a six-year-old investment house that eventually grew into Shearson Loeb Rhoades Inc., which itself was bought by American Express Co. in 1981. At Hayden Stone, Cohen hit his stride.

The four principal partners in the firm—Marshall S. Cogan, Roger S. Berlind, Sanford I. Weill, and Arthur Levitt, Jr.—were known as CBWL, or "Corned Beef with Lettuce." Cogan later purchased the "21" Club, Bob Fomon's favorite restaurant. Berlind went on to produce such Broadway hits as *Amadeus* and *Sophisticated Ladies*, and Levitt later became chairman of the American Stock Exchange. As for Weill, he ascended to the presidency of mammoth American Express and then, in 1984, took over Commercial Credit Co., where, in 1987, he would make an aborted run at E.F. Hutton.

Cohen turned down a $24,000-a-year offer to stay at Reynolds in order to accept the $12,000-a-year post as an analyst at Hayden Stone. "It was a very young firm," Cohen would later tell the *New York Times*, "and I perceived an opportunity to grow." Grow he did. By the end of his first year, he'd earned some $42,000, thanks in large part to a profit-sharing bonus. The next year he took home $81,000. At Hayden, Cohen had a reputation for getting things done. He also was known for having an exceptionally short fuse.

In 1973, Sandy Weill, who was then chairman and chief executive officer of Hayden Stone, tapped Cohen—thirteen years Weill's junior—as his new assistant. Soon the firm embarked on a succession of mergers. Most were arranged by Weill, then turned over to Cohen to coordinate. In 1973, Hayden Stone purchased H. Hentz & Co.; in 1974, it acquired Shearson Hammill; and in 1976, the Lambson Brothers of Chicago. In 1977, it acquired Faulkner, Dawkins & Sullivan. Meanwhile, Cohen was also helping to run the company, which was now known as Shearson Hayden Stone. By 1975, he had become executive vice president and a director of Shearson.

In 1978 he succumbed to a job offer from Republic National Bank of New York, joining the firm as executive vice president and chief administrative officer. But he stayed only a year and returned to Shearson as senior executive vice president and administrative officer. Cohen later said he missed the "day-to-day anxiety" of the investment-banking business. Back at Shearson, he could be his old hot-tempered self.

In 1979, Shearson merged with Loeb Rhoades Hornblower & Co. to become Shearson Loeb Rhodes, and Cohen—now chief operating officer—helped call the shots. Two years after that the company that had grown large by swallowing so many other firms was itself swallowed by American Express. Cohen stayed on, and in January of 1983 he reached the pinnacle of his profession. He was elected chief executive officer of Shearson, replacing his mentor, Sandy Weill.

Cohen arrived at the first board meeting in his new role carrying a big brown paper bag. Out of it he pulled an emperor's crown and mace, and, as a sign of respect, ceremoniously handed them to now American Express President Weill. Next he pulled out two oversized shoes to show how large were the ones that he, Cohen, would have to work to fill. For years, those shoes rested on the mantel in Cohen's office. A year later, in January of 1984, he was given the additional title of chairman.

For his office at Shearson Cohen added two sculptures—one of a chain saw, the other of a man's legs sawed off at the knees— symbolic of his willingness to be merciless with his opponents on Wall Street.

In 1986, Cohen spotted a target—two, in fact. He called his attorney, Jack H. Nusbaum, at Nusbaum's office at One Citicorp Center in midtown Manhattan.

A partner in the Wall Street firm of Willkie Farr & Gallagher, Nusbaum had known Cohen since his days at Hayden Stone, and over the years the two men had become friends.

"We've decided to expand our retail sales operations," Cohen told Nusbaum, "and we want to do it by acquiring a brokerage firm with a big retail sales franchise." Cohen was considering two possibilities—E.F. Hutton and PaineWebber—and he wanted Nusbaum to take a look at both. Right away, the attorney promised.

In his investigation—dubbed Operation Fruit Salad—Nusbaum turned up nothing negative about Hutton, which was known as Plum, or PaineWebber, code-named Peach.

Cohen decided to talk first to Hutton, because he believed, according to Lee Kimmell at Salomon Brothers, that of the two firms, Hutton was the better business and had the better sales force.

On September 22, a rainy day in Manhattan, Cohen dialed Rittereiser—the man he assumed was really in charge at Hutton. "Rittereiser," says Kimmell, "was heralded as the fresh new face, as the management of the future. So, if you are a good salesman, and Peter is a good salesman, you coopt him."

"Bob," Cohen said, "I've got an idea I'd like to broach with you."

Rittereiser agreed to hear Cohen out. Cohen chose a time that suited him (early) and a place that suited him (a luncheonette near his East Side apartment).

WEDNESDAY, SEPTEMBER 24

41 5/8

At the dreary luncheonette at the corner of Madison Avenue and Ninety-second Street in Manhattan, Peter Cohen and Bob Rittereiser met. They sat at a table alone, interrupted only by the waiter who took their order—two cups of coffee.

Cohen got right to the point. "I think the potential of a combination of Shearson and Hutton could be a very exciting, powerful firm in the industry," he said.

Then he outlined what he thought were Shearson's strengths and explained why combining the two firms made sense all around. Shearson was a powerhouse in investment banking, Hutton in retail brokerage, so the firms complemented one another.

Rittereiser responded by listing Hutton's other strengths—its research department, for example, and its ability to market special products, such as tax shelters.

Although he had not seen Hutton's books since the Chrysler

offer, Cohen told Rittereiser that he was prepared to begin talks at a share price of around $50. "If you're interested," Cohen concluded, "we're interested in exploring a merger."

Rittereiser conceded that Cohen's idea had merit. "It's terrific from a strategic point of view. But," he hedged, "I don't know whether it is really doable."

The big question, in Rittereiser's mind, was how the brokers at Hutton would respond. The firm had emerged from the check scandal whole but fragile. Rittereiser worried that the heavyweights of the retail sales force would jump ship at first mention of a merger with Shearson.

Rittereiser promised to get back to Cohen shortly, and the two men parted, with Rittereiser saying, "Why don't we think about this for a few days?"

FRIDAY, SEPTEMBER 26

42 ⅛

Bob Rittereiser phoned Peter Cohen before taking off for a two-week vacation in Bermuda. Cohen was also planning on leaving town. "We ought to have another conversation before I leave," Rittereiser said.

Cohen agreed, and the two men decided to drive uptown together later that day and talk in the backseat of Cohen's gray Lincoln Town Car.

Just before 6:00 P.M. Rittereiser made his way from his twelfth-floor office at One Battery Park Plaza to the nearby corner of Bridge Street. A few minutes later, Cohen's limousine edged up to the curb, a back door swung open, and Rittereiser climbed in.

During the forty-minute ride uptown, he tried to give Cohen a sense of Hutton's operations. He identified Hutton's key executives, and outlined their duties, so Cohen could get an idea of how the firms might fit together organizationally.

At the time, however, Rittereiser didn't ask Cohen for any job guarantees for Hutton people—including himself—in the combined firm. And Cohen didn't offer any.

"Part of the problem," says one former senior Hutton executive, "was Bob's attitude. His discussions with Cohen were an intellectual exercise. He didn't realize how serious Cohen was." That meeting, Rittereiser counters, focused only on the logistics of the conversations that would follow.

In any case, the conversation ended on a street corner uptown—at Ninetieth Street and Fifth Avenue—not far from Cohen's apartment. The two men stood together for a few minutes, talking, Rittereiser towering above the cigar-chomping Cohen. They agreed to speak further while Rittereiser was on vacation.

MONDAY, SEPTEMBER 29

42 ¾

While Bob Rittereiser was away, his management team uncovered a hidden time bomb. Potentially, Hutton was in more serious trouble, exactly the kind the firm didn't need. Senior managers learned that during the early 1980s Hutton had marketed tax-exempt securities under erroneous claims. Brokers had given customers literature that left the impression that floating-rate industrial revenue bonds—or upper floaters, as they were sometimes called—would behave like certificates of deposit. That is, the principal value of the bonds would not fluctuate. But in fact upper floaters were no different from any other bond: Their value moved up and down with the market. The mistake in the marketing literature wasn't uncovered until long after some $700 million of bonds had been sold.

Subsequently, ratings dropped on $250 million worth of the bonds issued by three companies: USX, National Steel, and Cleveland Electric Illuminating. When the ratings fell, so did the bonds' market value. Many of the people to whom Hutton had sold the bonds could be expected to complain.

The management committee quickly arranged an investigation—which ultimately proved to be another nail in Hutton's coffin.

TUESDAY, OCTOBER 7

41 ⅝

The self-governing British colony of Bermuda is—plain and simple—the quintessential tourist spot. A fish-hook-shaped chain of nearly 300 islands, it is anchored in the Atlantic Ocean 640 miles due east of Cape Hatteras, North Carolina.

On October 7 Peter Cohen boarded a private jet and headed for St. George—Bermuda's first capital—which sits at the far eastern tip of the islands. There he met with the vacationing Bob Rittereiser. Rittereiser's wife, Pat, joined the two men for lunch, then left them alone to talk.

Again, they discussed the possible merits of a merger. Rittereiser went into detail about changes in Hutton's back-office operations—that is, its order-processing department. But Cohen said little in response.

Cohen knew that Shearson's own back office could handle all of Hutton's transactions—and that Shearson could therefore eliminate Hutton's back office. This economy of scale was one of the things that made the merger look attractive to him.

Then Cohen described some of Shearson's personnel needs. Next, he outlined how Hutton executives might fill those slots and others as well. Norm Epstein, he said, could probably find a home at Shearson, but not Ed Lill nor Steve Friedman, because Shearson already had a chief financial officer and a general counsel. But, he stressed, he could make no definitive judgments until he met these people and others.

Rittereiser told Cohen, "I understand the idea, the issues here. If this is something you want to pursue, the right way to pursue it is to discuss it with Bob Fomon. That's the best way for you to handle it and the best way for me to handle it." In fact, says

Rittereiser, that's exactly what happened. "I wasn't in any position to decide this on my own."

The meeting ended with no decisions—or promises—made, but Cohen and Rittereiser did agree to proceed to the next step. Cohen would approach Bob Fomon, who still knew nothing about Cohen's conversations with Rittereiser.

WEDNESDAY, OCTOBER 8

42 3/4

True to his word, Cohen had phoned Fomon's office on October 8 to arrange a lunch date. The Shearson chief agreed to meet Fomon the next day on Fomon's own turf, the executive dining room on the twelfth floor of Hutton's world headquarters.

At the center of the dining room stood a pink granite table surrounded by four sleek stainless-steel-and-leather chairs, all by top furniture designer Gardner Lever. At the table, Cohen put forth the same idea to Fomon that he had to Rittereiser—in almost the same words.

"I think the combination of E.F. Hutton and Shearson would be very great," he said, "and, if Hutton is interested, Shearson would like to explore a merger." Again, he mentioned a $50-a-share starting point for negotiations.

Fomon, cautious, leaned forward. "I'd like to discuss it with Rittereiser," he responded and that was where the discussion ended. Fomon, too, thought Shearson would make an excellent merger partner—if the price was right. But, he says, he had no idea at that point that Cohen and Rittereiser had already talked in Bermuda. In fact, he says, he didn't learn of those talks until more than a year afterward.

Later that week, Rittereiser called Cohen from Bermuda to see if he had spoken to Fomon. He also told Cohen that he was coming home that Saturday and would speak to Fomon and to some others in the firm about the merger possibility.

He then hung up, promising to phone Cohen on Sunday.

SUNDAY, OCTOBER 12

Market Closed

Late Sunday afternoon, when he still hadn't heard from Bob Rittereiser, an anxious Peter Cohen called Rittereiser. Rittereiser told him he hadn't yet had a chance to speak to many of the Hutton executives and would get back to Cohen later.

At 10:00 P.M. Cohen's phone rang. It was Rittereiser. "I'm still trying to get in touch with Hutton executives," he said, "so I have nothing to report." On Monday, Rittereiser phoned Cohen again. "Still nothing to report," he told Shearson's tough-talking boss.

MONDAY, OCTOBER 13

47

Bob Fomon and Bob Rittereiser chatted briefly about Fomon's lunch with Peter Cohen.

"Shearson has a strong strategic interest in Hutton," Fomon said, "and it's something we ought to consider."

Rittereiser nodded. "At a minimum," he replied, "we ought to begin talking this through with the people on the management committee."

Fomon agreed, and the conversation ended.

TUESDAY, OCTOBER 14

46 ⅞

In the meantime the management committee met in the morning with the Shearson deal on the agenda. Scott Pierce, a member of the committee, knew very little about the deal in the making. He did know that Shearson had been making lots of public announcements during the fall, when Hutton's stock was soaring into the 50s. Shearson let the business media know that it wasn't talking to Hutton but would love to act as a white knight, in the event other suitors were after the brokerage.

At this juncture, whether or not to do a deal with Transamerica was still an open question. Not until that evening, when the group reconvened, would a decision be made not to proceed with the giant insurer.

After a two-hour discussion, the committee decided that the company wanted to remain independent, that they did not want to consider an offer from Shearson.

Jerry Miller and Norman Epstein were the most opposed to a potential merger. They both felt that the people in the field—the brokers—had loyally stuck with the company through the darkest days of the check scandal. Now the company should stick with them.

Most members of the management committee didn't even want to talk to Shearson representatives. Shearson, they thought, had breached its contract with Hutton earlier in the year. When, in its capacity as Chrysler's investment banker, it had received confidential information from Hutton, Shearson had signed an agreement saying it would not use this information in any way for two years. Now the company was using the data to see whether the brokerage wanted to merge. Some members of Hutton's management committee felt this was dirty pool.

WEDNESDAY, OCTOBER 15

48 3/4

Finally, three weeks after Cohen had first approached him, Rittereiser informed Cohen that Hutton had decided to end the merger discussions. "We pretty much want to go our own way as a firm," Rittereiser said.

Hutton's senior management committee met for its usual Tuesday session. Now that Hutton had spurned Shearson, would Shearson attempt a hostile takeover? The firm's senior managers chewed on the question for a while. It certainly seemed possible. Anything was possible, so wouldn't it make more sense to reopen discussions with Shearson rather than waiting for an unfriendly move?

The group agreed that it would. So, after the meeting, Rittereiser dialed Peter Ueberroth and summarized the discussion.

Ueberroth, without Rittereiser's knowledge, then phoned Jim Robinson, chairman of American Express, and told him Hutton's executives now were willing to reopen the merger talks. He suggested Robinson call Rittereiser, which he did; then Robinson dialed Cohen at Shearson.

Robinson told Cohen that he should call Rittereiser and resume discussions, and Rittereiser and Cohen agreed to meet for dinner on Thursday.

At this stage, the investment bankers at Salomon Brothers thought the possibility existed for a hostile bid. "Our own interpretation of some of the press reports toward the end of the previous week," says Rittereiser, "was that American Express seemed strongly interested in a hostile bid. We didn't believe Peter [Cohen] was going to do anything hostile. But a lot of the press comments were made by so-called unnamed American Express officials. And the tone of those comments really made us wonder."

Salomon Brothers suggested that the Hutton executives have some direct discussions with Jim Robinson, so "if this thing is closed down, it's closed down," says Rittereiser. In other words, the Hutton CEO, at this point, wanted to know that if Hutton and Amex agreed not to pursue a merger, that would be that. Amex would not come back later and pursue a hostile takeover.

THURSDAY, OCTOBER 23

46 ¼

Rittereiser, Cohen, and one of Cohen's associates, George L. Sheinberg, gathered at Cohen's apartment on Manhattan's Upper East Side.

The three men discussed Shearson's business and the investments that both firms were then making in new technology. Cohen asked Rittereiser what he thought Hutton was worth. Rittereiser declined to comment.

The three men also discussed a possible organizational structure for the merged firms.

Rittereiser left the session confident that he would serve as cochairman with Peter Cohen of the combined firms, although Cohen never made him an offer of any kind. He did say to tell Rittereiser, "If you want a role with the company, you'll have a role with the company." So, says Rittereiser, "I think that Peter was prepared to accommodate me in any way that was appropriate."

The men agreed to speak again, and Cohen reported the results of the meeting to Robinson.

MONDAY, OCTOBER 27

46 ½

Peter Cohen reached out and answered the telephone. "More time," Rittereiser said, "I need more time."

He explained that Hutton's board was slated to meet in a little more than a week, and he wanted to discuss Shearson's overture with it. He also wanted to discuss the merger further with members of Hutton's senior management. Cohen said he understood.

TUESDAY, OCTOBER 28

47 ⅛

Hutton's management committee held its regular session and again discussed the possible merger. For the most part, the senior managers were opposed to the move.

Later that day, Fomon telephoned Jim Robinson at American Express and suggested the two meet over the weekend. They agreed to have dinner at Fomon's apartment on Sunday. Fomon also informed Robinson that the more specific Shearson was about a merger, the better the discussion would be.

Rumors that Shearson would acquire Hutton swept through Wall Street. As a result Hutton's stock soared to a fifty-two-week high of $47⅛—up $4.875 in composite New York Stock Exchange trading. Volume was a hefty 2.7 million shares, and trading in the stock opened late, because buy orders exceeded sell orders.

THURSDAY, OCTOBER 30

50 ¼

The *Wall Street Journal* reported that serious merger talks were under way between Shearson and Hutton. It also gave signs that Hutton may have been headed for trouble. It quoted investment bankers as saying that Hutton's total capital of $1.14 billion on January 1 was inadequate for a major securities firm to compete in the marketplace.

Bigger and more powerful firms, such as Merrill Lynch and Goldman Sachs, the newspaper reported, were taking steps to bolster their capital. Also, the *New York Times* pointed out, a merger of Hutton and Shearson would "put out of work hundreds of Hutton's staff employees, brokers, and executives."

Meanwhile, Hutton's discussions with Transamerica ended quietly. Fomon knew he could do better than the stock swap

Transamerica offered. Ueberroth, for his part, wanted to know what Hutton was really worth. So, a former Hutton executive remembers, the baseball commissioner asked Rittereiser for "a rock-solid, no bullshit evaluation." The answer was a paltry $6 a share.

Rittereiser does not remember Ueberroth asking for an evaluation of the company. But one was performed—by Salomon Brothers. The bankers were asked to evaluate what they thought Hutton would be worth to American Express. Their answer was $56 to $60 a share. "In other words," says Rittereiser, "if American Express could have acquired Hutton even up to $60 a share, the benefit to their bottom line could be huge." Rittereiser communicated the results of the Salomon Brothers study to the board.

SUNDAY, NOVEMBER 2

Market Closed

Bob Fomon is a man of genuine good taste. His apartment at 2 East Seventieth Street, across from the Frick, is a classic of English style. With its elegant Chippendale furniture, fine English oil paintings, and antique orientals, it is both intensely rich and intensely masculine.

On a wall in the hall hangs a tiger skin, symbolizing Fomon the hunter. What Fomon doesn't tell people is that the tiger lived its entire life in Las Vegas and died of old age. After its death, its owner decided to keep the skin, and Fomon picked it up at a shop in Vegas.

On November 2, Peter Cohen, Jim Robinson, and Bob Rittereiser met for drinks at Fomon's apartment. Fomon showed them into the living room.

The meeting lasted about an hour and a half.

Again the men discussed the pros and cons of a possible merger. Cohen passed out a paper, detailing the potential merits of a merger, then another, a proposal laying out terms for an initial discussion, then an organizational chart, and finally a draft press release that sketched out an announcement of the combination.

The sheet outlining the terms of the deal included a $50-a-share cash price. It also spelled out incentive compensation arrangements for the sales force; severance arrangements for employees; the possible names of a combined firm; the timetable for the transaction; and possible titles and job descriptions for senior people at Hutton.

Rittereiser would be named cochairman of Shearson, but he would be responsible only for retail sales activities, asset management, and real estate. In other words, Rittereiser later told Fomon, "I'd end up with Jerry Miller's job."

Fomon—concerned about the survival of the Hutton name—asked Cohen what the combined firm might be called. Cohen suggested Shearson Lehman Hutton as a possibility, but made no commitments. Fomon, satisfied, pursued the matter no further.

Fomon and Rittereiser promised to take up the matter with the board on November 7, its next regularly scheduled meeting, and get back to Shearson. At this stage, Fomon favored the deal with Shearson; Rittereiser wanted to discuss the matter with the board before he made any decisions. "I was still concerned about [the deal's] doability," says Rittereiser. "And I did not believe that Fomon was in touch with how [the brokers] would react." "Fomon," says Morgan Stanley's Whittemore, "was willing to go down with the *Titanic*, but the rest of the guys didn't want to be standing on the deck when the water came over. They wanted a job."

TUESDAY, NOVEMBER 4

53 5/8

Hutton's management committee met. The mood, befitting the topic, was serious. Should Hutton merge with another firm was the question at hand. Ken Wilson of Salomon Brothers was present to offer his professional advice. The senior managers could come to no clear consensus. Some wanted to sell, others didn't. And some still didn't know which course to follow. Rittereiser asked Wilson if he thought Hutton could remain independent. Probably not, Wilson replied, not given its current financial condition.

"Ritt was confused," says Wilson. "He had assembled a new management team and wanted to pursue an independent course. On the other hand, he had met the enemy and knew it was Hutton."

As Wilson recalls the meeting, most of the senior managers were inclined to sell. "Kessenich didn't want to," he says, "Friedman was unsure. Lill didn't say anything. Dick Locke initially didn't want to sell out. At the time, I don't think Epstein wanted to sell."

Fomon had to leave the meeting, so it was adjourned early. At 5:30 P.M. the group reconvened at 800 Fifth Avenue, one of the apartments Hutton maintained. Fomon came in and fixed himself a drink. According to Wilson, the Hutton chairman was already "totally trashed."

"While the debate raged on," he says, "you hear the clink of ice cubes in the glass." Fomon, Rittereiser says, was particularly angry at Norm Epstein, whom, for reasons that weren't clear, he called a greenmailer.

Soon, says Wilson, Fomon started to walk out, saying, " 'Oh, you guys are all crazy. You are all full of shit. Let's sell this damned firm.' Norm Epstein, who was sitting next to me," Wilson says, "stands up and was about to take a swing at Fomon. I grabbed Epstein and pushed Fomon away. The place was beginning to look like a mad house."

It turned out to make no difference what the management committee thought. Hutton's board made the ultimate decision on its own.

Through this entire week, with the board meeting coming up on Friday, Rittereiser spoke to Wilson almost hourly during the working day. He was trying to put together a new business plan as an alternative to selling the firm. The board, explains Rittereiser, "had nothing to look at to enable them to make a judgment. The business plan would give them alternatives to consider."

At that stage Rittereiser, was, in Wilson's view, naive about a lot of things having to do with mergers. "He had no idea of his confidentiality obligations, of the structure of a transaction," Wilson says. "That wasn't his background at Merrill." By the following year, though, when Shearson actually succeeded in acquiring Hutton, Rittereiser had gained considerable sophistication in these matters.

FRIDAY, NOVEMBER 7

48 ³/₈

All this activity generated more widespread press activity, and by Thursday, November 6, Hutton executives were swamped with telegrams and telexes from their brokers expressing concern about the fate of the firm.

On the Friday following the meeting at Bob Fomon's apartment, Hutton's board met for a long, tense session at the company's headquarters. The meeting wouldn't adjourn until after 7:30 P.M. It began with some routine business, but once that was dispensed with, the meeting moved on to the real agenda for the day. Ken Wilson from Salomon Brothers and an attorney from Hutton's outside law firm were asked to sit in. From the outset, says Wilson, "it was very clear that the shit was going to hit the fan. This was going to be an all-day affair."

Soon after the meeting got under way, Wilson excused himself, went into an adjoining office, and dialed his boss, John H. Gutfreund, the canny, demanding chairman of Salomon Brothers. "Get over here," Wilson said firmly and hung up. Gutfreund, cigar in hand, arrived about a half hour later.

After everyone was gathered, Rittereiser laid out his plans for

Hutton. "I thought," he says, "since there had been no discussions at any time about the strategic direction of the company, it would be a good time for me to talk about other possibilities for the firm."

But Rittereiser wasn't allowed to make his presentation. Instead, the board insisted that it dive right into a discussion of a possible merger with Shearson.

"I gave them too much credit," Rittereiser says, "in terms of them being smart businesspeople. I was trying to do what I would have expected from line management if I were a board member, [which was to give] them enough information so they could make an informed decision."

Soon after the discussion of Shearson began, the outside directors asked Fomon, Rittereiser, and Pierce to leave the room. A half hour later, Gutfreund emerged with some questions.

Had Cohen and Robinson handed out any paper at the meeting on Sunday? Gutfreund wanted to know.

"Yes," Rittereiser replied.

"Could you get me a copy?" Gutfreund asked, and Rittereiser nodded that he could.

Did Rittereiser think that Shearson had made an actual offer for Hutton? Rittereiser said he did not think that they had.

The board then asked Fomon to rejoin the meeting. What did the chairman think of the Shearson proposal? What did he think the board should do?

Fomon sat quietly for a moment. "I knew that if I told them that we should definitely do the Shearson deal," he says, "then they would have done it."

But Fomon was worried about the employees. In the days preceding the meeting, he had been deluged with wires and letters pleading with him not to merge with Shearson. "Out of a sense of loyalty to the employees," he said, "I decided not to endorse the Shearson deal."

"It's up to you guys," Fomon said, then got up and walked out.

Next the board summoned Pierce. He, too, was asked what he thought of the Shearson offer. "We were going to put five thousand employees out of work, and I didn't think that was the right thing to do," Pierce says, so he urged the board to vote no.

When the board members zeroed in on Rittereiser, they asked him what he thought the risks of a merger were. Losing retail brokers, was Rittereiser's reply.

He also thought, probably with some justification, that if Shearson had a chance to initiate due diligence, its offer would drop. So if the board wanted to go through with the deal, Rittereiser told them, they'd better make sure they had a bulletproof contract.

Then Rittereiser and Pierce were asked to rejoin the meeting. The outside directors informed them that they had instructed Gutfreund to let Shearson know that they would entertain an offer of $55 a share for Hutton stock.

The board imposed other conditions besides price on a sale. Any merger agreement, Ueberroth recommended, had to be "bulletproof" and executed by the opening of trading on November 10.

Also, Shearson had to agree to integrate Hutton's management and employees into the merged firm. It was a dubious proposition at best, and Gutfreund knew it.

After the meeting adjourned, Gutfreund reached Jim Robinson by telephone at about 8:00 P.M. Robinson listened politely to Hutton's proposal, then dialed Cohen at home and laid out the terms. The kiss of death, as far as Cohen was concerned, was Hutton's insistence that the deal be executed by Sunday night with an airtight contract—no "due diligence outs," meaning Shearson couldn't call off the deal if it found any surprises in Hutton's books.

Robinson asked Cohen what he wanted to do. Not surprisingly, Cohen wanted to walk away. "I'm going to the beach," he said.

Cohen knew that his firm couldn't enter into a bulletproof deal to buy Hutton at $55 a share without having access to Hutton's books or performing due diligence.

Cohen told Robinson flatly that they simply couldn't proceed, and Robinson said that Cohen should expect a call from Gutfreund.

A few minutes later, Gutfreund phoned Cohen and again outlined Hutton's conditions. "John," Cohen said, "I appreciate your help in this matter, but we have no interest in pursuing a transaction on that basis. Have a nice weekend. Good-bye."

Immediately after Friday's long meeting, Peter Ueberroth pulled Rittereiser aside and told him, firmly, that he and Fomon could not continue their fighting. Puzzled, Rittereiser asked Ueberroth what he meant. The board, Ueberroth explained, "wanted a recommendation from Fomon himself that he step down." It was up to Rittereiser, said Ueberroth, to explain to Fomon "where we are." In other words, the board wanted Fomon to step aside, but they wanted Rittereiser to deliver the message. The assignment was, Rittereiser says, "almost a test of my manhood."

During the time that Rittereiser, Fomon, and the other executives had left the meeting, Gutfreund had told the board that it had to make up its mind who was going to be in charge of the firm—Fomon or Rittereiser. The outside board members were already angry at being kept ignorant of Chrysler's and Transamerica's interest in Hutton. Ueberroth learned about one of the potential deals only because he also served on the Transamerica board.

Rittereiser arranged to meet Fomon for lunch the next day before the reconvened board meeting.

SATURDAY, NOVEMBER 8

Market Closed

At 1 P.M. on Saturday, Bob Fomon met Bob Rittereiser for lunch at the Polo Club. The Polo in the Westbury Hotel at 840 Madison Avenue (between Sixty-ninth and Seventieth streets) is known for its opulent English club–style setting, its high prices, and its heavy French food. The two men walked past the portrait of Prince Charles in the vestibule into the handsome dining room with its dark mahogany walls and horsey prints.

They had barely taken their seats before Fomon lit into Rittereiser for giving the board information without first checking with him. Rittereiser listened briefly, and then stopped the older man. "Look, Bob," he said, "we're not going to go on like this anymore."

It was Fomon's turn to be puzzled. Rittereiser then summarized what Ueberroth had told him. "The time has come," Rittereiser said, "for you to step down as CEO." Now Fomon was stunned. A few minutes passed. Would Rittereiser mind if he stayed on as chairman? Fomon finally asked. He wouldn't, Rittereiser said, so long as Fomon clearly understood that Rittereiser would be the boss.

At 1:50 P.M. the two men walked to Rittereiser's Jaguar and drove together to Hutton's headquarters for the board meeting—Fomon not at all his usual self.

By nature Fomon is an irritable man. If his dinner isn't ready on time or people don't follow his orders, he often, as one associate puts it, "loses it." But when there is trouble—real trouble—his irritability disappears and a steely calm takes over.

That was Fomon's demeanor the day he stepped down as CEO. At 3:00 P.M., the morning showers now ended, Hutton's board convened at the firm's headquarters.

Around the table sat the people—Ed Cazier, Jim Lopp, Dina Merrill, Scott Pierce, Bob Rittereiser, and Peter Ueberroth—who would soon call a halt to Fomon's sixteen years as chief of Hutton. Also in attendance were Steve Friedman, Ed Lill, John Gutfreund, and Ken Wilson.

Gutfreund spoke first. Shearson, he reported, wouldn't meet the board's demands of $55 a share for Hutton's stock. The merger talks were off.

Next, Fomon spoke. Later, some people would say they saw the blood drain from his face as he addressed the board. "It is time," he told them, for a new CEO, and he nominated Rittereiser. The vote was unanimous. Fomon was now only the nominal head of Hutton, a figurehead chairman. "I didn't try to change their minds," Fomon says, "ask why and all that. I have too much pride to do something like that."

Scott Pierce, sitting across from Fomon, took heart from the ouster of the man who had hired him eleven years earlier. "Now," Pierce told himself, "we can get on with business. We can go off, rebuild the firm, and get it going again." He didn't know that his days—and the firm's—were numbered, too.

The board meeting continued for another two hours. Fomon left the room briefly a few times, but except for reminiscing occasionally on his part in building the company, in developing the "When E.F. Hutton talks, people listen" ad campaign—except for those understandable interruptions, he was quiet and remained at the meeting until the end. He was not, so far as anyone recalls, drinking.

When Sadoa Yasuda, general manager of the international investment department at Japan's mammoth Sumitomo Life Insurance Co., was nominated for a seat on the board, Fomon voted for him. Within a few months Sumitomo would purchase a 2 percent interest in Hutton, and rumors would sweep Wall Street that the Japanese giant was making a bid for the firm.

Then Ed Lill outlined his plan to raise capital by selling Hutton's life insurance subsidiary. Fomon voted in favor of that move as well. After the meeting, Cazier pulled Fomon aside. "We really didn't expect you to move that fast. I thought maybe six months from now, at the annual meeting. . . . " Fomon brushed aside his old friend. "You told me you wanted Rittereiser to be CEO. Now he's CEO."

Because the merger talks had broken down, Hutton issued a terse statement to the press, saying that preliminary discussions with Shearson had ended and that no further talks were planned. The news made its way into the papers on Monday. Hutton, the stories concluded, was now "in play."

"Either they will find someone else who'll pay more," one investment banker told the *Wall Street Journal*, "or they will come back to Shearson." Another predicted that Hutton's management was fighting a losing battle to keep the firm independent. Both bankers would turn out to be right.

Also, in its press release, Hutton declared that "no formal offers were made in the course of the discussions." That statement would later cause serious trouble for the firm. By month's end, the Securities and Exchange Commission would initiate an investigation into whether Hutton had adequately disclosed merger talks. And the following year, when Shearson would swallow Hutton whole for a paltry $29 a share, stockholders would cry foul. Why, they would demand to know, hadn't Hutton sold out when it could have for $50 a share? Why hadn't management foreseen the decline in the value of the company?

Still, almost everyone at the top of Hutton—the board members, Rittereiser, high-priced senior managers—was oblivious to the dangers that lay ahead. The bond and stock markets were booming, so there didn't seem to be any urgency to make dramatic moves at Hutton.

Within weeks after Hutton brushed Shearson aside, rumors started circulating that Jerry Miller had fed information to Shearson during the latter's takeover attempt. The same rumor would circulate when Shearson finally took control of Hutton in 1987. "It's hard to believe," says Fomon, "but he was the only senior guy offered a job at Shearson."

MONDAY, NOVEMBER 10

46

It didn't take long for word to circulate that Bob Fomon was out as CEO. On Monday—a cold, windy day in Manhattan—one of Rittereiser's men cornered Bob Witt.

"Fomon should have left five years ago," the man said. But Witt defended Fomon, his friend and mentor. "How," Witt asks now, "do you leave a company you have been with for thirty-five years, and you haven't reached retirement age? It's kind of hard to do."

Steve Friedman pulled Rittereiser aside on this, his first day in the CEO's job. He should do something to establish his authority, Friedman advised, something with great symbolism to demonstrate that he was firmly in control of the company.

"If you really want to make a statement," the $600,000-a-year-plus corporate counsel ultimately suggested, "change all the art on the twenty-eighth floor [of the new headquarters building]. People would know you are in charge."

Rittereiser decided to let the art stay as it was. He took a big chance, though, in ignoring the spirit of Friedman's advice. Rittereiser continued to involve Fomon in the firm's business. He felt guilty about pushing the man out.

The new CEO had planned to meet with each of his senior managers. Individually they would brief Rittereiser on the 1987 operational plans for their respective departments. He wanted Fomon in on those meetings.

"I was trying to continue to include Bob in the organization," Rittereiser says. "I had a conversation with him, and I said, 'Bob, I'm going to conduct meetings for a whole week.' I said, 'I want you to be part of this, but I don't want you picking on these guys. I don't want you bringing up old problems from the eighteen hundreds.' I said, 'If you think someone is trying to put one over on me, don't say it in front of him. Get me aside later, and you guide me. If you want to ask questions, ask them, but I'm going to ask you to be disciplined and businesslike and to pay attention to how important this is. If you want to stay involved, you gotta behave right.'

"The meetings lasted five days. People came to me that third day and said, 'What the hell did you do to Bob Fomon?' Fomon asked questions, and they all went right to the heart of the business, right to the issue. . . . He learned as much about the business that week as I did." Late on the third day and over much of the fourth, however, Fomon reverted to type. On the fifth day he didn't show up.

The Dow Jones Industrial Average reached its high for the year—1955.57.

Bob Rittereiser had spent twenty-six of his forty-seven years in the paramilitary organization of Merrill Lynch, and it showed in the way he ran Hutton. He believed in structure, he believed in order, and he liked everything written down.

In early December, Rittereiser set general counsel Steve Friedman, who had as much experience in the law as Rittereiser had in brokerage, to work drafting sample minutes for the firm's management committee meetings. The executive committee didn't maintain minutes, and Rittereiser thought the group should have a record of its deliberations. The sample minutes that Friedman worked up—outlined in a December 4 memo—were virtually identical in form to the ones maintained by Hutton's board of directors. "I don't want to make too much of this," one former executive complains, "but it was work any of the secretaries could have done."

No question that the job was a waste of the high-priced attorney's time. But more to the point, the incident got some people at Hutton wondering where Rittereiser's priorities lay. The firm had serious problems. Did he want his chief legal adviser spending his time drafting forms?

TUESDAY, DECEMBER 9

40 ½

Rittereiser was determined to sweep Hutton's troubles into the past. As part of his plan, he would propose to the board that Hutton use a large portion of its cash to establish a $130 million reserve. Intended to cover a number of the firm's more embarrassing financial obligations, the reserve's biggest chunk—$70 million—would go to buy back the upper floaters that Hutton had marketed with false claims in the early 1980s. Under Rittereiser's plan, Hutton would let the market set the price of the bonds, but it would buy them back from the original investors at face value. Hutton, in other words, would swallow the difference between the market value and the face value. The remaining $60 million of the reserve would pay for a variety of obligations—from litigation over tax shelters to severance payments for departing executives.

Setting up a $130 million reserve was an expensive proposition for the firm that would end its fiscal year awash in red ink. And some management committee members—Norm Epstein and Jerry Miller among them—argued vehemently against the move.

"You're telling me," Epstein, the head of Hutton's operations, said, "that our most sophisticated account executives sold these bonds to our most sophisticated clients, and they were surprised when these bonds—bonds from steel companies—declined in value. Come on."

But the situation with these bonds was not as straightforward as Epstein depicted it. The staff in the fixed-income area in New York, for example, continued to give quotes on the bonds, not at the market price but at the price that Hutton promised to hold. Besides, there was the error in the marketing literature to take into consideration.

The decision to take the write-off, says Rittereiser, was not an easy one. "We had nothing but financial bad news that we had delivered to the marketplace," he says. "Now to have to come out and take a write-off was not something that we were anxious to do."

Rittereiser was determined to go ahead, and, in the end, Epstein and Miller reluctantly agreed. Then Rittereiser ran through the rest of his game plan.

He and his senior managers knew that Hutton's lenders and the ratings agencies would question whether the firm could withstand a $130 million hit to its bottom line. So Ed Lill, chief financial officer, was to speak with the agencies and the lenders before the board meeting. His task was to reassure them of the company's strength and of management's confidence and resolve. That, Rittereiser reasoned, would forestall any problems.

Halfway through the board meeting, Rittereiser left to meet with the ratings agencies. He came back with the news that the agencies weren't happy and intended to put Hutton through another review. "But," says Rittereiser, "we did what we had to do to maintain our credibility with them."

One ugly incident marred the otherwise businesslike air of the session. Bob Fomon walked in. He was the chairman, so he had every right to be there—perhaps, one might argue, an obligation. He stayed just long enough to get the drift of the conversation, which at the moment dealt with the serious problem of the year-end reserve. "If you guys are going to talk about this shit," Rittereiser remembers him saying, "I'm getting out of here." He left as abruptly as he had arrived. It was classic Fomon, not wanting to hear about something he didn't want to face. "I don't know what he was like years earlier," says Rittereiser, who suspected that he wasn't dealing with the same Fomon who had run Hutton in the 1970s.

Appearances matter a lot to Bob Fomon. That's why he had personally approved every visible detail of Hutton's new headquarters building. He had even designated the address of the building. It could have been Fifty-second Street or Fifty-third Street, the edifice being equally impressive from either street. But Fomon had picked Fifty-second Street, because it was also the address of the exclusive "21" Club. A Prohibition speakeasy that was now operated as a private men's club, "21" was one of Fomon's favorite haunts.

On December 15, Hutton finally moved into its new headquarters. The entire twenty-eighth floor of the building contained just twelve opulent offices, each built for a man—there were no prominent women here—of executive stature. Fomon had also designed an unusual boardroom, which he intended to look like a lecture hall with tiered seating. The room was never finished, says a former Hutton investment banker, but the stage had been built and he could see what Fomon had in mind.

"He would sit on the stage, holding court, and have his admiring directors listen to him." The idea was, says the investment banker, "staggering."

Fomon's own work space, its two-story, slanting glass walls facing south and east over lower Manhattan and toward the harbor and Brooklyn, was distinguishable as the grandest of all. The floor above contained nine—quiet and dignified—private dining rooms.

Rittereiser looks back and sees the new Hutton building as a symbol not of the once mighty firm's success, but of his own missed opportunity. "If there is one thing I would do differently," he says, "it would be this. If somehow I could have had the political skills to come in and shut this building down on the day I started, to take the number-one project away from the chairman, I might have succeeded in turning Hutton around."

Some referred to the building as "Fomon's folly." But punsters dubbed the edifice "Fomon's last erection."

TUESDAY, DECEMBER 16

39 ¾

Steve Friedman's latest headache was Brock Hotels, a subject he addressed at Hutton's regular Tuesday management committee meeting. Bob Rittereiser, Norm Epstein, Ed Lill, Dick Locke, and Jerry Miller listened attentively as Friedman recounted the details of the Brock fiasco.

The long and short of it was that Hutton had sold industrial revenue bonds for Brock and Brock had gone belly up. In the end, the group decided that Hutton would acquire all the bonds it had sold to its clients—for an additional $22 million hit to the bottom line.

WEDNESDAY, DECEMBER 31

37 ⅞

For the first time in the firm's illustrious eighty-two-year history, Hutton reported for the year a loss—$90.3 million, or $2.90 a share, on total revenues of $2.8 billion. Still, Hutton managed to pay its shareholders a decent dividend—88 cents a share, 6 cents more than it had paid in 1985, when it had earned a profit. And its book value rose from $26.48 a share in 1985 to $27.14 in 1986.

Despite the gloomy financial news, the mood at headquarters was cheerful, even buoyant. Rittereiser and his men were confident they could turn Hutton around. "We were prepared to do what we had come to do," Steve Friedman remembers, "which was to rebuild E.F. Hutton." What Friedman didn't know was that 1987 would be a year that no one on Wall Street—particularly the men at E.F. Hutton—would enjoy. In fact, the year could hardly have turned out worse.

1987

The Dow Jones Industrial Average fell to its low for the year—1927.31.

For all the promise of Hutton's new management team, 1987 turned out to be disastrous for the firm. Still, the year began on a hopeful note. A buyer had been found for Hutton's life insurance subsidiary. Capital Holdings Corp. of Los Angeles would pay $300 million for Hutton Life. It was a cash infusion that the firm badly needed.

In just three years, Robert Weingarten—a plump, intense, onetime insurance salesman—had built Capital Holdings from scratch into a $493 million mutual fund and insurance empire. Only twenty-one months later, in September of 1988, Weingarten would cash out of the company. With unintended irony, he would sell his 15.5 percent stake in Capital Holdings to Shearson—which by then would be Shearson Lehman Hutton.

January 6 was another wintry morning in Manhattan. Hutton's senior management committee—Bob Fomon, Bob Rittereiser, Steve Friedman, Mark Kessenich, Norm Epstein, Jerry Miller, and Dick Locke—assembled on the twenty-eighth floor of the firm's impressive new headquarters. They were there to prepare for a meeting of the Hutton board on Friday, January 9.

Rittereiser and his men were determined to put the firm back on a straight-and-narrow path, and Rittereiser intended to brief the board fully on the plan—which included the establishment of the $130 million reserve—that he had so carefully crafted.

TUESDAY, JANUARY 13

42 ¼

Making amends for past mistakes was the theme that rang through the halls of E.F. Hutton's headquarters during the first half of 1987. Rittereiser was determined to sweep the firm's troubles into the past and start the year with a clean slate. "We were bruised and battered," Ed Lill remembers, "and we lived in fear of reading the morning paper, because we thought we'd see Hutton's name there."

Part of the huge job Hutton's senior management faced was to build a proper organization out of a confederation of idiosyncratically ruled fiefdoms. At 9:00 A.M., Hutton's management committee met and agreed that Steve Friedman would coordinate the compilation of a manual of the firm's policies. This hardly seemed a drastic step. But one of Hutton's long-standing problems had been that no one wrote anything down. There were simply no company policies and procedures.

Take the matter of compensation. Bob Fomon had always controlled salaries and bonuses himself. The management committee wanted to rationalize the compensation system and gain control over raises and promotions. For instance, members decided that they would review all salary increases to make sure they complied with a new 5 percent cap.

They also decided that, as a matter of policy, the title of executive vice president would be awarded only to "employees with significant management responsibility." Hutton, obviously, had quite a lot of catching up to do with even rudimentary management practices.

Then there was the matter of lunch. The committee ruled—as an exception to the policy that had sprung from Fomon's passionate preoccupation with appearances—that employees who had to remain in their offices during the lunch period would be allowed to eat at their desks.

Appearances had counted for so much at Hutton that back in the 1970s Fomon, upset that employees weren't dressing properly, had opened a retail store in the company's headquarters building where "proper" clothing would be sold. It was a good deal for employees—they could buy at cost. Having the store would prove handy years later. After its acquisition of Hutton, Shearson raided the store's inventory of tote bags—blue ones with the E.F. Hutton logo on the side. It handed them out—free—to Hutton employees it laid off, with instructions that they pack their belongings and clear out fast.

FRIDAY, JANUARY 16

40 ¼

Since he was a child, Peter Ueberroth had felt the need to be in charge, and age and experience had not changed him. The blue-eyed, sandy-haired Ueberroth had joined the board of E.F. Hutton in 1984 and immediately seized control. Everyone had taken a back seat to Ueberroth—even Bob Fomon. Ueberroth, says Ed Lill, "has an ego that is just a bit bigger than this building," referring to one of the twin towers of the World Trade Center.

If conversations at board meetings dragged on too long to suit him, Ueberroth would simply cut them off. Once, while Ed Lill was giving an oral report on the firm's financial condition, Ueberroth kept looking at the giant gold Rolex that encircled his left wrist. "Can we do this in five minutes," he said finally, adding, "some of us have schedules."

When Ueberroth was in attendance, board meetings rarely lasted long and the gathering on January 16 was no exception to this rule. Quickly and without much discussion, the board approved the $300 million sale of Hutton Life. It also endorsed the establishment of the $130 million reserve that Rittereiser wanted. Within a few hours, press releases went out announcing both actions.

The response from the financial markets—and the financial community—was mixed. Hutton's common stock fell only $1 a share. But Standard & Poor's downgraded the credit rating on $200 million of Hutton senior debt—the debt that had first claim on the firm's assets in the unthinkable event of liquidation. The agency contended that the reserve was "continued evidence" of management weaknesses that had damaged Hutton over the past few years.

The business press wasn't as critical. "This one-time assault on the bottom line," *Business Week* proclaimed, "may well mark a crucial turning point in the firm's troubled recent past. Hutton may finally be on the rebound—at least that's the fervent hope of the company's beleaguered management."

Who could have known then that the creation of the reserve and the sale of Hutton Life would turn out to be just as futile as other, later attempts to stave off the firm's demise?

TUESDAY, JANUARY 27

40 ½

Bob Rittereiser was becoming increasingly wary of Bob Fomon. He had cut most of the chairman's contacts with senior management—the men Rittereiser had brought on board—but he hadn't yet succeeded in isolating Fomon from the rest of the firm.

In Rittereiser's opinion—and in the opinion of most of the men on his team—Fomon's days were numbered and his importance to the running of the firm had evaporated.

Rittereiser remembers one meeting that seemed to sum up Fomon's place in the firm. Hutton's senior managers were discussing the $130 million write-off when in came Fomon and his art director. The two men held up a painting against a wall in the conference room to see how it looked.

"It was," says Rittereiser, "a scene right out of a Peter Sellers's movie." Fomon, Rittereiser notes, was involved in every aspect of the new building. "But we were letting him do it," Rittereiser maintains, "because it was better than anything else he was doing as far as business was concerned." In other words, Fomon, when he was involved with the building, was out of everyone's hair.

But old-timers, people from outside the senior management circle, continued to seek favors from Fomon, which he graciously granted. After all, Fomon figured, he was still chairman, still the number-one man, with the power and authority to do as he pleased. That was how he had always run the business, anyway.

The gulf that had opened between the two men in November, when Rittereiser had been promoted to CEO, leaving Fomon with only the title of chairman, was growing wider and increasingly difficult to paper over. Fomon's actions annoyed Rittereiser no end. How could he keep a tight grip on the firm with the older man dispensing largesse as if there were no problems? Fomon, for his part, was no longer successful in hiding his growing disdain for Rittereiser. Certain adjectives would slip into his conversations when they concerned the new CEO—*weak* and *indecisive*, for instance.

Within the management committee of Hutton, however, Rittereiser could and did exercise control. During this Tuesday's committee session, with Fomon not yet in the room, the group decided it would soon finalize its compensation recommendations, an area Fomon had always made his personal fiefdom, and determine title recommendations.

The top managers also decided that each committee member would prepare a presentation on his 1987 business plan for the March board meeting and that the full budget presentation would take place during the February board meeting.

MONDAY, FEBRUARY 2

41 5/8

Fomon's young assistant, Jay Moorhead, who had no previous investment-banking experience before joining Hutton in 1984, enrolled in the management development program at the Harvard Business School. He went with both Fomon's and Rittereiser's blessing. They could still, after all, agree on something.

The firm picked up Moorhead's expenses. He was the first person Hutton had sponsored to attend the program. At the end of his three months in Cambridge, Moorhead returned to Hutton as the investment-banking division's director of business development.

TUESDAY, FEBRUARY 3

39 1/2

Bob Fomon deeply resented the way *his* firm was being run. He resented it so strongly that he now saw Bob Rittereiser and his new team as the enemy, although this hadn't been the case when Rittereiser had first arrived at Hutton. As long as Fomon had been his boss, as long as Rittereiser's team had been Fomon's team, everything had been fine.

But when Fomon lost the CEO's job, the situation shifted, and Fomon himself began to turn on anybody he saw collaborating with the new chief executive—his old friend Jerry Miller, for one. Fomon and Miller went back about twenty-five years together, but Miller, named by Rittereiser to head Hutton's retail sales, was a friend no longer.

Fomon, says one senior executive, would pull each of Miller's subordinates into his office and criticize their boss. He would hint that he was going to get rid of Miller and that he was thinking of naming as Miller's replacement the man to whom he was talking. It was classic dirty corporate politics. (Miller maintains that this story is apocryphal. Fomon "wouldn't do something like that," he says.)

On February 3, Rittereiser decided he would try, once again, to get the situation under control. So he spoke to Ed Cazier, a Hutton board member and longtime friend of Fomon. Cazier, however, kept making excuses for Fomon's behavior—Fomon, Cazier maintained, wasn't drinking *that* much.

"You're supposed to be his friend," Rittereiser told Cazier, "and this guy is destroying himself the way he is behaving. If I were his friend, I would deal with it a lot differently than you are. I would sit down and have a conversation with this guy."

In the end, though, Rittereiser knew his intervention was one more futile gesture. He had succeeded only in antagonizing Cazier. "I know," Rittereiser says, "that I didn't win any points with him."

THURSDAY, FEBRUARY 12

40 ⅞

Hutton's board convened in the elegant boardroom on the twenty-ninth floor at 31 West Fifty-second Street. Scott Pierce—the man Rittereiser had demoted in 1986—spoke first. "It is difficult," he told the board, "for the firm's new management to function with Bob Fomon in the same building." Pierce then outlined the problems with Fomon in the most general terms. He had examples ready, in case he needed them, but it wasn't necessary to go into details.

"I had no problem with him remaining as chairman," says Pierce, "as long as he wasn't an operating person. But Bob was trying to get his power back."

The board concurred with Pierce. Fomon, board members decided, could hold on to his title, but he would have to move his office elsewhere. Although Rittereiser suspects that Fomon had already decided to get out, the meeting was an ordeal for the chairman. He didn't know how to stop the campaign to oust him, so he didn't try.

"I built the building we were sitting in," Fomon remembers. "I felt like I owned it, so it was like I was being thrown out of my own home." But self-pity quickly gave way to self-interest. He refused to vacate the premises until he had negotiated his severance contract. Those negotiations began right away.

MONDAY, MARCH 2

39 ⅞

A change of players took place at Hutton on March 2. Scott Pierce, then fifty-six years old, had resigned as vice chairman of the firm effective March 2. He had seen the handwriting on the wall. "Rittereiser, in effect, demoted Pierce into a phony job," Bob Fomon remembers, "and Pierce said, screw it."

Pierce himself remembers feeling that "there wasn't anything more for me to do, so I'd better get out. I felt that they would have let me hang around there. But I would have had diminishing responsibility, and I felt I was too young to play that role. I guess my pride was hurt a little."

To Jerry C. Welsh, Hutton was neither large nor unwieldy. A veteran of mammoth American Express, he had served as executive vice president of worldwide marketing and communications for the travel-related-services company, and was used to giant organizations. Welsh joined Hutton on March 3 as senior executive vice president for marketing and strategic development, replacing Bob Witt, whom Rittereiser had finally forced out. Welsh, according to Fomon, had helped Peter Ueberroth with his Olympic duties, and Ueberroth, in turn, had introduced Welsh to Rittereiser. But Rittereiser says that Welsh was referred to Hutton by an executive search firm.

Witt himself had been with the company twenty years, signing on as a broker and working his way to the top of the retail sales force, then moving on to the post of marketing director. What Witt knew was selling, not marketing, and Rittereiser wanted a professional in the job—someone sophisticated, with proven experience in the art of marketing and advertising.

Rittereiser picked Welsh. As was his practice, he didn't consult with anyone at Hutton about the hire, a fact that Jerry Miller, for one, found more than a little objectionable. "I've got to work with this guy every day," Miller told Rittereiser. "Don't you think that I should talk to him before you hire him?" Rittereiser shook his head no. "I want to keep this quiet," he said.

(Rittereiser says the Miller had other reasons for wanting a say in Welsh's hire. Rittereiser had first asked Miller to find someone for the post of marketing director, since, at the time, the job reported directly to the head of retail. Then Rittereiser decided to upgrade the post to a level equal to Miller's, and called Miller off the search.)

Henry Mortimer, a longtime Hutton vice president, saw Welsh as a "comedian, a buffoon. That's all he was. He stood on tables, putting on plays, talking to himself in his high-pitched voice." By anyone's standards, Welsh was flamboyant, an outspoken man with a Tennessee accent. He set to work immediately to overhaul Hutton's marketing department. One of his first tasks was to try to break the firm's contract with comedian Bill Cosby.

After the check scandal, Hutton had abandoned its successful and long-running advertising campaign. "When E.F. Hutton talks, people listen" somehow seemed inappropriate in the wake of the adverse publicity with which the firm had been inundated. Instead, Hutton was running television spots featuring Cosby. Fomon, thinking that Cosby's "clean" image would help remove the tarnish from Hutton's own, had personally picked the popular entertainer to spearhead a new campaign. Fomon liked the Cosby commercials and thinks they were a hit.

With his usual largesse, Fomon had agreed to pay Cosby $12 million over three years. The contract called for the entertainer to be available to Hutton four days a year, and he got paid whether or not he taped any new commercials and—if he did—whether or not they ran. This added up to expensive advertising for a firm in Hutton's position. And Cosby—or, in any case, Cosby's agent—wasn't willing to throw in any extra time, even for a worthy cause.

Dina Merrill, who was active in raising money for New York's homeless, asked whether, as a favor to Hutton, Cosby would appear at a benefit she was staging. Sure, Cosby's agent, Norman Brokaw, said, but the appearance would count as one of Hutton's "days." At $1 million a day, Hutton told Brokaw, thanks but no thanks.

Welsh never was able to crack the agreement with Cosby. The Cosby commercials aren't running, and Shearson Lehman Hutton is still paying the entertainer.

Other Welsh efforts didn't fare any better. Rittereiser had lured Welsh to Hutton with the promise that he could be the first to apply the principles of consumer marketing to Wall Street. His initial attempt—a coloring book that was intended to communicate the firm's problems to its retail sales force—would be an unmitigated disaster and major embarrassment to Hutton.

Even before that incident, though, Welsh was coming in for his share of criticism. While the new marketing chief heaped scorn on Hutton's decision to shell out $12 million for Cosby, Ed Lill points out that Welsh himself took a backseat to no one when it came to spending. Welsh spent millions, Lill says, on consultants and marketing studies. True, Lill concedes, "with marketing studies, you're investing in the future. But first you have to make sure you are there in the future."

TUESDAY, MARCH 10

39 ⅛

As chief financial officer of a firm that was hemorrhaging at the bottom line, Lill's most important job was to bring costs down—fast.

The financial services industry is cyclical. It rises and falls with the market. So, inevitably, every few years financial services companies go through a period when they have to cut costs. That was why Tom Lynch, Lill's predecessor at Hutton, used to keep a folder in his desk marked "Cost Cutting." When times got tough, he'd pull out his folder and start slashing costs, usually across the board.

But that was not the way Lill wanted to do it now. He and Rittereiser wanted to make sure that the "right costs" were cut. So Lill proposed to the management committee on March 10 that instead of cutting spending, Hutton undertake a study on *ways* to cut spending. Someone in Lill's department had dubbed the project NOVA—National Overhead Valuation Analysis.

NOVA was the same kind of study that the consulting firm McKinsey & Co. had performed for a number of other financial services firms—among them, Merrill Lynch, Citibank, and American Express. But Lill decided that his department would undertake the project without outside help. A do-it-yourself study would be cheaper, he figured, since an outside firm would have charged about $10 million. Also, he didn't think outsiders could get the project to work.

Lill assigned teams, each of which would examine a particular section of the company. Each team consisted of a person who worked in that section balanced by an employee from outside the area, who had no personal stake in the status quo. "A project like this usually takes two years," according to Lill, "and we were doing it in six months."

NOVA ultimately identified several areas where waste was rampant. One was the new building, which Hutton didn't even own, but rather leased. Another was printing costs. "Our printing budget was something like seven million dollars a year," says Lill. Finally, Lill wanted to target advertising and public relations costs.

Lill still maintains that his program fulfilled one of its objectives, which was to identify the costs that needed to be cut. But, he says, "in hindsight, NOVA was criticized as being too little too late." The critics were right, he concedes. Hutton's problems were too acute to spend valuable hours mapping the firm's costs structure. "We didn't have time to look at costs intelligently," Lill says. "We just had to get costs down."

In Tuesday's meeting, committee members zeroed in on this always delicate topic of Hutton's expenses. Rittereiser, too, was determined to cut costs—before NOVA was completed. Lill first distributed a March 10 memo on the cost of operating the firm's aircraft. Then he circulated a memo that detailed location expense budget reductions. The group decided that division heads should meet individually with Lill to review expenses for consultants, temporary help, use of corporate automobiles, and other special items.

MONDAY, APRIL 6

39¹⁄₄

Only one man at the top of Hutton openly expressed his doubts about the viability of the firm, and that was Kendrick R. Wilson III. Wilson had come late to the struggle to save Hutton. A managing director at Salomon Brothers, he joined Hutton on April 6, as senior executive vice president and head of the firm's corporate finance department. But even before he signed on, he had a good idea of the depth of Hutton's troubles.

His specialty at Salomon Brothers had been financial services institutions. He had raised operating capital for them, and it was in that capacity that he had taken Hutton on as a client in 1985. The brokerage firm had needed cash, and he had raised it through a stock offering. Subsequently, Wilson had, of course, been involved in Hutton's merger talks with Chrysler and later with Shearson.

At Salomon Brothers, Wilson had a reputation as perceptive, sophisticated, and evenhanded. Forty-six years old, and a graduate of Exeter, Dartmouth, and the Harvard Business School, he was also admired for keeping his cool under fire. Wilson left Salomon Brothers to join the brokerage for the same reason that Rittereiser had left Merrill Lynch. Each thought that one day he would have a shot at running Hutton. "I am ready," Wilson told his friends, "to have a shop of my own."

His colleagues at Salomon Brothers tried to talk him out of the move—Hutton was too much of a mess, they argued—but his ambition got the better of him. In time, Wilson figured, the board would oust Fomon, promote Rittereiser to chairman, and tap Wilson as the new CEO. The problem with that plan, Wilson realized once he joined the firm, was that Hutton was even more troubled than he had thought. It was *so* troubled that it wasn't likely to outlast Rittereiser.

"Hutton," Wilson says, "was already down the chute."

His first day at his new job, Wilson reported early for work only to find two of the firm's most senior investment bankers waiting in his office. They were resigning, they said, immediately. It was Wilson's first hint—but not his last—that the situation was more dire than he had imagined.

Wilson discovered that Don Sanders, the Houston broker duped by George Aubin, remained at Hutton. No one had fired him. "I was shocked that Sanders was still there," Wilson says, "but that shock was second to knowing Peter Detwiler was still there." Detwiler, an investment banker, had been featured on the front page of the *Wall Street Journal* for his $900,000-a-year expense account.

Fomon defends Detwiler, claiming the whole story was built on misinformation. "Rittereiser claimed that Detwiler ran up expenses of $900,000," he says. "It was an outright lie. Detwiler had some legal fees that were reimbursed as part of his expenses. Detwiler's total expenses were near $100,000." And, Fomon insists, they were all legitimate.

On Wilson's third day at Hutton, Rittereiser asked him to attend a two-hour briefing on NOVA. That afternoon, Wilson sat Rittereiser down. "NOVA," he stated flatly, "is a total crock of shit. It's never going to work. It doesn't address the real problems." Rittereiser tried to convince Wilson otherwise.

"Give me time," he said to his new hire. Wilson, Rittereiser says, "didn't know what I knew. His perspective was different. We had to force everyone through a gut-wrenching [reevaluation of the firm] or the marketplace would clean our clock a year from now."

A week or so after his encounter with Rittereiser, Wilson spied Jerry Miller sitting in his office with the two senior executives from the Hutton retail sales division. They were surrounded by wine bottles. Wilson stuck his head in. "What's up?" he asked. The three men were selecting wines as sales recognition gifts for Hutton stockbrokers, they explained. "That was their whole morning's work," Wilson remembers.

It was a key moment. Here was Wilson, realizing he had to scramble to prop up Hutton, while, to the other men at the top of the firm, it was business as usual. With their attitudes, Wilson suspected, Hutton was doomed. But he never considered bailing out. "It would have been embarrassing to leave," he says. "So my biggest concern was to get Hutton sold." It was, he concluded, the only way out—for him and for the firm. "I didn't want to be tarred with being part of the team that took Hutton over the hill."

To Bob Fomon, says Fred Whittemore, a friend and managing director of Morgan Stanley, "Hutton was more than a brokerage house. It was his entire life." In February, Fomon had agreed to move his office elsewhere, but he insisted that he wouldn't budge until he completed negotiating the terms of his eventual severance agreement.

When Hutton's board met on May 6, Fomon announced his retirement as chairman of Hutton and nominated Peter Ueberroth to replace him. Fomon had asked Ueberroth to take on the assignment before the board meeting. "I still cared about Hutton," Fomon says, "and I thought Peter could handle the job. I knew Rittereiser couldn't."

Rittereiser, of course, didn't see it that way. "I let the discussion go," Rittereiser remembers. "And Cazier, in his usual fashion, gave a sanctimonious speech about how, as open and responsible men, we should give this idea consideration. Then he turned to me, and said, 'Bob, what do you think? How do you feel about this?' "

Rittereiser responded with his own impassioned speech.

"As far as I am concerned," he told the group, "the time has come to cut the bullshit. Peter Ueberroth is a nice man, but he can contribute virtually nothing to the day-to-day management of this company. In fact, the entire organization is sitting out here hoping that I will not make them do what they must do to make this business succeed.

"What they want is someone at the top to appeal to who doesn't know the business. They will hope and pray that I go away. I already am on the line for this goddamned company. I don't need another title."

Rittereiser told the board, "the day of running this company for the benefit of individuals instead of the company is over."

When Rittereiser was finished, Ueberroth declined to take on the new assignment.

Fomon's response to Ueberroth's refusal wasn't theatrical. It was typical. "You wimp," he said, glaring at Ueberroth. "You wait," he continued, shifting his steely gaze to Rittereiser, "I'll sell this firm out from underneath all of you." Then Fomon stalked out.

An investment banker who knows Ueberroth says that Ueberroth actually wanted the job, having decided earlier in the spring. "He started looking at all the perks, at what went along with a couple million dollars a year cash. But," the banker says, "he was too subtle and he took too long." Ueberroth's refusal at the board meeting was a ploy, according to the banker. "He wanted someone to twist his arm. If you don't have your arm twisted, you don't get the best deal."

But no one twisted his arm, not even Fomon. Later that day, in a speech, Fomon told the firm's employees, "I have really considered myself prime keeper of the good name of E.F. Hutton."

After Fomon's departure, Rittereiser began to argue forcefully that he be made chairman. When Rittereiser had finished and others had had their say, the board took a curious path. It chose no one as chairman but decided that members would take turns chairing the board meetings. "The idea," Scott Pierce says, "was that Rittereiser would become chairman—once he proved that he could do the job. Talk about a vote of no confidence—this was it." Ed Lill agrees with Pierce. "When Fomon was pushed aside," Lill says, "so was Rittereiser. Even though no one made Ueberroth chairman, he functioned as chairman."

In one of those empty concessions to propriety that characterize corporate life, Hutton's 1986 annual report, issued several months later, contained admiring words about the defrocked Fomon. "Bob Fomon," Rittereiser wrote, "was responsible for bringing E.F. Hutton into the 1980s as a major firm with tremendous stature. His was a remarkable achievement. All of us who are undertaking to build on that impressive base owe him enduring gratitude." There was a picture of Fomon, smiling, seated in front of a portrait of the firm's founder. The picture was cropped in such a way that it cut off old Mr. Hutton's head.

Rittereiser had no second thoughts about praising Fomon in the annual report. "As my mother used to say to me," Rittereiser says, "you don't have to be rich, but you do have to have class. The right thing was to honor Bob for his years at Hutton."

That night, after the board meeting, Fomon had a few drinks with some old Hutton hands. "It was sad to see him deteriorate so badly," says one of them, an account executive. "He was tough, he was honorable, and he had a great love for the firm. . . . He talked about his successes, his failures. He was a pathetic man. His whole life was wrapped up in Hutton."

It was, says Rittereiser, during this period—from November 1986 to May 1987—that Hutton was lost, largely because too much time was spent dealing with internal politics and not enough was spent on Hutton's problems.

Hutton's new leaders, in the meantime, found themselves confronting problems that made the ouster of Bob Fomon look easy.

TUESDAY, MAY 12

36 ½

At times, Ken Wilson felt as helpless as a weatherman in a wind storm. He knew what was happening, but he could not control events. He simply didn't have the power to turn Hutton around. In his view, he didn't even have the information he needed.

At one management committee meeting after another—such as the one on May 12—he complained about the lack of data. Where exactly did Hutton stand now? Where was it going? He couldn't tell from the material Ed Lill prepared and distributed.

General counsel Steve Friedman shared his concerns. "We never had a good management information system," says Friedman. "There was never a set of agreed-upon indicators of how the business was doing and if we were moving in the right direction." But Wilson's complaints didn't impress or upset the other committee members.

In his own department, Wilson began to do what he could to shore up the bottom line. He fired some of the old guard—men he regarded as incompetent—and brought in a new team. And he adopted a strategy.

Hutton would provide corporate finance services only to a few specified industries—airlines, for example. But the services it would provide would be of high quality. Wilson knew that Hutton needed the revenue from a profitable corporate finance department, because it could not, as it had in the 1970s, rely on retail sales alone to drive the firm. As a realist, however, Wilson was well aware that Hutton's tiny department couldn't compete directly with the big operations at Morgan Stanley, Goldman Sachs, and Salomon Brothers. It had to find itself a niche and serve the industries that the other firms neglected.

"Kenny," says Jerry Miller, the head of retail sales, "had the right idea. His niche strategy was the only way to go about building a corporate finance business without throwing millions of dollars at the business. It was the only way we could have succeeded." (Ironically, the strategy Wilson chose was the same Fomon had adopted in the 1970s. Building a strong investment-banking arm had always been one of Fomon's dreams. He was on his way to achieving it when the check scandal threw him off course.)

It wasn't obvious to Miller or Wilson or any of the other men at the top of Hutton, but Bob Rittereiser's power had already begun to deteriorate—and not just with the board. Some of the men he had hired—Steve Friedman, Ed Lill, and Jerry Welsh—would sometimes complain about his indecisiveness to others. "He's no leader," Welsh told Bob Fomon.

Jerry Miller also had become an openly voluble critic of Rittereiser. He had started out as a fan, but his admiration had cooled. No one could credit Miller with subtlety. He couldn't afford it. Nine men made up Hutton's senior management committee, and only one, Miller, represented the retail side of the business. His sales force thought the deck was stacked against them. But Rittereiser himself sometimes joked that "it's eight to one, and sometimes Jerry takes on the eight and wins."

Rittereiser, for his part, expected the criticism. "I predicted it," he says. "I told everybody in June of 1986 that 'by the middle of 1987, you should all hate me, because you won't agree with me on some things. There will be a point where you will all be pissed off at me.' " Now, he adds, "it was getting tough."

What changed Miller's mind about Rittereiser was the CEO's vision of what Hutton's retail sales force should become—smaller. Rittereiser wanted fewer salespeople handling more high-volume accounts. In Miller's mind, the more salespeople the better. (Today, Miller protests that he was willing to do what Rittereiser wanted, but he wanted to do it gradually. "If we did it at one time," he says, "we would lose the revenues before we could shrink the cost basis and [we'd] throw the firm into deficit earnings.")

Hutton's sales statistics made Rittereiser's concept look attractive. Three-quarters of the company's retail accounts had generated less than $500 in commissions in 1986. Forty-eight percent generated less than $100, and fewer than 1 percent accounted for between $500 and $25,000 in commissions.

Looked at another way, high-net-worth customers represented 28 percent of Hutton's total customer base and 71 percent of its revenue base. By contrast, low-net-worth customers represented 72 percent of the customer base and just 28 percent of the revenues.

Moreover, Hutton customers split their portfolios more frequently than did clients at other firms. A full 32 percent of Hutton customers also had accounts at other brokerages—double the percentage at Merrill Lynch and PaineWebber.

These numbers are especially interesting in light of Hutton's own view of itself as the Tiffany's of brokerage businesses. In fact, Hutton's market share of low-net-worth customers was second only to that of Merrill Lynch, Rittereiser's old firm.

MONDAY, JUNE 1

40

Reasonable people could disagree about which of Bob Fomon's alleged excesses was the worst—subsidizing his son's rent in company-leased apartments, having affairs with young women who worked for the firm, or using the company jet to ferry him and his friends wherever they pleased.

For the record, Fomon claims that he sometimes reimbursed the company for personal trips in the jet, that sometimes Rittereiser told him he didn't have to pay because "that was business," and that stories of him and his friends once trashing the inside of the plane so badly that it had to be returned to the manufacturer for repairs are untrue.

His son, he says, paid the same rent to the firm for the use of the apartment as the firm paid, and in eighteen years, Fomon says, he hired only two women with whom he was involved. And both of those, he adds, saved the firm a great deal of money. One was the head of advertising, who, he explains, showed him how Hutton's ad agency was ripping the firm off. The other was a hotel school graduate who had been the banquet manager at the Metropolitan Club in Manhattan. Fomon had hired her to arrange dinners and lunches in the firm's dining rooms. That saved money, he explains, by encouraging Hutton's investment bankers and other top executives to eat in instead of dining out in expensive restaurants.

Such frugality notwithstanding, there were nonessential expenses at Hutton that could be shaved, and on this rainy Monday, Hutton's management committee—Bob Rittereiser, Mark Kessenich, Ken Wilson, Jerry Welsh, Dick Locke, Jerry Miller, Ed Lill, Steve Friedman, and Norm Epstein—met to address some of those extravagances. Lill took the floor and outlined the topics for discussion: the corporate apartments in New York City, San Francisco, London, and Paris; and the corporate jet.

The committee decided to keep the firm's eleven leased apartments at 800 Fifth Avenue—including the one in which Fomon's son, Robert Jr., had lived for a time. Hutton actually had a good deal there. The firm was paying just $2,000 a month each for apartments right on Fifth Avenue. The men did agree, however, to develop a stricter policy for their use. Rittereiser, Lill, and Friedman were assigned to the task.

The committee also decided to retain the forty apartments that Hutton kept at 3 Hanover Square, in lower Manhattan. It was common gossip around Hutton that these apartments were used regularly by Fomon's cronies and their girlfriends.

In 1983, a secretary, with whom Fomon acknowledges he was involved, paid $400 a month to occupy an apartment that would normally have rented for $800. Fomon argued that the rent was reasonable. It was, he says, equal to Hutton's lease payment on the place. That same year, the company paid the woman a $10,000 bonus. She deserved it, Fomon says, because she was more an assistant than a secretary.

The committee discussed the fact that Hutton had originally leased the Hanover Square apartments to house account executives and other employees while they participated in the firm's training programs. Henceforth, the group decided, that would be their sole use.

As for the San Francisco apartment, the committee voted to unload it. Likewise, the London apartment would go if a review by Lill revealed it wasn't needed. The committee also decided that Fomon could take over the lease to the apartment in Paris—as long as the lease was of no economic value to Hutton. "He had a personal interest in the apartment," Lill would later say. "One of his girlfriends lived across the hall."

Then the men turned to the corporate jet. Lill reported he was negotiating with a corporation to assume the lease on the plane. He'd already sold the firm's propjet for more than $1 million.

Ken Wilson later complained that the committee had been neither bold nor timely in dealing with these costly excesses.

"These were things that should have been done months before," he says. "They should have gotten rid of the jet the day Fomon left."

Lill also told the group he was working on a travel and entertainment policy. Senior vice presidents, the group decided, could travel first class—even as Hutton's losses mounted—if the trip required three hours or more.

The meeting adjourned at 6:30 P.M.

FRIDAY, JUNE 19

40

In the spring, Sumitomo Life Insurance had begun purchasing blocks of E.F. Hutton stock. By the middle of June, it had accumulated 694,200 shares, or a 2 percent stake. Rumor had it that Sumitomo was going to make a hostile takeover attempt. Nothing, however, could have been further from the truth.

Sumitomo wanted only to acquire a minority interest in Hutton. That is, it wanted to invest in Hutton the same way other Japanese insurance companies had invested in other American financial institutions—Goldman Sachs and PaineWebber, for example. "In other words," says Scott Pierce, "the Japanese would have a substantial amount of equity in Hutton without controlling it."

Bob Rittereiser had spurned this overture from Sumitomo and others that would be made as late as August of 1987. "I suspect," says Pierce, "that management [meaning Rittereiser and Ueberroth] was suspicious of Japanese ownership, that they didn't understand that it is the custom in Japan to invest ten percent or so in their friends. It was awful that they didn't take advantage of this [offer]." Rittereiser, Pierce says, also felt that a Japanese investment might discourage other potential suitors from taking a look at Hutton.

(Rittereiser claims that the Japanese never expressed an interest in buying more than 2 to 3 percent of Hutton stock. If they had wanted a larger stake, he says, he would have been happy to consider the proposition.)

Meanwhile, morale at Hutton hit an all-time low. On June 19, a group of fourteen salaried employees in Hutton's Syracuse, New York, office wrote Bob Rittereiser an angry letter. They had just learned in that morning's *Wall Street Journal* of further reductions Hutton planned to make in its support staff.

"Last Christmas," the employees wrote, "we were advised that there would be no bonuses for any of the support people. This seems ludicrous when you consider the fact that in 1985 support people received a bonus in spite of the fact that Hutton had some problems during that year.

"In 1986, when Hutton had a very good year, we didn't receive so much as a Christmas card. All of this, added to the fact that our annual salary increases have been severely limited, leaves us wondering just how important the support person in the branch office really is.

"We can't help but wonder if Christmas bonuses would have been given if Hutton hadn't decided long before the Christmas season to sign Mr. Kessenich to a $4.7 million, three-year contract. And Robert Fomon certainly got his, didn't he?"

The Syracuse employees—and everyone else in the firm—knew the details of the Kessenich contract, as well as amounts paid to Fomon and other top executives, because these deals were spelled out in documents Hutton filed with the SEC.

"What retirement benefit plans," the letter continued, "does Hutton plan to offer salaried employees in the future? Are there any incentives offered to us for being in the office every day from 8:30 to 5:00 (sometimes longer) servicing the account executives' clients?

"We recall that one of your objectives was to cut back costs. Yet, the only noticeable cuts in the branches are those affecting salaried personnel. In addition to all of this, salaried people are working even harder due to the hiring freeze."

The employees were referring to a freeze that had been imposed in April. When Ken Wilson had arrived at Hutton and saw what bad shape the firm was in, he had urged Rittereiser to lay off 2,000 to 3,000 of Hutton's 17,000 employees. Rittereiser had declined the advice and opted for a hiring freeze instead.

At the same time, the CEO had tried to impose a wage and salary freeze. The sales force was furious. Rittereiser didn't know it, but Jerry Miller had not only already told a number of his people that they would get raises, but also told them exactly how large those raises would be. Rittereiser had decided that it would be unfair to rescind raises already promised and equally unfair to award raises to some people and not to others. So he'd backed off. But the hiring freeze remained in effect.

"We believe what this boils down to," the letter concluded, "is 'The more diligently the account executive works, the more he/she is rewarded. The more diligently a support person works, the less anyone at the top cares.' " All fourteen employees signed the letter.

THURSDAY, JULY 2

40 ⅜

Everything had gone so badly for Bob Fomon. After seventeen years as chairman and CEO of Hutton, he was now virtually persona non grata at company headquarters.

Fomon blamed Rittereiser, the man who had ousted him, for his fate, and he was anxious to avenge what he perceived as a wrong. So in early summer he made a decision—to make good on his promise to sell Hutton out from underneath everyone who remained at the firm, including Rittereiser. Retribution aside, Fomon was also worried about the falling value of his 250,000 Hutton shares.

As a first step, he invited Peter Cohen, the chairman of Shearson, and Cohen's boss, Jim Robinson, the chairman of American Express, to join him for breakfast on July 2. Since Cohen and

Robinson had seriously pursued Hutton the year before, Fomon figured they might still be interested in acquiring the firm.

The three men gathered in the huge formal dining room of Fomon's luxurious Fifth Avenue apartment overlooking New York's Central Park. Fomon sat at the head of the beautiful antique mahogany table; Cohen and Robinson on each side. Fomon's French chef, Richard, served bacon, toast, orange juice, and coffee. "No eggs," Fomon says. "I never eat eggs."

Although Fomon had spoken to Cohen and Robinson a few times, the three men had not met face-to-face since merger talks between Hutton and Shearson had broken off in 1986.

Hutton, Fomon began, was now ripe for a takeover. There was no way, he argued, that current management could return the brokerage to a position of financial strength. Although he was no longer associated with the firm—and he was not Hutton's investment banker—Fomon said, he could help facilitate a merger with Shearson. What he meant, Fomon says, is that he could have facilitated the merger by arranging a meeting of Cohen and Hutton's board. Were Cohen and Robinson interested? he wanted to know.

The two men promised that one of them would get back to Fomon with an answer. They shook hands; then Cohen and Robinson departed. On the drive downtown in Cohen's gray Lincoln, they discussed Fomon's proposal. They resumed their conversation again during the weekend at Cohen's house in the Hamptons.

For his part, Cohen wasn't enthusiastic. In fact, he flatly told Robinson he had no interest in exploring a merger. The bull market was bound to end soon, he said, and the financial services industry would head into a "negative period." Anyway, he would have plenty of work to do at Shearson without taking on the added problems of a merger partner, especially one as troubled as E.F. Hutton.

Robinson didn't agree, but he decided to go along with Cohen. After all, Cohen was the one who would have to live with the decision day to day.

MONDAY, JULY 13

40 ⅞

The telephone conversation on July 13 didn't go the way Fomon wanted. Shearson, Cohen said, had no interest in E.F. Hutton—at least not now. Fomon was annoyed and depressed. It was clear that Cohen and Robinson weren't going to bite; he would have to look elsewhere for a buyer.

FRIDAY, JULY 17

40

Payouts to brokers—the percentage of their commissions that brokers actually pocket—were higher at E.F. Hutton than at any other major firm. Big producers got to keep as much as 50 percent of the revenues they brought in.

For months, Bob Rittereiser had told Jerry Miller that he was going to have to do something about this situation, that he was going to have to cut payouts. And for just as long, Miller had demurred. If he cut payouts, he insisted, his brokers would defect to the competition—en masse. Asking Miller to cut payouts, Rittereiser says, was like asking him "to move the Empire State Building from Thirty-fourth Street to Forty-second Street."

Finally, though, Miller had given in. He had no choice, if he planned to remain in his post at Hutton. Says Rittereiser, "I think [Miller] knew it had to be done and he'd talked to the regional managers about the necessity to do it." Miller told Rittereiser that he would announce a new payout schedule, but not until January. He needed time, he argued, to prepare his sales force for the bad news. For the firm, the cost-cutting measure turned out, once more, to be too little too late. Hutton would be swallowed by Shearson before Miller got around to slashing the amounts his brokers received.

242

Miller didn't know it at the time, but Hutton's top producers had already met and secretly decided that they would accept a cut in payouts. They weren't going to volunteer, though; they wanted someone to ask them. "The feeling of the producers," says one who was in on the meeting, "was that it was necessary to cut commissions, because upper management was pissing away the firm."

Hutton was changing under Rittereiser's management, and Jerry Miller, for one, was uneasy with the pace that change was taking. In Rittereiser's vision of the future, Hutton would become a financial services boutique, providing high-quality, high-margin services to fewer, wealthier clients. He wanted, in other words, to see Hutton serving the high end of the market—something the people at Hutton thought they had been doing all along.

That was not, however, what the firm's customer research showed. Those numbers confirmed that most Hutton accounts generated little revenue—and were unprofitable. As Rittereiser saw it, Miller consistently took the position that the more customers, the better—never mind the high overhead.

It was just that kind of thinking, Rittereiser argued, that had made Hutton what it was at that point—a brokerage firm in deep trouble. Steve Friedman and Ed Lill agreed. "Jerry," says Friedman, "believed in filling the empty seats. He wanted to fill the seats at Hutton's branch offices, because he wanted to increase revenues."

As far as Friedman and Lill were concerned, Miller's brokers were running him, not the other way around. Miller, Tom Lynch says, "was always terrified" of the sales force. It was a Hutton tradition. "I've never seen a company," Rittereiser says, "where people were more expert at managing their bosses." Says a former senior executive, "Jerry was overly concerned about the reaction of the sales force. He didn't provide enough leadership."

Rittereiser's plan for Hutton might have been reasonable, but it couldn't succeed, says Stephen A. Schwartzman, president of the hotshot Blackstone Group. "Bob Rittereiser's plan," insists

Schwartzman, "required three things—time, which he didn't have; money, which he could not have gotten; and confidence on the part of people internally and the world externally, which he never earned."

Rittereiser did realize that if E.F. Hutton's new retail strategy was going to work, it would be because its retail brokers made it work. So he planned a meeting of retail branch managers to be held in Washington, D.C. There, he and his senior lieutenants would explain the strategy and whip up enthusiasm among the managers, who in turn would carry the message back to the brokers in their own shops. The meeting was scheduled for Friday, July 17. Rittereiser and the management committee arrived a day early and met that afternoon to review their plans for the event.

"At the end of the meeting," recalls Jerry Miller, "Rittereiser said, 'We have a surprise for everybody.' I said, 'What kind of surprise?' He said, 'We have to solidify our thinking and the thinking of the managers and let them know the firm is in trouble, and we have a unique way of getting this across to them.' He said, 'Jerry [Welsh, the new corporate marketing head] has come up with an idea to have a coloring book to do it.' "

Miller asked to see a copy. Welsh shook his head no. "It will be attached to everybody's door in the morning in a plastic bag," Welsh said firmly. "You'll see it when they see it."

Miller's face flushed with anger. He asked again to see the book. "You're giving a coloring book out to my managers," he insisted. "I want to see it before they see it." Welsh reluctantly relented.

If Miller had been unhappy before, he was apoplectic after examining what Welsh intended to give his branch managers. "I went crazy," he concedes. "I said, 'You guys gotta be kidding. This is a disaster.' "

The Hutton Neighborhood Coloring Book contained thirty-four pages. Most were just silly, but two were simply suicidal in a publication intended for wide distribution. One, showing an insignificant structure wedged between two imposing mansions, conceded that "we're no longer the nicest house on the block. We're not even close. In fact, we're in big trouble." Another page showed a moving van in front of the house. "If we don't fix our problems *soon*," the text said, "someone could even take away our home. (Color this gloomy.)"

"Do you know," Miller demanded of Welsh, "what my competitors are going to do to me? You're admitting that we're not as good as everyone else. And I'm supposed to attract people in from other firms and not lose my people to other firms?" Others in the room—Dick Locke and Mark Kessenich, among them—also became upset, according to Miller. Rittereiser, however, told the retail head that he was "too negative."

What most disturbed Miller was not the foolish comic book itself but the fact that it had been slated for distribution to his people without his ever having seen it. If that weren't bad enough, Rittereiser and Welsh were deliberately publicizing an internal situation that Miller considered an egregious embarrassment.

But "at that point," Miller recalls, "we couldn't stop it." Welsh and Rittereiser had already granted an interview for the next day's marketing column of the *Wall Street Journal*. The story included a drawing of Rittereiser sitting with the book on his lap.

The next morning the coloring book hung on everyone's door-knob. Miller went down to the meeting. "It was worse than I thought it was going to be," he says. "Here these managers are away from their offices and, by this time, their account executives have read the *Wall Street Journal*. They haven't seen the coloring book but have read about it."

The managers asked him, "Jerry, how could you let this happen?" He apologized but protested his innocence. "If you want to talk to the people who knew about it," he told them, "talk to Welsh and Rittereiser."

Aside from this fiasco, the meeting went well. "It was a good meeting," says Miller. "We outlined where we were going and what we had to do." The comic book fallout continued, though. One Hutton branch office conducted a book burning outside the offices. "The retail sales force hated it," says one former senior executive. "People were ridiculing them. Clients were calling: 'What kind of firm is this? Is this the firm I trust my money to?' "

"The coloring book was not just any minor little fiasco," says a former Hutton executive. "It was a disaster to the soul of the firm. I do resent the Who-killed-Hutton stories with Fomon's picture. I think they've got the wrong man. It should be Rittereiser's picture."

Rittereiser admits he could have handled the situation better. "I accept responsibility for blowing that one," he says. "The design of it, the idea of it, was good. It was the implementation of the idea that was wrong. There wasn't enough sharing of it up front.

"If I did it at all today," he adds, "I would have done it differently, and chances are I wouldn't have done it at all."

Welsh later held another meeting in Washington to discuss marketing plans. People were still angry about the comic book. " 'You are all going to see how wrong you are,' " Welsh said, according to one senior executive's recollection. " 'Five years from now at the Harvard Business School, this is going to be used as an example of marketing genius.' "

"Welsh," the executive insists, "knew nothing about the brokerage business."

TUESDAY, JULY 21

38 7/8

Jerry Miller and Mark Kessenich were not pals. At management committee meeting after management committee meeting—and the one on July 21 was no exception—they fought bitterly. Miller wanted the retail sales force preserved—as is—no matter what the cost. Kessenich pushed for deep cuts in the brokerage operation.

(Kessenich claims that his disagreements with Miller were not so much about the size of the sales force as about whether retail or Kessenich's group would handle sales to institutional clients.)

The ill will from those disputes lingered, and Bob Rittereiser, for one, was fed up. In fact, he was beginning to have serious doubts about Miller *and* Kessenich. "Both of them," he says, "had yet to prove to me" that they were up to the tasks at hand.

WEDNESDAY, JULY 22

39 ½

On a humid day in July, Hutton's stockholders gathered for their annual meeting at the firm's pink-marble world headquarters. They didn't know it at the time, but when they next convened, it would be to approve Hutton's merger with Shearson.

The stockholders didn't make the meeting easy for Bob Rittereiser. One man—an elderly gentleman from Long Island—rose to take issue with the CEO. Why, he demanded to know, hadn't Hutton sold out to Shearson when Shearson offered to pay $50 a share for the firm? Rittereiser corrected the man. Shearson, he said, had made no *formal* offer for the firm. Several other stockholders chimed in before Steve Friedman intervened. The issue of whether Shearson had made a formal offer for Hutton was under litigation, he said, so Hutton executives could make no comment. At the time, outside criticism of Rittereiser and his regime was scarce. But the stockholders' comments were a harbinger of events to come.

After the shareholders' meeting, Hutton's board convened for a five-hour session. It was the first board meeting that Bob Fomon had not attended. Rittereiser had the agenda mapped out. Each member of the senior management team would outline the problems his department faced and his proposed solutions. "It was," Rittereiser says, "the first really comprehensive top-down briefing the board had ever received."

At the end of the meeting, Peter Ueberroth walked over and handed Rittereiser a piece of notepaper. On it, he had written the names of each executive and how long he spoke. His message was clear: Rittereiser had told the board that each executive would speak for a specified amount of time. The meeting ran about a half hour over the scheduled time because of questions, and Ueberroth now was chastising him. Rittereiser could only shake his head in disgust. Here we are, he thought to himself, trying to turn Hutton around, and all Ueberroth is interested in is making sure we don't take up too much of his time.

TUESDAY, AUGUST 18

41 5/8

Hutton's management committee gathered for a regularly scheduled meeting, although by now almost nothing was routine at the troubled firm. Bob Rittereiser's warts as a chief executive were becoming all too apparent to those who worked for him. "Bob," says one senior executive he hired, "doesn't come across like George Washington as a leader." His frequent use of sports analogies, a benign habit in happier times, was getting on everyone's nerves. "Bullshit!" says operations chief Norm Epstein. "We weren't playing basketball here."

Rittereiser, Fomon observes, "is one of those guys who is so inarticulate that he can talk for ten minutes and no one will understand what he is saying. He is completely obtuse." Adds a former senior executive, a man Rittereiser hired, "Bob Rittereiser is not worth a shit at getting anything done. At least Fomon could make a decision. Maybe it was wrong," he adds, "but, goddamn it, he made it."

Often, it was the difference between Rittereiser's concepts and their execution that was so striking. Sometimes, says Steve Friedman, he would have ideas that were brilliant, then would implement them ineptly. "An example," recalls Friedman, "was Jerry Welsh. Bob's notion was that one of the problems of the securities industry was that it had not really understood marketing as opposed to selling." That, Friedman claims, was a "powerful and important" judgment.

But Rittereiser's subsequent logic, he thinks, was seriously flawed and led to incredibly bad results. Rittereiser, Friedman explains, decided to reorganize the firm to make it more market driven. He also realized that in a market-driven firm, the company's objectives and those of its employees and the sales force had to be aligned. That, Friedman allows, was smart thinking, too.

Then, however, Rittereiser blundered. He decided that the way to align these forces was to put marketing director Welsh in charge of human resources. "On the conceptual level," Friedman says, "he [was] probably right. The problem is that Jerry Welsh is not the type of person you would want to put in charge of human resources." Welsh, Friedman points out, hated detail and wasn't interested in managing large groups. "For Bob to put Jerry in charge of human resources," he says, "was a terrible decision." But the incident said a great deal about Hutton's strengths and weaknesses under Rittereiser's management.

The retail sales force was growing increasingly unhappy with Rittereiser, who wasn't at all like George Ball. Rittereiser seldom returned their phone calls. He insisted that they go through channels. In short, he didn't pamper them as Ball had. Using an analogy that Rittereiser himself might otherwise have used, a former top account executive complains, "He was a minor league player in a World Series game."

A "nice man" is the strongest compliment Lee Kimmell of Salomon Brothers can pay Rittereiser, who, he goes on, is nonetheless "not without guilt. But, he bears the guilt of a man who wasn't qualified to have the job under the best of circumstances, much less under the worst."

Bob Rittereiser didn't know it, but he was now a marked man. By Labor Day, the consensus among Hutton board members would be that he had to go. Two and a half years had passed since he had joined the firm, and in that time he had been unable to turn Hutton around. The firm remained financially shaky.

Board members expected better, but none of them—not even the outspoken Ueberroth—ever said anything to Rittereiser. "Such cowards," Rittereiser now says.

In late October, though, Steve Friedman would get a glimpse of the board's loss of confidence in the Hutton CEO when he met with the compensation committee to discuss Rittereiser's unsigned employment contract. "I was surprised," he says now, "how far and fast the dissatisfaction had spread." Friedman was then in an awkward situation. As general counsel, he represented the board. As a Hutton employee, he reported to Rittereiser.

The terms Rittereiser wanted were those Fomon had outlined orally when he hired him. Unfortunately, either Friedman didn't get around to the chore until late in the summer of 1987 or Rittereiser only thought he had given him the assignment. In either case, by the summer of 1987 the board was ready to sack Rittereiser, and members weren't interested in his employment contract.

Although the board informally agreed that Rittereiser would have to be replaced as CEO, in typical Hutton fashion very little thought was given to a successor. In a desperate gesture, the job had been offered to George Ball, chairman and CEO of Prudential-Bache and onetime president of Hutton. Ball, not surprisingly, had turned it down.

September proved to be the calm before the storm. On an overcast Tuesday, members of Hutton's management committee gathered in the tasteful conference room on the twenty-eighth floor of the firm's corporate headquarters.

They listened politely as Hutton Comptroller Mike Castellano updated them on NOVA. The report, Castellano said, would outline $40 million in cost savings. Not enough, Ken Wilson knew, to make a difference. "No one seemed to realize it," Wilson remembers, "but we were already in deep shit."

Most of the savings, Castellano told the group, would come from an increase in fees. For example, the firm would charge customers for whom it held securities. But expenses would be cut in some areas—for example, operation of the executive dining room would be scaled way back.

Rittereiser, though, had more up his sleeve. He planned to reduce the firm's twelve regional offices to four, realign some back-office systems, make more efficient use of company-owned real estate, drop some business lines, cut back on Hutton's 550 marketing people, and—always the most controversial proposal—cut Hutton's legendary commissions. He also intended to make steep reductions in the investment-banking staff (from 110 professionals down to eighty) and in public finance (from about 100 staff members to about forty or forty-five).

The management committee also heard Mike Rieff make his bonus estimates, and Tom Styles, Bob Barbera, and Jeff Applegate present their economic forecasts for the market and the economy. Mark Kessenich then took the floor and discussed his objectives for the fixed-income area.

Of course, no one in the room knew what Bob Fomon was up to. They would soon find out.

TUESDAY, SEPTEMBER 15

38 ³/₈

Fomon was fiercely determined to sell E.F. Hutton, and his best hope, he thought, was still Peter Anthony Cohen, the short, dark, intense chairman and chief executive officer of Shearson Lehman Brothers. So late Tuesday, sitting in his apartment overlooking the Seine, Fomon dialed Cohen's number.

Once again, Fomon told Cohen that the time was right for Shearson to buy Hutton. And, once again, Fomon said he could be helpful in engineering a deal. Still, Cohen wasn't interested. Fomon, dejected, hung up.

THURSDAY, OCTOBER 15

33 ⁵/₈

The rumor that Hutton was about to go belly up caught Bob Rittereiser completely off guard. A man who identified himself as a reporter for the *Philadelphia Inquirer* dialed some two dozen Wall Street firms. At each one he left the same disturbing message for the head of research. The man said he had heard that Hutton planned to declare bankruptcy over the coming weekend, and he wanted to know if there was any truth to the rumor.

Rittereiser and his men scrambled to find the source of the rumor. Was someone trying to drive the price of Hutton's stock down? Probably. Was the *Philadelphia Inquirer* reporter for real? Probably not. But the Hutton executives could prove nothing. In the meantime, the rumor drove Hutton's stock down some $6 a share.

FRIDAY, OCTOBER 16

17 3/8

Peter G. Peterson is a star in financial circles, a man who has a reputation not only in New York but in Washington, London, and Tokyo as well. A summa cum laude graduate of Northwestern University, president of Bell & Howell at thirty-four, Peterson served as secretary of commerce in the Nixon administration until political infighting with Treasury Secretary John B. Connally did him in. "He comes across as a little daffy but he isn't," says an investment banker who knows Peterson well.

Brusque, imperious, and self-absorbed, Peterson went on to become chairman of Lehman Brothers Kuhn Loeb, where he remained until Shearson acquired the firm in 1985. Then Peterson joined forces with two other former Lehman Brothers partners— Roger C. Altman and Steve Schwartzman—to form The Blackstone Group. Peterson assumed the title of chairman; Altman, vice chairman; and Schwartzman, president. The three had never worked for—or even with—Hutton, but their firm would figure prominently in Hutton's shrinking future in two important ways.

On October 16—three days before the market collapse—Rittereiser joined Peterson, Altman, and Schwartzman for breakfast in the salon lounge of the elegant European-style Mayfair Regent Hotel at 610 Park Avenue, just up the street from Blackstone's Park Avenue offices.

The initial purpose of the meeting—in Rittereiser's mind at least—was to explore the possibility of Hutton's investing in Blackstone's new leveraged buyout fund. The Blackstone people thought they were there to discuss the possibility of Blackstone's acquiring a minority interest in Hutton. In the end, the conversation came around to what Blackstone could do for Hutton.

"Everybody got along very well at the breakfast meeting," Schwartzman says. He and the others found Rittereiser "honest, straight, a nice man, a solid guy who knew where he wanted to go with Hutton."

But, as it turned out, Friday was, as Bob Rittereiser says, "not what you would call a good day on Wall Street." When the market closed that afternoon, the Dow Jones Industrial Average had plunged 108 points, losing more than 10 percent of its value.

SUNDAY, OCTOBER 18

Market Closed

Each fall in Palm Beach, Florida—the winter refuge of the wealthy and well connected—hundreds of utility industry executives assemble for their annual meeting. E.F. Hutton has lots of utility companies as investment-banking clients. So each year, as part of that gathering, Hutton and Dina Merrill, who maintains a Palm Beach home, host a dinner.

This year, the annual event was held on October 18 at a Palm Beach country club. Early that day, Bob Rittereiser and his wife boarded a plane in New York and headed south. That night, they attended the black-tie affair. Rittereiser gave a brief speech, then mingled with the crowd. "The mood," Rittereiser says, "was that the market would fall further still."

MONDAY, OCTOBER 19

23 ⅛

The next morning, after a breakfast meeting, Rittereiser and his wife set out for the Palm Beach airport to make a scheduled 9:30 A.M. flight. As it turned out, however, the flight didn't leave until 11 A.M. In the meantime, Rittereiser dialed his office in New York. The market, he found out, was in a free-fall. He put Ed Lill in charge until he could make it back to the office, which turned out to be not until 2:00 P.M.

When the stock market crashes, more than money can be lost on Wall Street. Reputations, careers—even entire firms—can crumble. What was most striking, though, about the crash of October 19, 1987, was how little it *seemed* to affect Hutton. By the end of the day, the firm's operating losses amounted to less than $1 million. (Bad debts on margin accounts would later add up to some $20 million more.)

Ken Wilson, however, knew that first impressions could be deceiving, that the crash would affect Hutton dramatically. In his mind at least, on October 19, "the shit really hit the fan." In fact, it turned out to be the final nail in the coffin.

That evening Rittereiser was scheduled to be honored for his work in behalf of nonprofit theater in New York, a commitment he decided to keep. So at 7:45 sharp, he left the office to attend the dinner. "At that point," Rittereiser says, "there was nothing else I could do." Besides, he reasoned, if he didn't attend the event, it might make people more nervous about the markets than they already were.

TUESDAY, OCTOBER 20

16 ¾

None of the men Bob Rittereiser hired had expected life at E.F. Hutton to be easy. But they had not expected it to be impossible, either. Other brokerage executives had crises to deal with on the day the stock market collapsed. But Hutton executives would have traded their problems for their counterparts' in a minute.

The morning after the crash, Bob Rittereiser summoned Ken Wilson and Ed Lill to his office. "You are a committee of two," he told them. "You will be working directly with me to figure out what to do next."

At the meeting, Wilson again argued forcefully for the sale of Hutton. "The main agenda," he told Rittereiser, "has to be to get the firm sold." As far as he was concerned, a simple infusion of capital would not be enough. But Rittereiser wasn't convinced, at least not yet. "I had to keep my options open," he says.

That day, the men who served as regional vice presidents in the firm's retail sales division were scheduled to come to New York for a meeting at which Jerry Miller would outline changes in the retail sales operation, primary among them the planned reduction in payouts.

At 10:00 A.M., the group gathered in the huge conference room on the twenty-eighth floor of Hutton's headquarters. Black Monday had left them in a state of shock. "It reminded me of Vietnam," says Wilson. "These guys were white. They looked like they'd just come out of a barrage of artillery."

At the end of the meeting, which broke up early that afternoon, Rittereiser spoke briefly to the group. "Look, fellas," he said, "we're doing the best we can, and you've got to do the best you can. I'm glad you came here, but everybody's got to go home and get back to work." His words did little to soothe them.

After he spoke, Rittereiser strode back to his office and closeted himself with Wilson and Lill. Then he called a board meeting—via telephone—for 5:00 P.M. "No one from the board had called since the market crashed," Rittereiser says, "but I thought I should advise them of what was going on." In the wake of the crash, Rittereiser told the board, there were simply no guarantees. The market might plunge further, and in any case chances were good that the firm's revenues would drop as small investors bailed out.

"We didn't have deep pockets," Rittereiser says. "We had no financial running room." The likelihood was strong, he says, that "there was going to be a period of time when investors would pull out of the market, go to the sidelines, and lick their wounds. During that period, we were going to be hurting." Hutton, Rittereiser added, must "do something from a capital point of view," must get an infusion of fresh money. And it could raise that capital in only one way—by selling all or part of itself to an outside party.

No one on the board commented on Rittereiser's remarks. Nor did they ask any questions. "They said, fine, thank you," Rittereiser says, "and that was it."

Then Rittereiser asked the board to endorse a stock buy-back plan designed to shore up the price of Hutton's common stock. On October 19, Hutton's stock price had plummeted to $17.00 a share—down from $30.38 on October 16. Most securities firms' stocks, of course, fell steeply during this period. But Hutton's had the dubious distinction of being the worst-performing stock among major securities firms since the crash.

Aware of these problems, the board authorized Rittereiser to buy back as much as 10 percent of Hutton's common stock if the price dipped below $15 a share. In the days ahead, though, the stock price would hold.

WEDNESDAY, OCTOBER 21

18 ⅝

James D. Robinson III, fifty-two years old, is a very private man who has climbed to the top of a very public company, giant American Express. On October 21, Robinson answered a phone call from Peter Cohen. The crash, Cohen began, has created turmoil in the financial services industry—"enough turmoil," he said, that the time may be right to pick up E.F. Hutton at a bargain price. Robinson's response was exactly what Cohen wanted to hear. "Whatever you want to do," Robinson said and hung up.

As it turned out, Cohen wasn't the only one on Wall Street eyeing Hutton in the long, anxious days following the stock market crash. Already, Bob Rittereiser had fielded phone calls from Fred Joseph, a Hutton alumnus now the head of Drexel Burnham Lambert, and Philip Purcell, the chief of Dean Witter Reynolds. If there is any way we can help, let us know, the two men told Rittereiser, remarks the CEO interpreted to mean, If you're looking to sell, we might be looking to buy.

Meanwhile, Rittereiser continued to deal with the doomsday rumors that were spreading about the firm. Of course, he knew that Wall Street was abuzz with talk about virtually every firm in the industry. Already, he had heard that the crash had sent Goldman Sachs and Merrill Lynch reeling. Still, Rittereiser knew that Hutton was among the more vulnerable firms on Wall Street. And the rumors—if they were taken as fact—could spell the end.

Early that morning, he picked up the telephone and began dialing. "I called anyone in the industry who I thought could hurt us," he says, including the credit ratings agencies and Hutton's bankers. Rittereiser, however, wasn't sure what good his efforts did. "I probably sounded somewhat self-serving," he admits.

THURSDAY, OCTOBER 22

17 ⅝

That morning Hutton and Blackstone executives met for a second breakfast at the Mayfair Regent. Rittereiser began talking about his plans for the company. "His comments," Schwartzman says, "all focused on expense reduction, excising some of Hutton's businesses that didn't earn money, and doing something about the fat payouts to brokers."

Peterson was also impressed. He had run a brokerage and had been preaching for some time that Wall Street firms had way too much overhead and were growing too fast. Rittereiser seemed to address those concerns. "There was a certain logic to what Ritt was talking about," says Schwartzman.

Rittereiser needed time to carry out his plan to lower costs, and an infusion of capital by The Blackstone Group—$200 million to $250 million in exchange for a 25 to 30 percent interest in Hutton—would have given the CEO the financial breathing room he needed.

Perhaps just as important, from Rittereiser's perspective, the proposed deal—and it never got beyond the informal, talking stage—also called for several people from Blackstone to be added to Hutton's board of directors. "It was," Schwartzman says, "an opportunity to reconfigure the board, to bring on more people who were knowledgeable about the financial services business."

The Blackstone people suspected that Rittereiser was in trouble with the board, but they didn't know how serious his problems were. "He wanted to change the board," Schwartzman says, "so obviously we knew that there was some history there with the board members."

At this point, no one at Blackstone knew the extent of Hutton's troubles, that its future might be in doubt. Blackstone's only concern was that the industry as a whole wasn't "as healthy as it might be," and, for the short term at least, its prospects weren't bright. "What we were looking at," says Schwartzman, "was not just how viable was Hutton, but how viable was the financial industry? Was the plan for Hutton a good plan? Was the industry going to make it?"

No one at the breakfast meeting knew it, but later that day the death watch for Hutton would begin. At 10:00 A.M., Lou Dobbs, a Cable News Network newscaster, reported that Standard & Poor's had placed a number of brokerage firms—Hutton, Bear Stearns, and PaineWebber, among them—on a credit watch list. Standard & Poor's took the action, the newscaster said, because of the firms' weak balance sheets.

Ed Lill learned about the report from an associate. He immediately picked up the phone and dialed his contacts at Standard & Poor's. "What's the story?" he demanded to know.

To his surprise, Standard & Poor's executives said they knew nothing about the report, but they set about to find out fast. Within the hour, a Standard & Poor's executive had telephoned CNN and explained that the firm had placed the brokerage houses on a credit watch in response to the crash. The move did not—as the newscaster had stated—reflect the quality of their balance sheets. The credit watch only represented Standard & Poor's concerns about the firms' future business prospects.

Later in the day, CNN issued a correction, and later that week Rittereiser appeared on the network to talk about the stock market in general and Hutton in particular. But the damage had been done. New rumors began to engulf Hutton. The firm had long suffered from mismanagement, so people assumed Hutton was failing and failing fast.

SATURDAY, OCTOBER 24

Market Closed

Earlier in the week, Ken Wilson had stuck his head into Bob Rittereiser's posh office. He had a question for the chief executive.

That weekend Wilson was set to fly from New York to Englewood, Colorado, for a long-scheduled meeting with Jack A. MacAllister, the unconventional chairman and chief executive officer of USWest Inc., one of the hot baby Bells. MacAllister, fifty-eight years old and a graduate of the University of Iowa, had moved USWest, an $8.4-billion-a-year telecommunications holding company, boldly into cellular mobile phone systems, equipment sales, commercial real estate, and financial services.

USWest had been a client of Hutton's investment-banking arm, and, Wilson asked, should he—in the wake of the crash—keep his appointment?

Rittereiser argued that he should, but that the agenda should change. The round-faced, bespectacled MacAllister had once expressed an interest in acquiring Hutton, Rittereiser said, so Wilson should see if he could rekindle that interest. "At this point," says Lee Kimmell of Salomon Brothers, "what Hutton needed was a sugar daddy."

At the meeting, MacAllister told Wilson that USWest—parent of Mountain Bell, Northwestern Bell, and Pacific Northwest Bell—needed time to weigh the proposition. So Wilson had to board his flight back to New York, hopeful but empty-handed.

Sanford I. Weill is a financial folk hero, the man who built Shearson (at that time called Hayden Stone) from scratch to the second largest investment house on Wall Street.

In 1985, he sold Shearson to American Express for $1 billion, then, a year later, jumped ship to Commercial Credit Co. He was succeeded at Shearson by his protégé, Peter Cohen. "Sandy Weill has all the charisma that Peter Cohen lacks," says an investment banker who knows them both.

Early October 26, Pete Peterson dialed Bob Rittereiser at Hutton's headquarters. Would Rittereiser mind if Blackstone introduced him to Sandy Weill? As Rittereiser understood it, Blackstone viewed Weill as a potential addition to Hutton's board—not as a prospective suitor. Still, Rittereiser begged off. He needed time to think, he said, and promised to get back to Peterson.

Rittereiser never did give Blackstone permission to contact Weill. (But, a few days later, Peterson phoned the Commercial Credit executive and explained the situation at Hutton. "Sandy," Schwartzman remembers, "sounded excited" about the possibility of becoming involved with Hutton.

What neither Schwartzman nor Peterson knew was that someone else would soon introduce Weill to Hutton's board of directors, and that someone else would be Bob Fomon. Fomon's agenda was not simply to add Weill to the board but to effect a marriage between Hutton and Commercial Credit. If such a deal went through, Fomon stood to receive—as agreed with Weill—a $2 million finder's fee.

TUESDAY, OCTOBER 27

14 ¾

Hutton's senior management committee had been scheduled to meet off site for three days beginning October 27 to review the results of the NOVA project. It wasn't confidentiality they were worried about in taking the meeting out of the office. They just didn't want to be interrupted. No matter. The meeting was off now, anyway. Rittereiser and his men had more pressing matters to attend to.

That day Standard & Poor's officials met with Ed Lill. The ratings agency reaffirmed its confidence in the brokerage house and in Hutton's A2 rating. But Lill was a realist. Like Ken Wilson, he was now convinced that he and the other executives must do what they most emphatically did not want to do—sell Hutton outright.

In the meantime, Jack MacAllister, in New York on business, stopped by for a brief chat with Rittereiser, and Rittereiser shared with him Hutton's business plan. At the end of the meeting, MacAllister invited Rittereiser, Lill, and Wilson to meet with USWest executives that coming weekend in Englewood. Rittereiser accepted the invitation with alacrity.

WEDNESDAY, OCTOBER 28

15

To add to the firm's woes, federal prosecutors recommended on October 28 that Hutton and a Hutton officer be indicted on money-laundering charges. The scandal involved Hutton's Providence, Rhode Island, office, and a Hutton broker, Stephen Fusco, who had died of cancer in December 1985.

Fusco, in a scheme known as structuring, had allegedly helped his customers get around the federal law that requires financial institutions to report cash transactions that exceed $10,000 to the IRS. Fusco, according to the prosecutors, told customers how to break down large sums of cash into amounts of less than $10,000. Then he deposited the money into their Hutton accounts.

To make matters worse, the prosecutors alleged that Fusco had done his money laundering for organized crime figures. The case surfaced in a roundabout way after the IRS audited a Hutton secretary. The secretary had paid $10,000 in cash for a bond and asked a bank to report the transaction to the IRS in her name and not Hutton's. In its audit, the IRS asked the woman how, given her salary, she could afford the bond. The details she provided triggered the investigation.

When Rittereiser heard from Steve Friedman that the prosecutors had recommended indicting the firm, he threw up his hands in frustration. "It reminded me of a football game," he says, "when after the tackle is made, a player piles on. When that happens, even the hometown fans boo.

"Who," he wondered, "were these people punishing? They were punishing the people who were trying to turn Hutton around."

SATURDAY, OCTOBER 31

Market Closed

Ken Wilson, Ed Lill, and Bob Rittereiser continued to search for a buyer for all or part of Hutton. "I wasn't worried about the other shoe dropping," Wilson remembers, "I was worried that there wouldn't be a shoe to drop. My concern was holding the firm together until somebody could come in and take it over. It was a scary time."

That snowy Saturday the three men flew to Englewood, Colorado, for their meeting with USWest. At the start of the session, Jack MacAllister apologized for the absence of one of his key senior managers—John C. Willemssen, executive vice president and chief planning officer. The man most in favor of USWest acquiring Hutton, Willemssen, was ill, MacAllister explained.

"It was a terrific meeting," Rittereiser says of the four-hour session. The Hutton executives flew back home full of hope that a deal could be done.

MONDAY, NOVEMBER 2

18 ⅝

USWest wasn't the only baby Bell that Hutton courted. Bell Atlantic's chairman and CEO, Thomas E. Bolger, had steered his $10.3-billion-a-year company into businesses such as cellular phones and computer maintenance, leasing, and financing, and he thought he might be interested in getting into the brokerage business as well. Months previously, Bob Rittereiser had scheduled a lunch meeting on November 2 with Ray Smith, Bell Atlantic's chief financial officer. He kept the appointment.

Was Bell Atlantic interested in acquiring all or part of Hutton? Rittereiser asked. The executive didn't know, but he would explore the matter with his superiors, he said.

In the meantime, Jack MacAllister called with bad news. John Willemssen, the executive who had been unable to attend Saturday's meeting, had died after a brief illness. "The guy was only forty-eight years old," Rittereiser says. "The management team out there was just devastated, and we lost the one man who was very much for the deal."

Rittereiser suspected—rightly, it turned out—that the man's death would spell an end to a marriage between Hutton and USWest. A few days later, MacAllister confirmed his fears. The timing was wrong for USWest to pursue a deal, he said.

264

23 ½

Soon after the World Series ended and a few days after the crash, Peter Ueberroth—commissioner of baseball, *Time* magazine "man of the year," and Hutton board member—had phoned Bob Rittereiser at Hutton's headquarters. Ueberroth was going on vacation and would be unavailable for the next two weeks.

"Where are you going?" Rittereiser had asked innocently.

Ueberroth's response was typical of a man with an outsized ego. "North America," he had replied.

"Well, that certainly nails it down," Rittereiser said and hung up. It's good, he thought to himself, when you can describe yourself in continental terms.

On November 6 Ueberroth returned from his trip, and Rittereiser phoned him at his office with some disturbing news. Bob Fomon, Rittereiser had heard, was—like Rittereiser—shopping around for a buyer for E.F. Hutton. As the story went, Fomon and some other people connected to Hutton had dined the previous evening with Sandy Weill and an associate to discuss the sale of Hutton. (Rittereiser would later find out that the "others" were Warren Law, Ed Cazier, and Dina Merrill and the meeting took place at Fomon's apartment.)

Any sale, Rittereiser argued, had to be controlled, managed. The sale of the firm had to be negotiated by one man—the current CEO—not the firm's retired chairman. Otherwise, events could spiral out of control.

"Fomon was undermining the firm," Rittereiser says. "What concerned me was that we were dealing with banks, ratings agencies, other firms. If I can pick up a rumor like that on the street, so can anyone else. I was afraid people would read this and think, Oh my God, things at Hutton are a lot worse that they've been telling us."

Now Rittereiser wanted the straight story from Ueberroth. Ueberroth said he knew nothing about the dinner. But, he said, he would try to find out if there was any truth to the rumor and would call Rittereiser back if he had anything to report.

Ueberroth never phoned back. As it turned out, the rumor was true. Fomon and the board members *had* met with Weill. And, over the coming weekend, Fomon, Law, and Cazier would fly to California to discuss the Weill deal with another Hutton board member, Tom Talbott.

Fomon also tried to arrange for Weill to meet Ueberroth, who was in Los Angeles at the time. For months, Ueberroth had been urging Fomon to find a buyer for Hutton. "You know," Ueberroth told Fomon, "Rittereiser is no leader. We should just sell and get out of this mess."

In Los Angeles, Fomon dialed Ueberroth's number. Sandy Weill, he explained, is interested in Hutton. Ueberroth, Fomon says, "thought it was a fabulous idea."

But the baseball commissioner was unable to find time to meet with Weill. "I thought," Fomon says, "that he had a girl, and he was shacked up with her at the Century Plaza Hotel. I couldn't think of any other reason he would be avoiding me."

Meanwhile, word got out about Weill's interest in Hutton. "It's like a divorce," says Steve Friedman. "People stop thinking about common interest and start thinking about their individual interests."

The parade of executives into Friedman's twenty-eighth-floor office was almost endless. Would their options be good after the sale? Would their contracts be honored?

Some of Hutton's big producers even hired their own attorneys, with a view to participating in the negotiations to sell the firm. Mark Kessenich proposed that the entire fixed-income group be sold separately. "It was," says Friedman, "par for the course."

(Kessenich says he made the proposal because he believed that 75 to 80 percent of the people in the fixed-income area would lose their jobs in a merger with Shearson—a prediction that turned out to be true.)

MONDAY, NOVEMBER 9

21 ½

Bob Rittereiser had spent the first week of November preparing for Hutton's critical November 9 and 10 board meetings, at which he intended to present his new business plan. He would outline the cost savings he had identified, his earnings projections, and his recommendations about the types of alliances Hutton might want to forge. These alliances, of course, included an infusion of capital by a friendly minority investor—Blackstone or Bell Atlantic perhaps.

On November 9, the compensation committee of Hutton's board—Peter Ueberroth, Ed Cazier, and Warren Law—met with Rittereiser at the firm's headquarters. Rittereiser's contract with the board was still unsigned, and, as he understood it, the board would not adopt the agreement until work was completed on Hutton's new compensation system—a system that governed bonuses for all Hutton executives, including Rittereiser.

So Rittereiser outlined his proposal to formalize the system. None of the three men asked any questions, and, an hour and a half later, the group adjourned to join Rittereiser and other members of the board, including Ueberroth, for a dinner meeting at a restaurant named—appropriately enough—the Boardroom Club, at 280 Park Avenue.

Rittereiser had begun to describe his plans for Hutton's future when he was interrupted. "Well, Bob," Ed Cazier began, "as you know, Sandy Weill is interested in buying this whole company."

Rittereiser looked startled. "Excuse me," he interjected, "but I don't know what you're talking about."

"Ed was supposed to call you," Ueberroth said. "Didn't Ed call you?" He didn't, but now Cazier went on to explain the deal with Weill, which involved swapping Hutton stock for Commercial Credit stock. Rittereiser was flabbergasted.

"Look," he said finally. "We're dealing with a very delicate situation here. I told you on the phone a week or two ago, *I* was going to explore these things. If *you* are going to explore them, fine. But do you know what you are doing? Do you know what the hell you are talking about?"

Rittereiser did not stop there. "Do you think for one minute," he asked, his voice rising, "that Peter Cohen is going to stand still and let Sandy Weill get back in the business by buying E.F. Hutton, a company he had wanted to buy?

"There's another problem," Rittereiser continued. "When a brokerage firm or a financial institution comes apart, it comes apart because people lose confidence in its underpinnings. You have a bunch of board members running around with a former board member trying to sell this thing. Let me tell you, if this firm unravels, it could be because of the way you people are behaving."

TUESDAY, NOVEMBER 10

20 ½

Early on the morning of November 10, Peter Ueberroth met with Bob Rittereiser in Rittereiser's office. The board, Ueberroth said, wanted Rittereiser to set up a meeting with Sandy Weill, and he should do so before the board convened at 9:30 A.M. "That way," Rittereiser says bitterly, "the board could see that I was carrying out their instructions." Despite his feelings, Rittereiser did as he was told.

Hutton's board convened as scheduled at 9:30 A.M. Gathered around the big conference table at company headquarters were Rittereiser, Ed Cazier, William G. Milliken (who had joined the board the previous year), Ueberroth, Warren Law, Tom Talbott, and Dina Merrill. Only Sadoa Yasuda was absent. Ueberroth acted as chairman.

Ed Lill, Steve Friedman, and Friedman's assistant, Joanne

Marren, sat in on the meeting, as they often did. The board, however, soon went into executive session—excluding everyone except board members and Friedman, the general counsel. The
reason for Friedman's presence soon became clear. He was peppered with questions about the board's legal rights and responsibilities in merger negotiations.

The board then invited the other executives to rejoin the meeting and authorized Rittereiser to conduct exploratory discussions
with Weill. Now Rittereiser was certain that someone was trying
to engineer the sale of Hutton to Weill. He was also quite sure
that the situation at Hutton was out of his control. Clearly he
was far from calling the shots. It was Bob Fomon who was in
charge.

Rittereiser was fed up. "I was disgusted to even be involved
with people like that," he says. In a conversation with Ken Wilson
that day, Rittereiser asked, "What do we do?"

"You're history," Wilson told him. "The best thing you can do
is get your contract worked out. You're going to get screwed."

That evening, Rittereiser met with Sandy Weill at Weill's apartment on Manhattan's Upper East Side. The session lasted a little
more than an hour. The two men agreed to get together again
later in the week.

WEDNESDAY, NOVEMBER 11

19 7/8

With Hutton now on the block, the board began to meet almost
daily. At noon on November 11, the executive committee of the
board convened with the familiar cast of characters—Bob Rittereiser, Ed Cazier, Bill Milliken, Peter Ueberroth, Warren Law, and
Dina Merrill. Ed Lill, Steve Friedman, and Joanne Marren sat in.
Bob Rittereiser acted as chairman.

There was more bad news to report. For one, because of the
late Stephen Fusco's unsavory activities in Rhode Island, Hutton

faced a potential indictment by the Justice Department on money-laundering charges. Worse, the ratings agencies had taken a dim view of Wall Street's fortunes since the crash. Standard & Poor's had met with Lill early that day, and now, despite previous assurances to the contrary, it wanted to review a possible downgrading of Hutton's rating. "That's when I knew it was over," Rittereiser says.

In the past year, with the debt the firm had piled up for the new headquarters building—more than $50 million so far—with the $130 million reserve it had set aside in 1986, and with the losses it was racking up in Kessenich's fixed-income trading department, Hutton had become especially dependent on commercial paper for its operating capital.

The danger of a lower rating on its commercial paper was this: Commercial paper works like a bank note that comes due every thirty days. A lower rating might prompt holders of Hutton's paper to bail out. That is, at the end of thirty days, the holders might say they wanted their money back. Hutton didn't have the cash to cover its $1 billion in outstanding commercial paper. "It was clear," Ken Wilson says, "that Hutton was on the fringe."

FRIDAY, NOVEMBER 13

20

Again, Rittereiser met Weill at the latter's apartment. Again, the session was brief—this time less than an hour. Weill told Rittereiser that he had planned to go away for the weekend but had canceled his trip. Could Rittereiser and members of his management team meet at Weill's house in the country on Saturday? Rittereiser said that they could.

SATURDAY, NOVEMBER 14

Market Closed

At about ten on Saturday morning, Rittereiser, Ed Lill, and Ken Wilson met with Sandy Weill at Weill's home in Greenwich, Connecticut. Rittereiser described Hutton's financial condition in detail. He also outlined his plans for the firm. At one point in the conversation, Rittereiser turned to Weill and said, "Do you think this merger can happen? Why won't Peter Cohen come in with a bigger bid?"

Weill didn't respond.

Late that afternoon the meeting wrapped up, and Weill invited Rittereiser and his wife to join him and his wife for dinner. Rittereiser picked up his wife, Pat, at their home in Franklin Lakes, New Jersey, then drove back to Greenwich to join Weill and his wife. "I had a very pleasant dinner with Sandy," Rittereiser says, "but, in the end, it didn't change anything. Whatever Weill offered for the firm had to be judged on its merits."

MONDAY, NOVEMBER 16

20 ¾

Once again, Bob Rittereiser, Steve Schwartzman, and Peter Peterson met for breakfast, this time at the Links Club. Rittereiser had a bombshell to drop.

Weill, Rittereiser said, had not been entirely straight with Blackstone. Soon after Blackstone had approached him about joining Hutton's board, Weill had begun discussing with Bob Fomon and members of the board the possible acquisition of E.F. Hutton.

Schwartzman and Peterson were not entirely surprised. That was, after all, the way Wall Street worked sometimes. The question now was, what to do next?

Weill had outlined to Rittereiser a proposal for a stock exchange worth about $18 a share, and Rittereiser had passed the proposal along to Schwartzman. "This deal with Weill doesn't make sense," Schwartzman said bluntly, referring to the fact that in such an arrangement the stockholders gain nothing. "Why are you doing this?"

Rittereiser was annoyed. "*I* am not doing this," he retorted. Rittereiser wasn't convinced the deal with Weill made sense either, but the situation was out of his control. Bob Fomon, he figured, would have more to say about it than he would.

Hutton was clearly in play. The entire firm would be sold to someone, Rittereiser knew, so the issue of a minority investment by Blackstone was dead, at least in his mind. Therefore, on the spot, Rittereiser hired Blackstone to serve as Hutton's investment banker. "The board's instructions to me," Rittereiser says, "were to *not* bring in any outside advisers. That's what I was told by Mr. Ueberroth speaking for the board."

How, Rittereiser had asked Ueberroth, can Hutton negotiate a merger without outside advisers? "Well," Ueberroth had replied, "we don't think we need them. We don't think we want them in at this point."

Rittereiser decided to ignore Ueberroth's orders. Some members of Hutton's board might be determined to sell the firm to Weill, but Rittereiser wasn't about to go along with any deal unless it was endorsed by outside advisers who were competent to evaluate the proposition.

The previous Sunday he had engaged Salomon Brothers, Wilson's old firm, to advise Hutton. He had called John Gutfreund, the Salomon Brothers CEO, at home, told him the situation, and asked if Salomon Brothers would serve as adviser to Hutton. He also let Gutfreund know that he planned to talk to The Blackstone Group.

"At this point," Rittereiser says, "I knew that if I followed their [the board's] instructions, I would look like a jackass. The stupid CEO would be out there all by himself. This group would do their usual fade into the woodwork, and I would look like the biggest jerk on two feet. Usually, in these cases," he adds, "it's the board that worries about management [not] behaving properly. I had to worry about a board that wasn't behaving properly."

Hutton's board convened at 6:30 P.M. Rittereiser and Peter Ueberroth remained at the company's headquarters, while Ed Cazier, Warren Law, Bill Milliken, Tom Talbott, and Sadoa Yasuda were connected to their fellow board members by telephone. Also attending the meeting were Steve Friedman, Ken Wilson, Joanne Marren, and James C. Freund, an attorney from the Wall Street law firm of Skadden, Arps, Slate, Meagher & Flom, which specializes in mergers. Friedman had retained Freund a few days earlier.

Rittereiser led off the session by reporting on his weekend meeting with Sandy Weill. Weill, he said, wanted to reach an agreement as soon as possible, but Rittereiser had refused to begin formal discussions until he met with the board.

Now Rittereiser strongly recommended that the board "seriously consider" selling Hutton in light of the "post-October nineteenth environment and certain potential problems with the ratings agencies"—but not necessarily to Weill. Rittereiser reported that he knew of other companies interested in Hutton, and he had retained Salomon Brothers and The Blackstone Group to assist in these talks.

"That's when the board got mad at me," Rittereiser says, "really mad at me, because I had cut them off at the pass. They knew damn well that they would never get the deal with Sandy Weill done with outside advisers involved. No outside adviser was going to tell them that the Weill deal made sense."

The reason was simple enough. Weill—in his informal discussions with Fomon and members of Hutton's board—had proposed a swap of Commercial Credit stock for Hutton stock. Bob Fomon liked the deal because the Hutton name and organization would remain intact—and he would pocket that hefty finder's fee. Rittereiser's comeuppance for not obeying orders would come two days later, when the board, in effect, appointed Ueberroth to head up the merger team.

After Rittereiser finished, Cazier asked Lill to provide more information about conversations between Hutton and the ratings agencies. Lill reported that Hutton's commercial paper could be downgraded. That action, he reiterated, would adversely affect Hutton's credit and liquidity. In other words, he told the board again, Hutton would be dead.

If any board members didn't yet know how serious the situation was, they could have no doubts after Friedman took the floor to warn them of their potential liability. It was critical, he said, that the board be fully aware of all the facts and circumstances of any proposed offers and have the benefit of legal and investment banking advice, which they did. He also emphasized that confidentiality was crucial.

At 7:30 P.M., the board meeting adjourned.

WEDNESDAY, NOVEMBER 18

20

Hutton's board reconvened the next day at 5:00 P.M. Rittereiser and Ueberroth were joined by Dina Merrill at company headquarters, while Cazier, Law, Milliken, Talbott, and Yasuda were again connected by telephone. Wilson, Friedman, Lill, Freund, and Marren once more sat in.

Ueberroth, who was serving as chairman, immediately turned the floor over to Rittereiser, who summarized the activities of the past two days. He had met with Salomon Brothers and The Blackstone Group, he reported, and had authorized Salomon Brothers to perform due diligence on Commercial Credit.

Rittereiser also said he was exploring Hutton's alternatives— within and outside the financial services industry. A company he refused to name—Bell Atlantic—was considering making a partial investment in Hutton, he reported. That news cheered Lill. Since Hutton was planning to seek a merger partner or additional capital,

Lill said, he didn't think the ratings agencies would move immediately to downgrade the firm.

Again, Friedman reviewed the directors' legal obligations. Directors owed shareholders, he said, "a duty of care and a duty of loyalty." If the board met both these duties, the directors were protected under what is known as the business judgment rule. Freund cautioned that no board member, or anyone else with nonpublic information, could now buy or sell Hutton stock.

Ueberroth then asked that everyone except members of the board and Friedman leave the room. When they did, the directors designated Ueberroth as "an independent director to work with management as a committee of one" of the board to explore all alternatives. The board also designated Tom Talbott to work with Rittereiser to explore a possible merger with Transamerica. (Ueberroth couldn't meet with Transamerica, because he was a member of both boards.)

"This was my punishment," Rittereiser says, "for bringing in outside advisers. What they were saying to me was, 'Goddamn it, if you're not going to follow instructions, we'll have our own committee.'"

Later Ueberroth would concede that bringing in outside advisers was "the smartest thing we ever did." Rittereiser would respond, "Peter, the whole time, I was only trying to protect you from yourself."

Now Rittereiser spent little time brooding about the slap in the face. "I knew," he says, "that I had already forced them down the right path by bringing in the advisers."

The meeting adjourned at 6:25 P.M.

THURSDAY, NOVEMBER 19

18 ⁵⁄₈

Thursday dawned cold and damp. Pete Peterson of Blackstone and John Gutfreund of Salomon Brothers met with Peter Ueberroth, who was now functioning—without the title—as Hutton chairman.

"Rittereiser thought it would be a good idea if we would see Ueberroth," says Steve Schwartzman, "to find out what the options were for Hutton." Rittereiser dispatched Peterson and Gutfreund to see Ueberroth, because it was clear to him that Ueberroth was firmly in charge.

One possibility Ueberroth raised was to bring in a large minority partner, but Peterson and Gutfreund put the kibosh on that idea. "Putting in capital wasn't going to be good enough," Schwartzman says. "You really needed an alliance with a large financial company." The markets, he points out, were fast losing confidence in Hutton. A merger with an outside institution "would show that there was something to rely on—not just a little bit of money but a large institution that could support Hutton if it got into trouble."

The bankers had put together a list of potential merger partners—both American and foreign, including some Japanese companies. Contacting the Japanese was Blackstone's idea. "Those guys at Blackstone," says one investment banker, "have Japs on the brain."

Ueberroth still thought Transamerica might come in as an ally. After all, Hutton had previous contacts with the giant conglomerate.

That afternoon, Lill informed Standard & Poor's that the brokerage was actively considering either a merger with another corporation or a partial sale. The ratings company agreed to postpone its next meeting with Hutton's management until the following Monday or Tuesday.

At 4:00 P.M., Hutton's board convened again. As soon as the meeting was called to order, Ueberroth asked Rittereiser to report on the day's events. Rittereiser said that he and Ueberroth had met earlier in the day with Blackstone to discuss Hutton's alternatives.

He also summed up the conversation with Standard & Poor's.

As far as Moody's, the other big ratings agency, went, he said, a December 17 meeting had been in the works for some time. Rittereiser concluded by reporting on contacts that he had made with companies outside the financial services industry.

When he finished, Ken Wilson and Jim Freund discussed Hutton's possible responses to approaches from other securities firms. Wilson was worried. If these preliminary contacts weren't kept totally confidential, he warned, Hutton could find itself in worse trouble than it already was, with other Wall Street firms recruiting its top producers.

The directors wrapped up their gloomy discussion at 5:10 P.M.

An hour or so later at Shearson headquarters in lower Manhattan, Jack Nusbaum of Willkie Farr bumped into Peter Cohen. "I hope you don't have too many Thanksgiving plans," Cohen said to Nusbaum. Why? Nusbaum asked. "I've heard that Hutton is going to put itself up for sale," he replied, "and I'm going to buy it."

FRIDAY, NOVEMBER 20

20 ¼

At 2:30 P.M. board members Bob Rittereiser, Peter Ueberroth, and Ed Cazier gathered around the conference table with Jim Freund, Steve Friedman, Joanne Marren, and Ken Wilson. Warren Law was connected by telephone, and Bill Milliken joined the meeting late. Tom Talbott, Sadoa Yasuda, and Dina Merrill were absent.

Again, Rittereiser—at Ueberroth's request—summarized the day's events. Ueberroth had met with Sandy Weill that morning, Rittereiser told board members, and Weill was interested in opening formal merger discussions. Rittereiser, meanwhile, had held a meeting with representatives of Transamerica.

Ueberroth then laid out the game plan for the next few days. Step one was for the firm's investment bankers—Salomon Brothers and Blackstone—formally to contact two companies outside the brokerage industry, Bell Atlantic and Chrysler, that had previously expressed an interest in Hutton. The bankers would let Hutton know by Monday whether the two were interested in a possible merger. Next, Rittereiser and Wilson would draw up a list of inquiries Hutton had received over the past month from firms in the securities industry.

Factors beyond Hutton's control, particularly the actions of the ratings agencies, Rittereiser added, would inevitably affect the process of selling the firm. And, he reiterated, problems with credit and liquidity made it uncertain whether Hutton could remain independent for the long term without shutting down some of its operations.

It would be a good idea, Ueberroth thought, for the full board to meet in New York on Tuesday. By that time, he said, Ed Lill should be ready to present a more detailed report on the effect of a downgrading.

The meeting adjourned at 3:15 P.M.

Meanwhile, Blackstone was also busy contacting potential suitors. The response so far was not favorable. The reactions, according to Schwartzman, were "Troubled company, troubled industry, financial systems in disarray. Don't think I want to enter this as an investment right now."

The problem, Schwartzman points out, wasn't peculiar to Hutton. In the highly charged after-crash environment, selling a major brokerage house was no simple matter. "This was an industry problem," he says. "Other brokerage stocks had collapsed. You have to look at this in some sort of context." Still, Schwartzman remained optimistic that the bankers would find a buyer for Hutton.

In fact, he figured even then that Shearson would ultimately buy Hutton. "Shearson had done this kind of deal before," he says. That is, Shearson had purchased other brokerages, retained the brokers—the people who bring in revenues—and laid off everyone else. To handle the paperwork generated by the extra brokers,

Shearson simply beefed up its own massive back-office operations. Shearson, it seems, also saw Hutton as a good deal. "The Shearson guys like bargains," Schwartzman says, "and it was clear that this was one."

Blackstone and Salomon Brothers weren't the only ones beating the bushes for a Hutton buyer. Ken Wilson was doing what he could to get Dean Witter to do more than talk about a deal. So, it turned out, was Peter Ueberroth talking to Dean Witter, and he was doing so without the aid of his investment bankers. "Peter Ueberroth," says one former Hutton executive, "thinks of himself as a man of high moral character, impeccable judgment, and extraordinary negotiating skills. So what does he need scumbag investment bankers for?"

When Lee Kimmell heard that Ueberroth had met with Dean Witter alone, he hit the roof. "You are out of your damned mind," Kimmell told Ueberroth, after he pulled the baseball commissioner into an office at Hutton. "If you don't trust me, say so. You can find someone else at Salomon Brothers, or you can replace Salomon Brothers, but I will not work in a vacuum."

Ueberroth's reaction was that of a man who is seldom confronted. He turned beet-red, but Kimmell's face was even redder. "Okay," Ueberroth said finally. "I don't like it, but I don't have a choice."

"You got that last part right," Kimmell shot back.

SUNDAY, NOVEMBER 22

Market Closed

It was on Sunday that a formal strategy to sell Hutton finally began to evolve. Hutton's investment bankers agreed to meet at 10:30 A.M. at the firm's headquarters. Ueberroth, who had been scheduled to go away for the weekend, didn't join the meeting until sometime after 2:00 P.M.

The bankers agreed that Hutton's best hope was to merge with another financial services company. "Hutton," says Lee Kimmell, "was always worth the most to the people already in the industry, because you could buy what was good and close what was bad." But, the bankers decided, they would keep communication open with companies outside the industry as well—just in case.

When Ueberroth joined the meeting, the bankers had to repeat their earlier presentations. While they did so, Ueberroth and Cazier whispered back and forth.

Around 4:00 P.M., Ueberroth and Cazier informed the bankers that they wanted to give Sandy Weill another shot, a chance to make a preemptive bid—even though the bankers argued against it. Ueberroth, however, prevailed, and a phone call was placed to Weill. A few hours later, he appeared with his management team in tow. If the conversations went well, Commercial Credit was prepared to begin due diligence immediately.

Weill, Ueberroth, and Cazier secluded themselves in a conference room, and Ueberroth asked Weill what his final price for the company was. "Okay," Weill said, "you guys tell me that I've got the company, and I'll tell you what my price is."

Ueberroth, of course, could make no such promise, so Weill was out of the bidding. Why was the board, represented by Ueberroth, so determined to sell Hutton to Weill? Rittereiser didn't know for sure. "But," he says, "I've heard all kinds of stories about how Peter Ueberroth would have been chairman and Cazier would have been on the board. The Hutton name would have been preserved, which would have made Dina Merrill happy, and Fomon would have been paid a fee."

MONDAY, NOVEMBER 23

27 3/8

It was the Monday before Thanksgiving. Rittereiser wanted the sale of E.F. Hutton to be controlled, but, by now, he knew it would be anything but.

He, however, planned to do what the investment bankers told him to do. His assignment was to notify his counterparts in the financial services industry that Hutton was to be sold. Early that morning he dialed Peter Cohen at Shearson.

"Peter," Rittereiser said, his voice sounding weary, "we are auctioning off Hutton. Are you interested in participating?" It came as no surprise when Cohen said he was.

Next Rittereiser phoned executives at Merrill Lynch, Prudential-Bache, Drexel Burnham, the Equitable, and Dean Witter.

Rittereiser's former colleagues at Merrill Lynch agreed to take a look. After all, Merrill had the most to lose—their standing as the largest financial services firm on Wall Street—by some other firm acquiring Hutton. Still, "the sense of urgency," said one investment banker later, "was what you would expect from Merrill, meaning there was no sense of urgency at all. Merrill Lynch is always limp."

At Drexel Burnham, Fred Joseph had started to get cold feet. He said that he couldn't risk an acquisition until his firm's problems with the SEC were cleared up. "Look," Joseph said to Rittereiser, "if you get into serious trouble, though, we are here to help. We have a lot of cash." But Joseph didn't say what, precisely, he was prepared to do.

That morning, Hutton issued a press release saying that it had retained Salomon Brothers and The Blackstone Group to represent it. The release let the public know, once and for all, that Hutton was officially shopping for a suitor. Meanwhile, the firm's bankers—with an increasing sense of urgency—were contacting Xerox, Ford, and General Motors.

WEDNESDAY, NOVEMBER 25

28

The auction was on. Hutton's financial advisers sent a letter to companies that had previously expressed an interest in a merger with Hutton. They should submit their bids no later than Tuesday, December 1, the letter said.

At Shearson, executives speculated on the reason for the tight timetable. "The more time anyone has to dig and do due diligence," they theorized, "the lower the price was likely to be."

In reality, Hutton's investment bankers feared the loss of the firm's most valuable asset. "If you can't move quickly," says Lee Kimmell of Salomon Brothers, "and if you can't keep the sales force intact, what the hell are you going to sell? Dina Merrill?"

THURSDAY, NOVEMBER 26

Market Closed

As part of their firm's due diligence process, Shearson executives pored over Hutton's books right through the Thanksgiving weekend.

FRIDAY, NOVEMBER 27

28 5/8

For the bankers at Salomon Brothers, the next few days were dominated by hand-holding. "There were a number of Hutton executives who were wondering what was going on," one Salomon Brothers banker remembers. "We had to calm them down."

Market Closed

Peter Cohen knew that if he wanted to acquire Hutton at a bargain price—which he did—he would have to ward off other potential suitors.

So he moved to head off the Hutton auction. At 6:00 P.M. on November 29 Cohen dialed Lee Kimmell at Salomon Brothers. Kimmell—like Cohen—is a canny deal maker. Negotiating for a company, he likes to tell people, "is no different than negotiating with a hooker on a street corner."

"Lee," Cohen began, confident as always, "I think Hutton is really making a mistake going forward with this auction process."

Cohen suspected that it was Ueberroth who had pushed Hutton into the auction. "It was consistent with his experience as baseball commissioner," Cohen had told his associates. "But there's a big difference between auctioning off television time and a business like Hutton."

"The stockholders in the company," Cohen argued, "would be better served by sitting down and having a negotiation with us now."

Kimmell asked why Cohen felt that way, even though he knew the answer. Kimmell himself, aware that auctions seldom produced top dollar, had tried to talk the Hutton board out of its plans.

"Look," Cohen replied, "due diligence shows us that Hutton has problems." Kimmell didn't ask Cohen what those problems were, and Cohen didn't volunteer any information.

"We might be the only ones to show up on Tuesday. And," Cohen continued, "even if someone shows up on the deadline for bids, they're not going to know enough to give you a firm proposal. You'll be into a dragged-out due diligence process, during which the firm will suffer substantial deterioration."

"We've done our homework," Cohen concluded. "We know what we're willing to do. I bet if we sit down, we could get something done fairly quickly."

"It makes sense to me," Kimmell told Cohen, "but I've got to check with Ueberroth." A half hour later, Ueberroth called Cohen.

"We're going to give Shearson a chance to be preemptive," he said, then suggested that they meet as soon as possible that evening. Cohen begged off. It was his wedding anniversary, and he had promised to take his wife and children to dinner.

Already, though, Cohen knew he had the upper hand in the negotiations. The tip-off was that Ueberroth was willing to discuss a preemptive bid at all.

MONDAY, NOVEMBER 30

27 ½

At 7:30 the next morning, executives from Hutton and Shearson gathered at the plush offices of Willkie Farr & Gallagher at One Citicorp Center. The Hutton executives would hear Shearson out but would make no promises in advance.

On one side of the table sat Peter Ueberroth, Bob Rittereiser, Ken Wilson, and Jim Freund, the attorney from Skadden Arps. On the other side sat Peter Cohen; Jeffrey B. Lane, president and chief operating officer of Shearson; and Jack Nusbaum of Willkie Farr.

Lee Kimmell came to the meeting late.

Ueberroth was a man Nusbaum—or at least his law firm—knew well. Willkie Farr represented major league baseball. "So," says Nusbaum, "we knew a little about his negotiating style. His tactics," he adds, "were not a surprise."

For the next hour or so, Cohen and his men outlined their view of Hutton's financial condition, which they saw as dire. "It is very plausible," Cohen argued, that Hutton is worth nowhere near the

$840 million stated on its balance sheet. In fact, he said, "Hutton is really very close to a desperate financial condition."

Then Cohen outlined two possible scenarios—one an all-cash offer, the other cash plus securities. With both offers, Cohen started at $22, then moved to $25 a share.

The Hutton executives called for a brief recess. When the group reconvened, they told Cohen that they were disappointed in Shearson's proposals.

What Hutton was looking for, Kimmell intimated, was an offer with the "number three in front of it." He meant between $30 and $35 a share. "That's a terrific goal," Cohen replied, "and I wish you the best of luck in getting it from somebody other than us."

The Hutton executives, hoping that another bidder would top Cohen's offer, let Cohen know that they would proceed with the auction.

Kimmell, the investment banker, knew better than to hold out hope. Cohen, he was sure, was Hutton's last, best hope. "Peter Cohen," he says, "was always the only place to sell this firm. The issue was not who was going to buy it, but how were we going to make Peter Cohen believe that he had competition."

TUESDAY, DECEMBER 1

27 5/8

Hutton's increasingly anxious board convened promptly at 9:30 A.M. Board members Rittereiser, Ueberroth, Milliken, Yasuda, Talbott, Law, Cazier, and Merrill, joined by Jim Freund, Jerry Smith (a Salomon Brothers banker), Ken Wilson, Lee Kimmell, Pete Peterson, and Steve Schwartzman, sat around the by now all-too-familiar conference table.

Ueberroth took the floor to bring members up to date on events that had occurred since the board's last meeting. Dean Witter, Ueberroth reported, had requested that the board grant the firm the exclusive right to negotiate for the purchase of Hutton. It seemed that Ken Wilson's behind-the-scenes discussions were going to pay off.

If these negotiations proved successful, Ueberroth said, Dean Witter was prepared first to sign a letter of intent, then to hammer out a definitive agreement. He also cautioned that Dean Witter wanted the negotiations kept confidential.

The rival brokerage, he added, had already hinted at the possible structure of the deal. The firm would probably offer Hutton shareholders a combination of cash, based on Hutton's "hard" book value, and Sears common stock. (Hard book value excludes the value of "soft" assets, such as leasehold improvements to Hutton headquarters.) Dean Witter, however, had not specified how much cash it had in mind. Nor had it indicated the amount of Sears stock it would offer. Instead, Dean Witter executives had proposed that they and Hutton first negotiate which items they considered in excess of hard book value.

If, at the end of negotiations, they came up with a book value less than that shown on Hutton's books, Dean Witter would reduce the amount of Sears stock they would issue. But any gain in the share price of Sears stock that took place after the signing of an agreement would be passed on to shareholders.

Ueberroth also reported that Dean Witter would consider paying a premium above the negotiated amount if an agreed-upon number of Hutton's account executives—that is, its stockbrokers—stayed on with the merged corporation during the transition period.

The board then adjourned briefly.

When it reconvened, Peterson summarized the investment bankers' opinions of Dean Witter's proposal. Hutton's financial advisers all agreed, he said, that the proposal to negotiate book value was ambiguous and likely to result in a delay.

But, he cautioned, the Dean Witter deal could turn out better than ones other potential acquirers had suggested so far. What was more, he said, the Sears stock part of the offer was a sweetener, since it gave shareholders some chance for appreciation.

At noon, Kimmell and Peterson telephoned Peter Cohen. There's no need for Shearson to submit a written offer, they said. The board is willing to give Shearson another chance to preempt the auction.

"Well," Cohen responded, "you're too late. The letter is already on its way."

"Why don't you tell us what it says?" Kimmell asked, and Cohen did. "Well," Kimmell replied, "that isn't going to do it. But we would be willing to sit down and discuss a transaction with you exclusive of all the others."

"We would be willing," Cohen said, "to come up there and sit down with the board, but only under certain conditions. We will come down if you agree that we won't get up until we have an agreement or we agree not to do a deal. And you will not have any discussions with any other potential buyers during that period of time."

Fine, Kimmell and Peterson said.

At about 1:00 P.M., Cohen, Jeff Lane, and Jack Nusbaum arrived at Hutton's midtown headquarters. They sat down with Kimmell, Wilson, Ueberroth, Peterson, and Smith.

Shearson opened with its offer of $25 all cash, then upped it to $27 a share, and finally settled on a combination of cash and preferred stock valued at $29.25 a share. The session lasted until 8:00 P.M. In the end, the men shook hands on the Shearson offer.

That night, the lawyers and investment bankers argued over the final details of the deal—among them, the valuation of the preferred stock. In a few days, Shearson switched to a combination of cash plus subordinated debt. But the share price of $29.25 held firm.

This new offer was, says Ken Wilson, "remarkable, when you looked at the proxy statement and saw the book value was down to just $7.63 a share."

"Hutton's balance sheet," he adds, "was just terrible."

But one of the investment bankers involved in the deal says that Peter Cohen was prepared to pay $33 to $35 a share for Hutton. Ueberroth, he maintains, blew it. "It was clear to Peter Cohen," the banker explains, "that he was the only serious player."

WEDNESDAY, DECEMBER 2

27 3/8

At a 5:00 P.M. meeting in their twenty-eighth-floor boardroom, Hutton's directors and executives from Shearson listened attentively as Wilson outlined the Shearson final offer. Then Ueberroth called for a vote. "All those in favor of the merger," he said, "raise your hand."

Every hand in the room shot up—including, oddly enough, Pete Peterson's. Peterson had been writing letters in the back of the room during the discussion, and, when he heard a vote called, automatically responded, even though he wasn't entitled to vote.

After the vote, the party. Everyone—the Shearson people, the Hutton people, the investment bankers—moved to the twenty-ninth-floor executive dining room for drinks and dinner. Hoisting champagne glasses, Rittereiser, then Cohen, toasted the deal.

Cohen spoke glowingly of the newly acquired firm. "We have always admired E.F. Hutton," he said. "We have always looked at Hutton as a role model for us."

All those present looked relaxed and seemed to be enjoying themselves, all, that is, but Steve Friedman, who felt sick. After the first round of toasts he excused himself and walked alone in the rain to his Park Avenue apartment.

"I didn't feel as if we had anything to celebrate," he says now. "I felt a real sense of failure. It is relatively important to me to be in control of things, and we were just totally out of control as a management group. That was a very uncomfortable, unpleasant experience."

THURSDAY, DECEMBER 3

27 ⅞

The day after the Shearson deal, Ken Wilson and a group of bankers from his corporate finance department gathered in Wilson's office.

"Rittereiser," Wilson says, "got on the hoot-and-holler system and gave a speech that so infuriated the retail system that we turned it off." Using the office-paging system, Rittereiser was doing his best to persuade his corporate troops that the merger with Shearson was in their best interests too. "It's going to be a great deal," he insisted.

Hutton employees were aghast at Rittereiser's remarks. Before Wilson turned off the speaker, he heard someone reply to Rittereiser. "You better hope your parachute doesn't open. You goddamned son of a bitch, you sold us down the river." The Hutton investment bankers knew that they would lose their jobs as a result of a merger. Shearson was already an investment-banking powerhouse. What did it need with them?

"It was such bullshit," says Wilson, who advised the people with him that each of them should think about his own situation. "It is not the time to get mad, it is the time to get even," he told them. He promised to help get as many of them as he could jobs at Shearson, and for those that he couldn't, he said he'd do what he could around the Street.

At 4:10 P.M., Hutton's board convened. Cazier, Law, Friedman, Freund, and Marren were connected with Rittereiser by telephone. Rittereiser acted as chairman, Marren as secretary.

The first item of business, Rittereiser said, was getting into shape the Schedule 14D-9 that Hutton had to file on December 7.

(A Schedule 14D-9, required by the Securities and Exchange Commission, lays out the terms of a merger.)

The board then voted unanimously to adopt a resolution granting Rittereiser, Friedman, Lill, and Marren the authority to take any and all actions necessary to complete the deal with Shearson. So, it was done.

Then, in a move that would further infuriate Hutton employees, the board voted to dissolve Hutton's employee stock purchase plan, retroactive to December 1. Rittereiser also pointed out that since Shearson wanted to move quickly on personnel decisions, Hutton would itself have to move fast to formalize a severance policy for terminated employees.

Shearson had requested that the board formally adopt Shearson's severance policy, a request that the board again approved. According to this policy, terminated employees would be paid one week's salary for every year of employment up to five years, and two weeks' salary for every year after that. But severance pay would never top a year's salary.

The board meeting adjourned at 5:00 P.M.

Meanwhile, at Shearson headquarters, Peter Cohen and several of his key executives met with ten of Hutton's top producers. "There were ten of them and ten of us," says one of the brokers who attended the session. "We were treated somewhat akin to captured officers in World War II. And, believe me, there was no question who had taken over whom."

MONDAY, DECEMBER 7

27 7/8

Shearson, using its own form of triage, divided Hutton employees into three groups for evaluation. The first group was offered jobs with Shearson. The second was asked to stay on board anywhere from a few weeks to a few months. The third group would be unceremoniously terminated.

The fired employees were notified by line managers at Hutton or Shearson and then presented with personnel packets, which contained information on outplacement services, forms to sign, and procedures to follow—among them, when to vacate the premises. The length of notice depended on people's jobs and responsibilities. But every terminated employee remained on the payroll through December 31.

After the check scandal, Bob Fomon had worried endlessly about what his legacy at Hutton would be. After Shearson swallowed Hutton, Bob Rittereiser brooded about the same thing. "You could hear it in the comments he made after the merger," says one former senior executive. "He was very concerned about how he was going to come out." Rittereiser, the executive maintains, was every bit as concerned as Fomon was about his image. In conversations, Fomon blames Rittereiser, and Rittereiser blames Fomon, for Hutton's demise.

"He'll tell you that when he got there things were so bad, and he didn't realize how bad they were, and that nobody in the world could have saved that firm," the executive says. But the executive doesn't agree with Rittereiser's evaluation. Still, "there is no question," he says, "that Rittereiser was somewhat blind when he came on board. I don't think he recognized the difficulties he was facing coming in."

Fomon tells everybody he made a mistake bringing Rittereiser in because the former Merrill Lynch executive couldn't make a decision. "I don't think this is black and white," says Jerry Miller, "that Rittereiser did everything wrong and brought the firm to its knees, but he might have done things differently [to reverse the situation at Hutton]."

TUESDAY, DECEMBER 8

28

Sumitomo Life Insurance announced it would sell its 2 percent stake—or 694,200 shares—in E.F. Hutton to Shearson Lehman Brothers.

Sumitomo had paid 4 billion yen, or $30.1 million, for Hutton shares purchased from April through June. It would take a $9 million bath on its investment.

THURSDAY, DECEMBER 10

28 ⅛

Shearson summoned another group of Hutton's top producers to New York for a meeting. They were not prepared for the treatment they received.

"With Hutton, we always traveled first class," says one broker who attended the meeting, a man who generates some $2 million a year in commissions. "Hutton always gave us a little suite of rooms in the hotel. Hutton always had us picked up in a limo. With Shearson, there were no limos. Just jump in a cab and get yourself down there. The hotel room they gave me was not in the front, not in the back. It faced the alley. I knew the party was over.

"When I came in the room there was this enormous arrangement of fruit, a bottle of wine, and some cheese. I'm thinking, This is really nice. So I opened the card and it says, 'Did you really think this was from Shearson? Regards, Tony.'" (Tony was another top producer at Hutton.) "I laughed," the broker says.

The next day this same account executive paid a visit to Hutton headquarters. Already he had decided to jump ship to Prudential-Bache, but he wanted one last look. "As I walked out the door, they wanted to inspect my attaché case," he remembers. "I said, 'Get the hell out of my way. I have been with this firm sixteen years.' There was no dignity left at all."

Meanwhile, on December 10, Hardwick Simmons, vice chairman of Shearson and head of the firm's retail sales unit, met in Los Angeles with about eighty Hutton and Shearson branch and regional managers. He gave them the bad news—5,000 to 6,000 jobs would be eliminated from the combined firm. But Simmons had some good news too—at least as far as brokers were concerned. Most of the cuts, he said, would come in New York and involve back-office personnel who processed brokerage orders. Also, most of the cuts would occur through attrition. Simmons promised that no account executives would be let go (and so far none have).

Shearson brokers would receive a bonus of 5.0 percent of their total net commissions for the first six months of 1988 for staying with the combined firm. Hutton brokers would be offered a bonus equal to 22.5 percent of their 1988 net sales commissions.

FRIDAY, DECEMBER 11

28 ⅛

Hutton's board convened at 11:00 A.M.

Rittereiser was joined by Friedman, Freund, and Marren gathered at E.F. Hutton, while Cazier, Law, Talbott, Ueberroth, and Merrill were connected by telephone.

Rittereiser announced that Shearson wanted to decide—sooner rather than later—who would stay, who would go, and who would help in the transition. The firm also wanted to notify the people involved as soon as possible.

Shearson had another condition too. It was looking for a way to trim the cost of the acquisition. So it wanted to reduce the size of Hutton's discretionary bonus pool and have Hutton seek its approval before bonuses were paid to Hutton employees.

Freund advised the board that responding to Shearson's request was an "appropriate exercise of the board's business judgment." Then Merrill, concerned about Hutton workers, asked Rittereiser to review the severance arrangements for terminated employees.

"Dina," says an investment banker who attended the meeting,

"was the only one who even *asked* about the employees. She was the only one who seemed to give a shit."

Rittereiser repeated the Shearson severance policy, then the board voted to do as Shearson had asked. Next on the agenda: Rittereiser's compensation.

His compensation package had been up in the air for months, and, Ueberroth said with unintentional irony, it was now time for the board to resolve the matter.

Rittereiser's compensation for 1987—salary, bonus, and so on—said Ueberroth, would add up to $1.2 million. In addition, under a draft agreement, Rittereiser would receive an additional payment of $1.2 million if he didn't stay on with Shearson. Finally, Rittereiser would receive a life insurance policy purchased for him by the corporation and a car the company had leased for him— again, if he lost his job. The board voted unanimously in favor of the draft agreement—pending its approval by Shearson—and the meeting adjourned at 11:45 A.M.

A few hours later, Shearson executives held a staff meeting attended by managers from more than forty Hutton divisions. Represented were several thousand employees in the institutional trading, sales, administration, and research departments.

As they had at other, happier, staff meetings, employees gathered in the auditorium on the second floor of Hutton's headquarters. Shearson executives announced that the combined firm would start laying off employees on December 15. Terminated employees would be expected to leave at once. They also announced that the firm would not commit itself to paying bonuses that year. Until that time, Hutton employees had counted on receiving their bonuses, which accounted for a substantial part of their annual incomes.

"The board," says an investment banker involved in the deal, "made a decision. They would rather have had the higher price share for the shareholders than the lower price and accommodate executives who had in effect run the business into the ground. Were they at fault? Who knows, but the fact is, the business was failing."

MONDAY, DECEMBER 14

28 ⅛

Shearson gathered more than 200 employees of Hutton's taxable fixed-income sales and trading desks and informed them that they were history. Vacate the premises by Friday, most were told. The fired employees made up about 80 percent of the professional staff in all Hutton's taxable fixed-income areas.

The 200 people were simply the first of many. In the end, more than 5,000 people would lose their jobs.

Many Hutton account executives decided to jump ship. Some telephoned George Ball, chairman of Prudential-Bache and former president of E.F. Hutton, seeking positions with his firm. Others were offered by other companies a signing bonus of 20 percent of 1988's gross commissions.

TUESDAY, DECEMBER 15

28 ⅛

The atmosphere grew increasingly tense as Shearson placed additional security guards at Hutton's offices in New York. Shearson wanted to make sure workers didn't spirit away Hutton files or information. Some employees were even asked to open Christmas presents for inspection. "It's like living in occupied France," complained one trader, whose job had been eliminated, to a reporter for *Securities Week.*

Meanwhile, the terminations continued. Hutton employees who were working under contract complained that Shearson was questioning the validity of their contracts or trying to squeeze them out. Traders and salespeople claimed that Shearson was offering them jobs that differed from their current positions.

THURSDAY, DECEMBER 17

28 ³/₈

A memo, originating from Hutton's midtown Manhattan head-quarters, circulated over the firm's in-house wire. Entitled "Radio Free Hutton," it encouraged Hutton employees to read the first three pages of the firm's Schedule 14D-19 filed with the SEC to see how Hutton CEO Rittereiser "and his band of rogues feathered their nests while putting Hutton under water."

It then listed various executives, their years of service—in some cases, zero—and the amount of compensation Hutton had awarded to them. Outraged employees read in the Schedule 14D that Bob Rittereiser was to receive cash compensation of $1.2 million (two years); Ken Wilson, $2.4 million (less than a year); Mark Kessenich, $1.4 million (one year); Jerry Miller, $975,000 (fourteen years); and Jerry Welsh, $643,000 (less than a year).

In Boston an account executive pulled out a copy of the July 1986 issue of *Manhattan, Inc.* and turned to the glowing article about Bob Rittereiser. Accompanying the piece was a picture of Rittereiser peeking over the back of an office chair. The broker clipped the picture from the magazine, then tacked it to an office wall with this caption: "Why is this man afraid to show his face? Because he sold out the company for his and his cronies' benefit."

Meanwhile, Dina Merrill and Ed Cazier paid a visit to Peter Cohen. Ueberroth, they argued, had played a pivotal role in the negotiations—a role that far exceeded his responsibilities as a board member. He deserved a fee for his services, and they suggested $500,000.

Cohen thought about it briefly. "Fine," he said. "You've got to remember," says an investment banker involved in the deal, "$500,000 is not a lot of money to Peter Cohen."

28 ⅝

Shearson sweetened the terms of its acquisition of E.F. Hutton to settle several lawsuits filed in the Delaware Court of Chancery. Under the new terms, Shearson would purchase 29.6 million shares of Hutton common stock, up from 28.1 million shares, at $29.25 a share.

1988

28 ³/₄

On behalf of a group of Hutton employees, Christopher J. Harris, a Hutton executive who was dismissed by Shearson on December 18, 1987, filed suit against the firm and Shearson Lehman Brothers Holdings Inc. The suit charged that the employees' "golden handcuffs" had disintegrated when the firms merged. One hundred employees, the group alleged, were cheated out of about $30 million of stock due them in the event Hutton underwent a "change of control."

The document—filed in U.S. District Court in Manhattan—also charged that Hutton and Shearson had conspired to manipulate the definition of change of control, and that they had denied payment of the shares to the employees by claiming that a change of control had not occurred. Further, the suit said, Shearson and Hutton had agreed to pay certain people their equity shares, including some senior officers. Harris's suit was just one of many that have been filed against Shearson, Hutton, and executives of the two firms by former employees, shareholders, and other executives.

FRIDAY, JANUARY 29

29 ⅝

Shearson Lehman Brothers Inc. officially changed its name to Shearson Lehman Hutton Inc.—effective January 29. It was the first time since 1904, when Edward F. Hutton had founded the firm, that the Hutton name hadn't stood alone.

Shearson didn't keep the name for sentimental reasons. Market research told Shearson executives that "Hutton" still had some goodwill value, so they decided not to chuck it.

SUNDAY, JANUARY 31

Market Closed

Steve Friedman, general counsel, was removed from Hutton's payroll effective January 31. Under the terms of his employment agreement, Friedman walked away with $1.5 million.

TUESDAY, FEBRUARY 2

29 ½

Shearson and Hutton won a temporary restraining order in New York Supreme Court barring Dean Witter Reynolds from recruiting Hutton brokers. Dean Witter had already hired away eighty-two Hutton brokers, including some of the firm's superstars. For example, Anthony Malatino, who had racked up some $3.9 million in gross commissions in 1987, joined Dean Witter's office in Albany, New York.

Dean Witter also grabbed Hutton's entire Wichita Falls, Texas, office; half of Hutton's brokers in Rochester, Minnesota; and thirteen of its twenty-nine brokers in Phoenix, Arizona. But Dean Witter wasn't the only firm to raid Hutton. Drexel

302

Burnham, PaineWebber, Prudential-Bache, and Donaldson, Lufkin & Jenrette also made Hutton brokers offers they couldn't refuse.

SATURDAY, MARCH 4

30 ¼

Mark Kessenich—the man whose hundreds of millions of dollars in trading losses had helped bring Hutton to its knees—went off Hutton's payroll effective March 4. Under his 1986 compensation agreement, he received a cash payment of $2,319,999—that is, the difference between the $2,380,001 he'd received to date from the company and the $4.7 million due him under his three-year employment contract.

FRIDAY, APRIL 29

30 ⅛

At 10:00 A.M. Hutton shareholders gathered at 33 Maiden Lane in New York and voted to approve the firm's merger with Shearson Lehman Brothers. Also on this date, Hutton filed documents with the SEC, disclosing—for the first time publicly—golden parachutes for Steve Friedman, Ed Lill, Mark Kessenich, Ken Wilson, and Jerry Welsh.

MONDAY, MAY 17

Shearson pleaded guilty on Hutton's behalf to three criminal counts of money laundering and conspiracy at Hutton's branch office in Providence, Rhode Island. Shearson was fined $1.01 million for the offenses, which had occurred between 1982 and 1984. The SEC, however, granted Shearson a temporary exemption from securities laws that would have barred it from acting as an investment adviser in Providence as a result of the guilty plea.

. . .

PERRY L. BACON, author of the smoking-gun memo, was named president of B. C. Christopher & Co. Inc., a subsidiary of the Central Life Assurance Co., in January 1988. A retail brokerage with operations in ten states in the Midwest, B. C. Christopher is based in Kansas City, Missouri. Before being tapped as president, Bacon served as a consultant to the parent company, Central Life, a midsized mutual life insurance company in Des Moines, Iowa. Separated from his wife, Susan, Bacon is now forty-two years old.

GEORGE BALL, who helped Bob Fomon build Hutton into a retail brokerage powerhouse, remains chairman and chief executive officer of Prudential-Bache Securities Inc., the firm he joined in 1982. Prudential-Bache is a subsidiary of the Prudential Insurance Company of America, and word has it that Ball has his eye on the top spot. He keeps a Manhattan apartment and a home in Short Hills, New Jersey. Now fifty years old, Ball remarried in September 1988.

PETER COHEN remains at the helm of the combined firm, Shearson Lehman Hutton. He lost out to Kohlberg, Kravis, Roberts & Co. in the bloody, $25 billion brawl for RJR Nabisco. He has not given up his cigars.

NORMAN M. EPSTEIN, Hutton's longtime head of operations, was recruited by Shearson soon after the merger. He holds the post of "consultant."

Robert M. Fomon, in the days following his ouster as chairman of E.F. Hutton, decided to set up his own shop. His one-man investment bank—Robert M. Fomon & Co.—specializes in leveraged buyouts. He's also a consultant to Shearson, in accordance with the terms of his severance contract, "but they've never once asked me to consult on anything," he says. Since Shearson swallowed Hutton, hundreds of angry Hutton employees have telephoned Fomon at his apartment to accuse him of engineering Hutton's downfall. He hasn't known what to say to them. "I did the best I could with Sandy Weill," he says, "but they still blame me. I had an uncle who . . . said, 'Bob, if in a lifetime you have five close friends, you can consider yourself lucky.' I think," Fomon quietly concedes, "he was right." Most of the people he thought were his friends no longer come around or call. "One of the things that you realize is that you thought you had real close friends, but they were just kissing up to you because of your position. It kind of shakes you up a little to learn that. . . . People are extremely loyal to you only when you can do something for them." Fomon, who received a $3 million severance payment from Hutton, was slated to wed Lewis Widener, a Palm Beach socialite, on April 22. The couple will make their home in Palm Beach. Widener is Fomon's third wife.

Stephen J. Friedman left Hutton in January 1988 and spent six months deciding what he wanted to do. "Net net," he says, "Hutton was a wonderful experience for me. I met and worked with a number of wonderful people. I felt that almost more than any other time in my career I was using everything I had to offer." In June, he joined The Equitable Life Assurance Society of the United States, the nation's third largest insurance carrier. At the age of fifty-one, he is now executive vice president and general counsel, virtually the same title he held at Hutton. Friedman, who lives in New York, will receive a retirement benefit of around $150,000 a year for the remainder of his life.

GENESEE COUNTRY BANK, which tipped the first domino in the line that finally toppled Hutton, has been a branch of Rochester's Central Trust Co. since 1984. NED CHATT still manages the branch. Genesee's former president, A. KEENE BOLTON, left the bank in 1982 to start Genesee Capital Inc., a small equipment-leasing and venture capital firm in Rochester, where he remains president.

JOHN HOLLAND, age forty-nine, is still a postal inspector living in Mechanicsburg, Pennsylvania. The Hutton case is the biggest so far in his career.

Congressman WILLIAM J. HUGHES, Democrat from New Jersey and the man who instigated the congressional investigation into Hutton's banking practices, is serving his eighth term in the U.S. House of Representatives. He is investigating allegations of illegal gun running and drug smuggling by individuals involved in the contra supply network.

MARK KESSENICH is now with Beekman Partners, a firm formed by eight people from Hutton's fixed-income group. The firm, which is entering into a joint venture with Nippon Credit Bank, will operate under the name Eastbridge Capital Inc. Kessenich says of his time at Hutton, "I wish that Hutton had been successful. I think it was a very interesting experience."

EDWARD J. LILL, Hutton's chief financial officer, returned to Deloitte Haskins & Sells, the Big Eight accounting firm. He resumed his post as the partner in charge of the financial services industry practice. "I'm here," he says, "and I'm staying here until I retire." Now fifty-seven years old, he occupies an office in the World Trade Center, which houses the New York banking commissioner's office, where Hutton first learned that it was under investigation for check kiting. Lill says he has no regrets. "I didn't meet a person at Hutton—including Fomon—that I could not have grown to like," he says. Lill will get a retirement benefit of about $50,000 a year for the rest of his life.

DINA MERRILL—because she is the daughter of Hutton's founder—was appointed a director of Shearson Lehman Hutton. She was the only member of Hutton's board who was asked to become a director of the newly merged companies. Her most recent movie is *Caddyshack II*.

JEROME H. MILLER, former head of the retail sales group, is a vice chairman of Shearson Lehman Hutton, the only top Hutton executive to remain with the combined firm. He codirects the domestic retail system with Joe Margolies, also a Shearson vice chairman.

JOHN U. MOORHEAD, formerly Bob Fomon's assistant, turned thirty-seven in the spring of 1989. He stayed on after the acquisition and is currently a vice president of investment banking and director of new business development for Shearson Lehman Hutton in New York.

ALBERT R. MURRAY, JR., the former federal prosecutor in Pennsylvania, age thirty-nine, resigned from the Justice Department in the fall of 1988 and is now in private practice in Monroe County, Pennsylvania. He is also involved in building a motel with his family. "What keeps coming out is the irony of the whole thing," he says now about Hutton. "A major player [on Wall Street] has actually been put out of business as a result of a series of [events] that [our investigation] started. What better punishment for a white-collar crime than going down the tubes?"

SCOTT PIERCE, onetime president of E.F. Hutton & Co., now holds the title of chairman of the Prudential Asset Management Co., a division of Prudential Insurance. "I think I was very fortunate to have left when I did," he says. Fifty-eight years old, he maintains an office in Newark, New Jersey. On occasion, he visits his sister at the White House.

THOMAS W. RAE, who retired as general counsel after the Griffin Bell investigation, practices law part-time with the firm of Kutak Rock & Campbell. When he sought membership to the Washington, D.C., bar, Judge Bell sponsored him. For a few months, his law firm shared office space with Robert M. Fomon & Co. Now fifty-eight years old, Rae says he's "enjoying life, smelling the roses, and doing a lot of fishing." He lives in Connecticut— "I'd rather not say what town"—with his wife of twenty-four years.

ROBERT P. RITTEREISER, Hutton's chief executive officer, remained at the firm but not in his office after the acquisition. He had to move from the twenty-eighth to the sixteenth floor, where he is still working on the transition. "Shearson needed help figuring out how to deal with certain things," Rittereiser says. He spends a lot of his time giving depositions in various still-pending suits. "I'm probably seventy-five percent of the way to figuring out what to do next," he says. He's had a number of job offers, but he's still considering the option of going into business for himself. Rittereiser is now fifty years old.

MICHAEL J. RYAN, who managed Hutton's Batavia brokerage office, also stayed on the job after the Shearson acquisition. Now sixty years old, Ryan retired as branch manager in early 1989 but remains a broker in the Batavia office, which has grown from four to seven people.

DON SANDERS, the Houston Hutton broker involved in the Aubin scandal, is now president of his own small securities firm, which does its trading through Prudential-Bache. Sanders and Prudential-Bache head George Ball are "still close," says an associate.

STEPHEN S. TROTT, who was associate attorney general during the Hutton investigation, is now Judge Trott, a member of the Ninth Circuit Court of Appeals since 1987. Trott will turn forty-nine this year.

KENDRICK R. WILSON III joined forces with Lewis S. Ranieri, the creator of the mortgage-backed securities market and ousted head of the Salomon Brothers mortgage and real-estate group. Together they formed the investment firm of Ranieri, Wilson & Co. "[Hutton] left an indelible mark on me," says Wilson. "It was a very sobering and maturing experience."

INDEX